HOW TO BE AN AUTHOR

36 Real Authors Talk Writing and Publishing

ASHTON CARTWRIGHT

Table of Contents

Introduction

Writing has given me more than I ever thought possible.

There is a type of satisfaction that you get when you create something, whether it be a book, an artwork, or a song, and you get to see and hear about other people enjoying it. You know that you've made an effect on someone's life, even if it's only in a small way. It's one of the best feelings in the world.

Writing has also given me a new way of looking at books that I read myself; I enjoy them more now that I understand a little bit of what goes into them, and I can relate to what the author must have gone through to get their thoughts to a point where another person can read them.

Lastly, becoming a professional writer has allowed me to make an income doing something I enjoy, and has given me a lifestyle that I'd never have been able to accomplish otherwise.

Particularly as a self-published author, I have a degree of freedom that I wouldn't have imagined 5 years ago. I get to work my own hours, I've been able to travel and do my work from my laptop anywhere in the world, and I can't remember the last time I needed to set my alarm clock.

That's not to say it's always been smooth sailing: it definitely hasn't been.

There have been plenty of times that I wanted to throw in the towel.

Occasionally you'll get a really bad review for something you poured your heart and soul into, and you'll thing to yourself "Why do I bother?"

I've had plenty of sleepless nights when a new book launch fails, or a major shift in the industry occurs, and I start to worry about how I'm going to pay my mortgage, or put food on the table.

Overall though, I've loved (almost) every step of the journey, and I wouldn't trade this job for anything in the world . . . and I think it's fair to say that almost every one of the 36 authors in this book feels exactly the same way.

Everyone who becomes a professional author does so for different reasons. They each face different obstacles, have different goals, and choose different paths. The more authors that a new writer learns from, the greater the chance that they'll find someone they resonate with, and that they'll discover something that can help them in their own career.

Some of the authors in this book (like myself) are self-published; others are traditionally published.

Some have worked with agents, and others have chosen to represent themselves.

Some authors in this book generate hundreds of thousands of dollars in royalties, and have been involved with the publishing industry for years, while others are just starting out with their very first book.

Some exclusively write fiction, some non-fiction, and some write a bit of both.

Some of us write just for the joy of writing, others for the money, and still others because they have a story that NEEDS to be told.

One thing that every author in this book has in common though is this: we've all published at least one book. Each of the authors that you'll read about has had an idea, and has worked at it, and persevered until that idea turned into something tangible. Every author here has struggled with the distractions of the real world, but has still made time to write down some words, and then turn those words into something special.

So, onto the book!

The format of this book is a little bit different.

We sent each of the 36 authors in this book a list of questions about writing and publishing. There was no word limit: each author answered with as much information as they felt they needed.

You'll rarely find a group of authors so willing to be open and honest about their mistakes as well as their successes, and hopefully this book will help you make less of the former and have more of the latter.

Happy reading.

Ashton.

A.C. Fuller

Tell us about yourself and your books!

I am the creator and host of the WRITER 2.0 Podcast and an English teacher at Northwest Indian College. Previously I taught journalism at New York University and worked as a freelance reporter. I live with my wife and children in the Pacific Northwest, where I write, teach English, and lead writing workshops for adults. My first novel—a media thriller called THE ANONYMOUS SOURCE—came out in June of 2015 and the sequel, THE INVERTED PYRAMID, will come out soon.

How long have you been writing, and how did you become involved in writing?

I wrote on and off throughout my teenage years and twenties, but I only got very serious about it in my early thirties. That's when I decided I was going to do it no matter what. I started treating writing like a job, like a career, and that's when things started rolling.

What are you working on at the moment?

The Inverted Pyramid, the sequel to my debut novel, The Anonymous Source. It follows reporter Alex Vane as he tries to uncover a plot to rig the 2004 U.S. Presidential election and stack the FCC.

Did you have any goals with writing, and if so, how well do you feel you've achieved them? What do you hope to achieve in the future?

My goal is to make a full-time living as an author, publishing around one book per year. I haven't yet achieved this, but I plan to.

How long does it take you to write a book?

It takes me around a year, but keep in mind that I'm writing full-length, complex thrillers.

What are the hardest parts of being an author for you?

Balancing the need to write and the need to promote and communicate with readers. For most authors these days, publishing is like running a small business, and although I like all the business aspects, they take a lot of time to do well. To write well I have to immerse myself in the story and characters deeply, and it's sometimes difficult to do this because I'm pulled in so many directions.

What do you enjoy most about being an author?

A lot.

1. The freedom to explore topics, time periods, and people that interest me.
2. The camaraderie among other authors.
3. The quiet time of actually writing.

What books or authors have had the most influence on you as an author?

A few writing books had a big influence on me: BIRD BY BIRD, by Anne Lammott, WRITING DOWN THE BONES, by Natalie Goldberg, ON WRITING, by Stephen King, and THIS YEAR YOU WRITE YOUR NOVEL, by Walter Mosley. Also, some fiction had a big influence on me: THE HOBBIT, by Tolkien, THE GLASS BEAD GAME and everything else by Herman Hesse. Also, most of the work of Kafka, John Steinbeck, and Virginia Wolf. But also thriller and mystery authors, like

John Grisham, Michael Conelly, Roger Hobbs and Robert Dugoni.

What did you find most useful when you were learning to write and expanding your skills?

Writing as often as possible and really struggling with it is the best way to get better. There's no way around this. If you're not willing to sit in the chair, write mediocre sentences, then work to make them better, there's no hope of being a good writer. Of course, you can be a successful author without being a good writer. It just depends on what your goals are.

I also found that writing conferences helped me a lot. Particularly the Pacific Northwest Writers Association Conference in Seattle every July, which I now teach at.

What author services do you pay for, as opposed to doing yourself? Things like cover design, formatting, editing, proofreading, etc.?

My publisher handles those, but I do pay for some promo services. If I were self-published, I would pay for all of them.

What technology/services/programs do you use as an author? (email subscription services, Dragon software, editing software, etc.)

Scrivener is my most important writing tool. I also use Dragon dictation on my iPhone for times when I have a short piece of writing I want to dictate. On my website I use an email subscription pop-up and a bunch of other plugins. For email I use Mail Chimp, which I love.

What are your thoughts about ebooks vs. print books?

I sell mostly ebooks, but paperbacks are quite important to me. Some thriller readers ONLY read paperback, so it's important for me to have a good paperback. I also do a lot of in-person events, so having a well-produced paperback allows me to sell at these events. Meeting people in person is a chance to make a real connection and find a fan for life, so even though I don't make much money on paperbacks at in-person events, I consider this is central part of my career. Personally, I prefer to read paper books, and always will. I look at a screen enough for work that I don't need to do so when reading.

What are your thoughts about self-publishing vs traditional publishing?

I could write for a long time on this topic. Here are a few of my thoughts. Anyone who says, categorically, that one is bad and the other is good does not know what he or she is talking about. It all depends on the situation.

Self-publishing is a wonderful option now, and I know multiple authors with great careers built entirely on self-publishing. But the rumors that traditional publishing is dying, and that publishers never give out advances, are false. I have friends making a good living who are 100% traditionally published. Another good option these days is to become a hybrid author: self-publishing some projects and traditionally publishing others. Some publishers are now even using strategic self-publishing in order to market an upcoming traditionally-published book. So, nothing is black and white here.

Personally, I went with a hybrid publisher, called Booktrope, which offers much of the freedom of self-publishing and many of the benefits of traditional publishing, mostly a professional team and great support.

For anyone consider publishing book, I'd recommend really researching all the options. Take your time.

How often do you write, and how do you find or make time to write?

I try to work on whatever book I'm writing every day, but it doesn't always work out. When I wrote THE ANONYMOUS SOURCE, I worked on it 5–6 days a week, ever week. My latest book has been a little different because of schedule changes, work changes, and so on. Sometimes I'll go 3–4 days without doing anything, then do 40 hours of work over 3 days. Because I'm not yet writing full time, I have to be flexible.

Do you plan your whole book out in advance, or just let it flow? What does your writing process look like?

I plan major elements of a book in advance. The main characters, the main storyline, the main plot twists and turns. But I leave a lot of room for things to change as I write.

What's a typical working day like for you? When and where do you write?

There's no typical day anymore, but when I'm writing a first draft I try to do the actual writing between 4:30 and 7 am, before my kids wake up.

Do you ever get Writer's Block? If so, how do you deal with it?

I do. Usually I try to just get something down, even if it sucks. I might skip ahead in the book and write a different scene. I might take a walk, or change something about my routine. I'll try anything. From time to time, nothing works and I just need a bit of a break. More info here: *http://acfuller.com/10-tips-for-when-writing-gets-hard-episode-74-october-30–2015/*

Do you read your own reviews? If so, how do you deal with bad reviews?

I did at first, but once I got over 100 reviews on my first book I felt like I'd learned what I could and I needed to move on. Now I don't. Sometimes I'll skim them, and I DO check whether new ones are coming in. I've been lucky to only have a couple negative reviews, and they don't really phase me. Every book has an audience, and as your audience grows, people are going to come across your book who aren't going to like it. No biggie.

Other than reviews, do you hear from your readers very often? What kinds of things do they say?

I hear from readers almost every day, mostly via Facebook and email. Honestly, I've been bowled over by all the nice things they say. Stuff like, "The book dropped on my face at 2 am because I tried to stay up all night reading." Or, "Amazing that this is your first book."

What are some ways in which you promote your books? What have you found most or least effective?

I try everything I can. I talk about it on my podcast, I share updates on Facebook, Twitter and Instagram. I have a small email list through my website. And I've used some of the promo services, like Freebooksy and Bookbub.

The three most effective things for me: Facebook, Bookbub and my email list. When I launched the book, my Facebook Street team, as well as friends and family, were a huge help. That led to the first chunk of sales, which led to reviews and more sales. After the book was out for 4 months, it was accepted for a free Bookbub Promotion. This led to 50,000 free downloads and a couple thousand paid sales after the promo ended. But I probably wouldn't have gotten the Bookbub promo without all the early sales and reviews. Finally, my email list, though small, has a been a big help.

How easy or hard is it to make a living as an author?

Very hard. Period.

What advice would you give to someone aspiring to be an author?

Get a good day job (or a spouse with one) that leaves you enough mental space to really focus on writing. Use your best hours of the day to write. If you're a morning person, get up early to write. If you're a night person, lock those hours away and use them to write. Treat your day job as casually as you can get away with and start treating your writing like a career long before you intend to publish.

How can readers find out more about you?

Website: www.acfuller.com

Facebook: www.facebook.com/acfullerauthor

A.G. Billig

Tell us about yourself and your books!

I am an explorer of the human soul, a dreamer, a traveler, a spiritual seeker and a citizen of the world. My mother is Eastern European, my father is French, and I was born in Bucharest, Romania.

Ever since I learned how to write, I never let a day pass without putting words on a blank piece of paper or on an empty screen. I've written poems, stories, plays, diary entries, a novel, press releases, interviews, articles, blog posts, presentation texts for the radio and TV shows I hosted. Some of the words are collected in books. "Four Doors and Other Stories" explores the nature and the breadth of love, not only in its most recognizable forms—sacrifice, forgiveness, and longing—but in its strangest: in distance, infidelity, jealousy, and isolation. "I Choose Love! Overcome Your Fears To Attract The Life You Want" is a non-fiction book, an Amazon bestseller that offers practical guidance on how to create a happy life through love.

How long have you been writing, and how did you become involved in writing?

I started writing fiction when I was eight. That's when I realized that I enjoyed doing the school composition assignments as much as playing with other kids.

My first "masterpiece" titled "Our New Blue Car" (the title speaks for itself) is included in my first collection of stories and poems available in hardcover. The sole copy, published under the pen name A.G. Billig, is to be found on a bookshelf, in my living room. My father who was the editor, the publisher and the illustrator of the book, typed it on glossy paper then had it bound in leather.

My parents were passionate about literature and art. They encouraged my appetite for reading and writing, and supported my endeavors. I joined a literary circle and entered writing competitions. Some of them, I won. By the time, I was fifteen my first novel was ready. To this day, it remains just a manuscript in my drawer.

My literary debut happened later in life, in 2012, with a collection of short stories traditionally published. It is related to The London Book Fair. As you probably know, The London Book Fair is not precisely the place where an author hopes to find a publisher, certainly without having an agent. Yet I took the advice of a good friend, compiled a portfolio and, without lending an ear to what people believed, I went there to try my luck. As I was walking around the stands on the ground floor, watched by a benevolent J.K. Rowling from a larger than life billboard, I realized that somehow I was walking in a circle. I kept coming to a small stand with beautiful covers.

Everything in life happens for a reason. I stopped, said hello and asked if they were interested in new authors. As a matter of fact, they were. They were looking for manuscripts that would appeal to women. Two days later I received a contract offer. In November 2012, MP Publishing released "Four Doors and Other Stories."

What are you working on at the moment?

I am currently promoting my newest book, "I Choose Love! Overcome Your Fears To Attract The Life You Want." It was released on the 20th of March 2016, and became an Amazon bestseller. Until November 2015, I've never imagined that I would write a non-fiction book. Until April, the same year, I've never imagined that I would self-publish. I've done both and it feels great. I have several ideas for novels and a new collection of short stories waiting for editing.

Did you have any goals with writing, and if so, how well do you feel you've achieved them? What do you hope to achieve in the future?

When I started, the goal was to be the best I can be, win the competitions, and to get published. I still want to give my best but I don't wait to be published anymore. I am my own publisher.

I believe that each human being has a gift. There are many things I enjoy — singing, photography, dancing, journalism, being a radio and a TV host, but somehow writing has been with me from the very beginning.

I don't write stories with happy endings. I write stories about transformation and change. My moral goal is to empower people, inspire them to find their gift and express it. Offer it to the world. Bring back the light in their eyes. I believe I've achieved it.

My next goal — while staying true to the moral one is to reach as many people as possible and make a life (not just a living) as a writer. I am also starting a service for indie authors that will include author branding, cover design, publicity and consultancy.

My dream life is to travel the world, discover untold stories and connect with my readers. I admit I have big dreams. The Universe supports the brave ones. I do believe that great books always find their way to the readers.

How long does it take you to write a book?

It depends on the book. I wrote my first novel in about year. I completed the collection of short stories (there are 21 in the Romanian version) in about six months. The latest book I wrote took me one month. The new collection of short stories took almost two years. But that's because I lacked focus and direction. Also, because I doubted myself.

What are the hardest parts of being an author for you?

The long hours on a chair, eyes glued to the computer screen are tough. I am a sporty, active person, who loves being outdoors. I recently started to use dictation for shorter pieces such as blog posts. I am also planning an exercise book for authors, with simple routines they can do at home. I have to admit, though, that when I am in the flow, time flies by. The "mission accomplished" sensation I get when the voice in my head silences, the joy in my heart, the makes me forget about the pain in my back.

What do you enjoy most about being an author?

Birthing new worlds. Feeling fulfilled in a sense that I know this is my life path and I am walking on it. The messages from readers saying they loved the book or how the book helped them see life from a different perspective. Connecting with other authors. The endless opportunities provided by the Internet, the access to global audiences.

What books or authors have had the most influence on you as an author?

Having a B.A. in English and French languages and literatures, I would say the great classics of these two larger-than-life cultures. Nevertheless, I never wanted to be the next Balzac, Dickens or Twain. On the other hand, contemporary writers such as J.K Rowling and Mark Dawson inspire me to follow my dream and be persistent. I prefer to keep in mind the few successful examples instead of the numerous failures. Overall, I am happy to be the most authentic and original A.G. Billig I can be.

What did you find most useful when you were learning to write and expanding your skills?

I didn't learn to write fiction. I never took creative writing classes. I believe that reading from early childhood helped a lot. Reading literary fiction, good literature, starting with Homer's "Iliad" and "The Odyssey" was the best writing school for me, just as it is for anybody who is a natural born writer.

Great and lasting literature comes from the spirit and the heart, and not from the mind. It is important to have the necessary vocabulary to translate the ideas that are whispered in your ear into fiction. To be present, observe, pay attention to other people—to their gestures, clothes, dialogue, is also crucial. The writer must be awake all the time. Love people. Love the craft.

What author services do you pay for, as opposed to doing yourself? Things like cover design, formatting, editing, proofreading, etc.?

For my self-published book, I paid for editing, proofreading and formatting. I would have also paid for the cover if a friend of mine didn't do it for free. An author who doesn't have many fans or a big email list should consider paying for promotion. I paid for being featured on free and bargain books websites. I organized my own book blog tour. If you are in it for the long run, it is important to build your author brand. Hire someone who can get you on podcasts, blogs, and traditional media. Promote yourself together with your book.

What technology/services/programs do you use as an author? (email subscription services, Dragon software, editing software, etc.)

The old, plain Microsoft Word. The dictation feature is great. I use WordPress for my author website and MailChimp to collect emails.

What are your thoughts about ebooks vs. print books?

Ever since I've got my first Kindle a couple of years ago, I use it for most of my reading. I think it is effective from many points of view—storage, books price, the possibility to read in the dark not to mention that it saves some trees. The only problem is when you are on a desert island with no power supply. I am in a phase where I am decluttering my life so the fewer objects I own, the better. I still have a house full of print books, I enjoy leafing through pages in bookshops but I believe that ebooks are as good as their print version. The writer's craft is the same, the content is the same. I am definitely not one of those people who miss the smell of ink.

What are your thoughts about self-publishing vs traditional publishing?

I wanted to have my literary debut with a traditional publisher, to have a seal of approval and I did. As long as a book looks professional and is well written, readers don't care if it is traditionally or self-published. Some bloggers and traditional media outlets, as well as writing contests, do.

Being traditionally published — at least theoretically offers the advantage of no upfront costs, being distributed in bookstores and having a strategic promotion plan. In reality, the top ones aside, the writer still needs to promote the book. And has very little control over his work. I am 100% in favor of self-publishing but I do believe that it is for those who are committed, consistent and persistent, who believe in themselves and have an entrepreneurial mind.

How often do you write, and how do you find or make time to write?

I've been a freelancer for the past few years with no fixed schedule. When I am working on a book, I write daily. I am a morning person and dedicate the first part of the day to writing. That's how I managed to complete my latest book in one month. I sit at my desk every day, even during the winter holidays, for a couple of hours. Once I stop, I have a hard time getting back in the flow during the same day.

Do you plan your whole book out in advance, or just let it flow? What does your writing process look like?

I have an idea of the theme or the plot, and then I let it flow. I always have an outline in my head before I start hitting the keyboard. For example, the working title of my debut short-stories book was "20 stories about love." Sometimes when I walk on the street I get ideas or I see something inspiring and I record a voice memo.

What's a typical working day like for you? When and where do you write?

I write in the morning (or I do other creative work that involves imagination and words), I go to the gym or for a walk or other outdoors activities at noon, I work on my freelance projects in the afternoon.

Do you ever get Writer's Block? If so, how do you deal with it?

To me, the writer's block signals not being in the flow. Letting the mundane aspect of life cloud the clarity within my spirit. A writers' block goes away with meditation and a good infusion of self-confidence.

Do you read your own reviews? If so, how do you deal with bad reviews?

Yes, I do. I know I cannot please everybody. Nor do I want to. I am grateful every time I find something useful that helps me to improve my writing.

Other than reviews, do you hear from your readers very often? What kinds of things do they say?

I get messages on Facebook or Twitter. Some people say they recognize themselves in certain characters or stories. Others say they loved a certain story. Somebody told me that my book was food for his soul. He bought two more copies for his best friends.

What are some ways in which you promote your books? What have you found most or least effective?

Some of the best online tools online are the interviews, blog tours, and guest posts.

In real life, I like creating events that blend arts. I had an evening of literature, music and wine. I also created a happening titled "Summer Story." I am thinking about creating a Kickstarter campaign and going on tour to meet my readers around the world. I think the mix of online and offline activities generates the best results.

I know that promotion is mandatory, but still, I do believe that once put out there, books get a life of their own. If the book is great, it will find its way to the readers.

How easy or hard is it to make a living as an author?

It is hard if you believe it is hard. It is easy if you believe it is. The outer world reflects our own thoughts, beliefs, and emotions. Make sure that writing is your gift, have undeterred faith in yourself and your gift, put in the time and energy, and it will pay off. The hard work will become easy.

What advice would you give to someone aspiring to be an author?

First and foremost, make sure that writing fiction is your best skill, your gift. Everyone who goes to school can write but not everyone is born a writer. Make sure that writing is that "thing" that you are passionate about, that makes your heart sing with joy. Treat writing seriously. Not as a hobby or amusement. Give it top priority and invest yourself in it 100%.

How can readers find out more about you?

Website: www.agbillig.com
Facebook: www.facebook.com/A.G.Billig

Aishah Macgill

How long have you been writing, and how did you become involved in writing?

Despite despising school, I was great at writing essays. Often I would get an A with little effort on my part, or so it seemed. It was easy for me to plump up the volume, impressing the teachers with my word count.

If anything, my essays were often too long and annoyed the teachers as they had to trawl though my diatribes. Often I would go off on a tangent and it seemed I was born with a penchant for left-wing politics and standing up for the downtrodden, always weaving some thread about an injustice to someone, somewhere in the world. Some hailed me as a lunatic, others appreciated the sentiment and always marked me highly.

When I left school I became a poet, largely influenced by the psychedelic era and Monty Python style stuff at first. As my mind turned to the meaning of life and 'what's it all about,' seeking the truth and again justice, was often a theme, and still is.

I continued to write poetry and short stories about daily life. Whenever I wrote a letter, it was usually at least ten to twenty pages of foolscap, that's old A4, handwritten. Often the recipients of my lengthy tomes remarked that I should be a professional writer and they enjoyed my letters immensely. Apparently I had a knack of making the everyday and banal interesting. I wonder if anyone out there still has any of my letters stashed away? My mum still has some postcards from me, stuck on the inside of the toilet door from 30 plus years ago.

I got a job with a magazine in my twenties for a while, I still have my very first article I wrote for them. But travel beckoned and writing took a back seat, though I continued to write poetry and stories about my travels along the way.

I began fulfilling my dream of novel writing in 2008 when I discovered Amazon and figured out how to publish a book all by myself as a Kindle eBook.

The catalyst for writing my first book, a memoir of my travels, was bought about when I read "Eat, Love, Pray." I thought her travel tale was relatively boring compared to my adventures. Who cares how much pasta she ate? Who cares if she put on a few kilos and was okay with it? Though many of my experiences mirrored hers, it was pretty bland overall as far as a travel adventure went. She took the safe route and obviously money wasn't an issue.

I thought, "If this trifle can be a best seller, I can do it too." Not that I have a best seller. Anyway, Elizabeth Gilbert had a contract to write the book and wrote it as she travelled. A luxury any budding novelist would love to acquire. Imagine having an advance payment, taking off and writing about what you are doing as you go. Wow.

What are you working on at the moment?

Presently, I have turned my hand to a Young Adult Fantasy. The idea came about when I was at a friend-of-a-friends 60th birthday party. I only knew one person there. The party was boring and full of old people. I berated myself for expecting something different, after all, it was a 60th!

It was in a small country town in the birthday boy's shed. Mind you, this was a palatial backyard shed, the envy of many-a-man.

It had a built in BBQ, a toilet, and a full size pool table. It was big enough to house farm machinery, which had been removed for the party. A top shelf sound system was also installed. After a few rounds of billiards, and a bite to eat, a sausage or two in bread, which I always swear I will never eat again, but the smell is irresistible, I settled in to chat with the most interesting person there who was under the age of 60. It turned out he was a farmer of sorts like most of the other people present. Only he was the farmer of a fantasy land.

In our newly found camaraderie, we managed to laugh the night away, becoming more and more outrageous over time, laughing so hard our stomachs were aching and we were gasping for air, much to the exasperation of the other party goers. We were completely sober and ignored the disproving looks and tut-tuts from the elderly women. One can safely assume they thought we were high on something.

The seed for my Young Adult Fantasy novel was born that night. Our conversations followed the most unlikely threads. He told me about the paranormal influences and his unorthodox lifestyle on his farm with his partner, also a farmer.

It turns out their farm was inhabited by a fleet of UFOs which regularly landed in their paddocks. Along with a mythical Bunyip, who haunted the area immediately around the house and the extensive verandah. The Bunyip sometimes came inside, usually when they were having an argument, leaving wreckage in its wake, and sometimes physical scars on their bodies. No one had ever actually seen the Bunyip in the flesh, but they said you could sense its presence, feel it touching you and see items being knocked over in its wake. It was mind boggling stuff.

There was no question in his mind about the truth of the existence of UFO's and the mythical creature. He also told me with a completely straight face that his boyfriend was an alien. His boyfriend was there at the party and I have to admit he did look like one. He had a peculiar protruding forehead with little bumps on it, like something straight out of Star Trek. He was very stocky with an unusual body shape, a bit apish, but moved with style and grace somehow.

When he could sense I was starting to suspect he was making it up, he called over the birthday boy to confirm one of his stories.

Apparently one night, the birthday boy and his wife popped around for a visit. As they were getting out of their car, they were knocked to the ground by a huge force of energy. The visiting birthday boy had cuts in a straight line through his jeans just below his knees on his shins. The Bunyip had given them a welcome they would never forget.

This unique chance meeting opened up all kinds of possibilities and trails of thought which led to the idea of the type of fantasy book I am currently writing. I only wish I could impart some of the humor into it from our first conversation about all things weird and wonderful.

Did you have any goals with writing, and if so, how well do you feel you've achieved them? What do you hope to achieve in the future?

Firstly, just finishing a book was the goal. Now I have finished 6 but not all of them are published. My memoir is far too personal and needs to be pared back before I would consider publishing.

My only hope for the future regarding writing is to keep on doing it. It's a kind of obsession when it kicks in. I can't not write.

How long does it take you to write a book?

The quickest I have completed a book is 6 months. I would call that a novella. Otherwise, 1 to 2 years per book. A book is never really finished. You can go on improving forever. At some point you just have to let it go and live with the shudders of embarrassment that seem to come and go. Many actors can't watch their own films later on. I feel that way with my books. After a couple of years, what I thought was genius seems naive and amateurish.

What are the hardest parts of being an author for you?

Nothing is hard about being an author. It is a constant joy.

What do you enjoy most about being an author?

Writing is a passion and completely fulfilling for me. The fact that someone else might read it and enjoy it is of little consequence when I am writing. I become completely immersed in the story, thinking about little else. Ripples of delight pass over me and through me when I am in the creative zone. If I do get tired and frustrated, I know it's time to give it a break.

What books or authors have had the most influence on you as an author?

Enid Blyton books were a childhood favorite. I loved the Faraway Tree and the Magic Wishing Chair. It's sad that she went out of favor. I know some stuff is now politically incorrect. But who wouldn't want to have the Faraway Tree in their back yard or a magic chair with wings?

I progressed on to Herman Hesse, Kurt Vonnegut and of course JRR Tolkien's Lord of the Rings. When The Hobbit came into my sphere of consciousness, there was nothing else around like it, it was mind boggling stuff.

Being a flower child, I delved into Carlos Castaneda, Timothy Leary and others who were way, way out there. Listening to music too took much of my leisure time. So much of the old music has amazing lyrics and cool album covers. We used to sit for hours, staring at album art and trying to figure out the meaning of our existence. The lyrics gave us clues. The art baffled and inspired. It was a popular hobby in the 70s to contemplate the meaning of life and nurse a desire to make the world a better place. Well, that has never stopped for me.

What did you find most useful when you were learning to write and expanding your skills?

I didn't learn to write, I just wrote. The more I wrote, the better I got. For me, the book writes itself. When I start, it's already finished in my head. I just put the words on to paper, so to speak. The story lives somewhere in another dimension. It already exists. I just give it form, polish and a voice. My voice.

What author services do you pay for, as opposed to doing yourself? Things like cover design, formatting, editing, proofreading, etc.?

I don't pay for any services as I am a publishing service provider myself. I format, design and publish books for self-published authors. I have done hundreds of books for other authors. The only thing I cannot do professionally is edit, but I have trusted editors who perform those duties. And an author should never edit their own books.

What technology/services/programs do you use as an author? (email subscription services, Dragon software, editing software, etc.)

I write everything in MS word. That's what editors want. Books written with Mac pages are a disaster for editors and formatters. Mac pages puts awful hidden glitches into the files.

Professionally I use Adobe suite. Photoshop, Illustrator and Indesign. They give the best results.

What are your thoughts about ebooks vs. print books?

eBooks allow me to trial a book or a new author as they are cheaper. eBooks enable me to buy many more books than I could before, print books in Australia are generally not cheap, around $30 plus for a good novel.

Generally, I will buy larger format books such as art or nonfiction in print. If I need to reference information, a print book is generally easier.

Who doesn't love to see where a book opens by itself?

What are your thoughts about self-publishing vs traditional publishing?

As a provider of self-publishing services, I love self-publishing. I do it differently to almost everyone else around, including the big corporates. I do everything for an author and they retain 100% of their royalty.

If a traditional publishing deal was offered to me, I would seriously consider taking it as long as they didn't want to tie up all my future books under their umbrella.

It's interesting to note that some successful traditionally published authors are turning their hand to self-publishing. Many more would probably love to, especially if their books always sell well. Many are probably contracted to an inch of their life to their publishing house, who will not easily relinquish control over a bestselling author. After all, publishing is big business.

What's a typical working day like for you? When and where do you write?

I generally write in the mornings in a cafe when I get the chance.

Do you ever get Writer's Block? If so, how do you deal with it?

I just don't feel like writing sometimes. Writer's block would probably more be an issue when facing a deadline, especially for journalists.

If I don't feel in the mood or simply can't get going, I leave the book alone for a while, even a few months. Fresh eyes make all the difference.

Do you read your own reviews? If so, how do you deal with bad reviews?

I haven't had a bad review, yet. Yes, I read reviews written about my books. Some authors don't?

What advice would you give to someone aspiring to be an author?

Write, Write, Write and read.

Revel in the love of being a creative.

If you are doing it just for the money, good luck.

How can readers find out more about you: (Fb, Goodreads, website links and such)

Website: www.aishahmacgill.com

Facebook: www.facebook.com/aishahmacgillauthor

Amanda Howard

Tell us about yourself and your books!

I am Amanda Howard. I am a true crime author and crime thriller writer. My first book was published in 2004 and I have been writing books ever since.

I have published 10 true crime books:

Rope: The History of the Hanged (2016)

Murder on the Mind (2014)

A Killer in the Family (2013)

Serial Killers: Being and Killing (2010)

Predators (2008)

Innocence Lost (2008)

Terror in the Skies (2007)

The Lottery Kidnapping (2007)

Million Dollar Art Theft (2007)

River of Blood: Serial Killers and their Victims (2004)

Three crime fiction novels:

Ritual: A Thousand Cuts (2015)

Ritual: The Elements of Murder (2013)

Ritual: The Blood of Many (2013)

A novella:

The Cicadas Roar (2013)

And two short stories:

Charlotte's One of A Kind Cakes (2013)

Writer's Block (2013)

I have also published dozens of articles in various journals, newspapers and online blogs covering subjects such as Jack the Ripper, serial killer suicides, local news and serial predators and child abduction.

I have been featured in international documentaries on serial killers, including Ivan Milat, David Birnie and Frederick Deeming as well as consulted on three others. I have appeared on national television programs including Sunrise and Studio10, and radio talk shows. To compliment my writing, I've studied criminology, psychology and law at University and am currently in the process of completing my Masters in Arts (Writing).

When I am not writing, I work full-time in an unrelated field, doing long hours that usually begin before sunrise, in a place where few know my 'true identity.' I also run a YouTube channel that examines serial murder, vintage horror and other strange and creepy facets of life. I like to spend my free time with my husband and two children, we dine out regularly so we can catch up and chat about life and the world. I am a lover of fine food and great wine, and enjoy spending evenings curled up in bed reading a good book or attending dance classes.

How long have you been writing, and how did you become involved in writing?

I fell in love with writing from an early age. The first story I ever wrote was a pretty bad screenplay based on the Beach Boys song Surfin' USA. I was only 7 at the time, and looking back it certainly had potential, if only I knew what I was actually doing. A year later I wrote an extensive story about a girl and her imaginary dragon. I agonized over it for weeks before finally given a deadline by my class teacher, meaning I had to finish it and hand it over, a feeling that all authors dread. I've been writing ever since—coming up to 35 years. I have numerous stories published over the years in school magazines and the like before I decided to try my hand at writing a book.

My first published book was released in 2004 it was an anthology of serial killer cases. It had been the culmination of about a decade of research and though at the time I was quite proud of it, I know now, it certainly wasn't up to my current standard. Since that first book, I was commissioned by a publisher in the UK to write a book on an Australian kidnapping that then turned into a commission for two further books. The rest, they say, is history.

What are you working on at the moment?

I have a number of current works in progress, at last count I had more than fifty works that were in various stages of completion. I always like to jot down notes or write out fully formed ideas, they may turn into stories or they may feature in something already in progress, regardless I have a pile waiting for love and attention. However, at the moment, my focus lies with:

A screenplay in the thriller genre. Since the awful Beach Boys screenplay of my tender years, I have not tried my luck in the screenplay format and it had always been something I wanted to try my hand at. The storyline for the play came to me whilst sitting at a school swimming carnival a year ago. The work started out as a novel manuscript, but it just doesn't work well, and I got stuck trying to force something that didn't want to come. Instead I did a little research and have changed it to a screenplay and now it now works well. It is about a third of the way through and I hope to complete it within twelve months.

Another true crime book: There is always a book or two on true crime on my to do list. After writing, *Murder on the Mind*, a book on a variety of types of serial murder, I penned another two books in a similar vein. The next volume is almost complete, it just requires a final run through, the final volume is sitting just under the three-quarter completion mark.

One of my earlier books, *Innocence Lost*, has always been a favorite, and back then, it didn't really get the publicity that my later books received. So I am currently working through the manuscript, and constructing an updated version. It should only take me about three months to complete the changes and then it will be ready for publication.

The fourth book in my Ritual series, as yet untitled: I travelled to London eighteen months ago, as part of my research on *Rope: The Story of the Hanged* and for my fourth Ritual book. The city was such an incredible amount of inspiration that the storyline I had planned didn't fit as well as I had hoped, so I have been slowly working on a new storyline since then.

Two stand-alone fiction works. *The Man with Shovel* is currently my favorite story to write. It is a slow, simmering thriller that has a few unexpected twists and turns. I thought it was going to be a novella, but after I surpassed the 15,000-word mark and there is still a lot more to tell, I know that the manuscript may end up a full-length novel. Of course only time will tell. The other, *The Relic* is definitely a short-story. It is already in a finalized first draft, so it's at the stage of pulling it apart, teasing it out, checking its pace and then polishing it. I think the first draft ends a little abruptly, so I want to work on that before I publish it.

I like to mix up my writing so I don't get stale working on one project. I find that if I am solely invested in one manuscript, that I get impatient and start to abandon my plans and that is when I find that my work suffers. By working on a few different projects, I can swap and change, altering my writer's voice and keep things fresh and exciting. It also allows me to ruminate over story ideas and characters.

Did you have any goals with writing, and if so, how well do you feel you've achieved them? What do you hope to achieve in the future?

Like most people, I wanted to publish a book. Just one. I wasn't greedy. We all have one book in us and I thought once I had done it that was it. Now I have to consciously sit down and count how many books I have written, as I sometimes lose count. That is a nice thing sometimes.

Once I had started writing my second, third and fourth books, I set another goal. 10 books by the time I turned 40, and I surpassed that. By the time my 80s fancy dress 40th birthday party came around, I had published 12 books. I was extremely proud of that effort.

Since I first started writing, I set a few goals, appearing on news programs, doing talks and book signings, appearing on film and publishing a screenplay. Some have come to fruition and others are works in progress. I think it is extremely important to set goals, I have pipeline dreams such as a book launch at the Guggenheim in New York, something that will probably never happen, but it is important to set lofty benchmarks. It can remind you want you want in life; it can also guide you towards greatness.

In regards to my daily writing, having such a busy lifestyle, I like to get as much done as possible, often when everyone is sleeping. 1,000 words a day is a great goal to have and is something I can easily do in less than an hour. Sometimes I easily surpass it, working for a number of hours, other times it's a struggle — often due to interruptions or a lack of inspiration, but I always aim to get something written each day. It may just be an idea on paper, or sometimes a fully-realized chapter, regardless, writing something each day is important.

How long does it take you to write a book?

This is one of those 'how long is a piece of string' questions. I wrote one of my books in three months. I admit it was hard to do and something I vow never to do again, particularly whilst working full-time, looking after a family and studying. I pushed beyond mental and physical limits to get it done in such a tight turn around and I actually ended up in hospital with exhaustion, but I got it done and the book was a fantastic success, becoming a best seller. Thankfully that is the exception rather than the rule. If I plotted out the time spent on each book, I'd say about 8–9 months per book from inception to completion (plus the publisher's time with artwork, editing etc), however, because I work on several books at once, that time is spread out, sometimes over eighteen months to a few years.

My non-fiction books are by far the easier projects to do—in that the story is already there, it is just about finding the sources, interviewing people, clarifying the facts and getting it typed up. From start to finish they take about six to nine months usually.

My fiction books take far longer as it's all from my own imagination, and like most authors that sometimes fails me. With my fiction novels once they are complete, I don't rush them off to the publishers like I do my non-fiction work. I often like to read it through, after the drafts are done, make sure the storyline is what it should be. My last fiction novel was completed a year before it was published, but I didn't like it's ending so I left it for a while, letting it ruminate in my mind, until a different ending came to me. It meant a lot of re-writing but my gut-instinct was right and the new ending—and the clues I needed to sprinkle throughout—turned out to be far better than the original.

What are the hardest parts of being an author for you?

I think the hardest part of being an author is trying to make sure you never make a grammatical error when speaking to people, and when using mundane things like social media. You always think you are being judged, and whenever I have typos in a status or comment I believe people are thinking "oh she's an author and she forgot an inverted comma in that sentence." It's a silly thing I know, but thankfully there is the edit button and so typos can be fixed, but it's a fear that is always there mocking you.

It is also tough being an author, working so long and hard on a labor of love and still making very little money. As soon as you say you're an author, people think you're as rich as JK Rowling, but in reality most authors have 'day jobs' away from their writing. It is not because they aren't successful, but it's because writing books isn't profitable. That $24.95 you pay for a book mostly goes to the printing costs. I usually make about $1–2 per book at the most, if the publishing deal is good.

It is also isolating being an author. It's not a shared job. Only you can do it, no-one is there to help you write it. It's about bashing away at the keyboard for hours on end, no interaction with others, there is no chance of someone coming in and writing the next part for you. It's all about you and your words. It can get pretty lonely, but then at the same time, you have a whole other universe to discover and that makes it all worth it. It can be exciting to visit places that no-one else has seen, and then invite your readers to discover it as well.

What do you enjoy most about being an author?

Writing is like breathing for me, if I don't write, I feel as though I am missing a part of me. Writing is freeing and allows me do things that I cannot do in my own life. The fantasy world in my brain is limitless and I enjoy being able to stretch the boundaries, see where it can take me. I enjoy having 'another family,' I talk to my real family about the characters I am writing about, they often help me tease out story ideas and help me with characterizations. It gives me an outlet, to try things that I don't think I could do. It also often challenges me to be braver. I have often found myself thinking about Kate Reilly, the protagonist from my *Ritual* series and I would say to myself, "Kate Reilly would face that without a problem. She's tough and she wouldn't let that upset her." I enjoy having my characters sometimes call me out when I am being fearful or afraid. They force me to be a stronger person.

I also love the fear that writing instils in me. I never think that it's an easy job. It certainly has never been easy and I hope it never becomes easy. I agonize over every word, every sentence, every idea and every storyline. I want it to be good, I want it to be what my heart and head see. I want people to read what comes from my imagination and love my characters and the stories I write as much as I loved writing it. Every time I sit down and write, I think about my reader, I write as though I am sitting across from you, telling you a story. I want it to be the voice of my characters. I want them to be believable, I want my reader to want to know more, to feel invested in their lives as though they were friends — or enemies. I had a reviewer of *Ritual: A Thousand Cuts* write that she had to look down at her own clothing to make sure that she wasn't splattered in blood after reading a particularly brutal murder scene. She could smell the blood, she could see the scene, and watch in horror as the killer murdered his victim. She was right there in the middle of the scene that had come from my imagination. That is what I love about being an author.

What books or authors have had the most influence on you as an author?

In the introduction to one of my recent books, I made mention of the authors who have shaped my life, and there are many writers that influence the way I write in my various author voices. For my non-fiction true crime, it was John Douglas and Mark Olshaker, the authors of Mindhunter who started me on my journey in true crime. This was coupled with multiple readings of Silence of the Lambs by Thomas Harris. These two books, plus a quote from my English teacher, about 'going to the source,' encouraged me to interview serial killers that later culminated in my true crime writing.

In regards to my fiction writing, I write in several genres, I like to write crime thrillers, short stories, novellas, horror and ghost stories, violent psychological pieces, as well as nostalgic yet eerie works. Therefore, I often read several authors in those genres for inspiration, particularly for my novellas and short stories. Stephen King is at the top of my list for bending genres and writing in numerous styles. I enjoy both his horror and his dramatic works. I have had a few reviews over the years that has liken my writing style to that of King, and it's a compliment that just makes me want to write more, dreaming that I could do him justice with my words.

My Ritual novels are face-paced crime thrillers and I like to write them in the short chapter style of James Patterson. I have been reading his novels since his first Alex Cross was released many decades ago, and he continues to inspire me. I find his work easy to read and well-paced, I take many notes from his action-packed pieces, particularly his Michael Bennett series. His books are pure pulp fiction, but there is a reason he is one of the top authors in the world.

When it comes to my other writing styles, I often look to the classics. The language of Ernest Hemingway, Sir Arthur Conan Doyle and Edgar Allan Poe are second to none. The books by these authors should be on the shelves of all true bibliophiles. The heroicism and true greatness of Hemingway's writing makes my heart sing, The Old Man and the Sea is a story I re-read almost every year. Hemingway's directness and lack of verbosity is still refreshing today. Doyle's Sherlock Holmes remains a beloved character and a recent re-reading of The Adventures of Sherlock Holmes, reminds me of why it has remained popular for more than a century, with its use of revealing everything to the reader without revealing anything at the same time. It is done with such skill that it creates a devilishly delightful dance that I continue to cherish decade after decade. I find great satisfaction in guessing the man's deductions before the final reveal, and enjoy the smugness that guessing the outcome brings. For true gothic greatness nothing will beat the poetic nuances of Edgar Allan Poe. I discovered Poe as a teenager, pouring over The Murders in the Rue Morgue and The Pit and the Pendulum. Every so often I return to Poe for inspiration when writing about the darkness of a man's soul and how sanity and insanity are often only a breath apart.

What did you find most useful when you were learning to write and expanding your skills?

The first and most important rule is knowing that there are no shortcuts. You can't skimp on writing. You need to write and you need to write well. I have spent many hours trying to find a way to do talk-to-text, I have begged family and friends to type up my scribbled notes, but all to no avail. It is something you have to do yourself and there is no easy way around it, but in saying that, the results of your hard work are always worth it.

I believe it's important to face your fears and put yourself out there, find challenges to your writing, don't sit in a safe zone with safe characters. Push the boundaries as far as you can. You've never written a non-fiction book/screenplay/poem/song before? It doesn't matter. Give it a go, you never know what you can achieve if you don't try.

When I began writing my first fiction novel, after writing non-fiction for many years, I was terrified. It took me about two years to write the first version, I had no idea what I was doing nor where it would end up. The first version wasn't great, but that is why revision is so important. Even Ernest Hemingway apparently said, "The first draft of anything is shit." It is important for new authors to remember that that first draft is basically you just getting the story down on paper/computer. It is not meant to be perfect, just bash it out, get it from your head and into a format that you can then improve on. It's about the journey from that point. I have so many writer friends who agonize over their first draft, they want to write more but get stuck fixing typos and grammatical errors, altering details and changing ideas. They wear themselves out before the story has been told. No-one is likely to ever read your first draft, so leave it raw, leave it with errors, with notes scribbled in margins, highlighted points and ideas. From your second draft on, you begin to polish it, you find better ways to say things, you describe what is going on, you adjust the story line so it is paced well and fits together and you also put the senses (sight, touch, taste, smell, sound) into the story.

I read many books about the 'rules' of writing, many of them talk about the formulaic pieces that fit into a manuscript, but I found that it can be detrimental to the thought process and the freedom of writing. Write what you want to write, break the rules, make up your own rules, don't ever let someone tell you that's now how you write a novel. Write what comes to you.

Another important point that I will touch on in the next question is that of ego and the need for editorial assistance. There are few writers who can edit their own work to perfection. We read what we expect to be there, and not what we have typed. We hear a sentence one way that when read in the style of another will sound clunky. It is important to realize that an editor's role is not to destroy a writer's work, but to enhance and nurture it. An honest relationship with a professional editor can make a good book great. Listen to their advice, discuss their points of issue and learn from their point of view. They may not always be right, but if they are good at their job, they make your job a lot easier. I have worked with some fantastic editors that enhanced my work with their suggestions and I have worked with some editors that were terrible and destructive to the finished product.

What author services do you pay for, as opposed to doing yourself? Things like cover design, formatting, editing, proofreading, etc.?

My publishers organize the artwork, internal photos, covers, editing and proofing, so this part is often the 'easy' part for me as I just give them my ideas regarding cover work and they do their magic. My publishers have always given me a few cover samples to choose from, and I am pleased to say I've never been disappointed with a cover yet. I think it takes a certain skill to do cover art and I am always grateful to the unsung artists who do incredible work.

I will admit though that I usually do most of the formatting before it gets to the publishers, I ensure that headings are done using the document's style templates. I do all my own contents tables, endnotes and other bits and pieces throughout that help cut down on the noise when it gets to the formatting department.

What gets to the publisher is often a final draft—often after, 10–15 draft versions and then the backwards and forwards with the editor begins, until I have final work that is as good as it can get. This process is often another 4–5 draft run throughs, though I did have one book that only required one edit. I think the drafting, proofing and editing processes are extremely important for any book and those who feel that they can edit their own work are probably, in most cases, doing themselves a disservice. A great book can be destroyed by errors that distract the reader from the book's storyline. I have read many e-books that could have been best sellers, if the author had not let pride get in their way and allowed an editor to go over their work. Some authors see an editor as a judge, in that they are there to find everything that is wrong with a manuscript, but in reality the editor is an author's best friend. Beyond the typos and the grammatical errors, they will see the potential and encourage the writer with suggestions and alterations. The best step an author can make is having a good editor go over their work.

What technology/services/programs do you use as an author? (email subscription services, Dragon software, editing software, etc.)

There are so many platforms for a writer's voice these days but sometimes it comes down to timing and my time is so limited that it would be hard to add more avenues to my writing career. I do talk to many readers via social media, with many followers on various platforms such as Facebook, Twitter, Instagram, Pinterest and Blogger. I also have a YouTube channel where my most popular videos are my "Truly Disturbing" montages of creepy vintage photos, horror stories, serial killers and all manner of macabre subjects. As I write this, my channel is about to click over 2 million views, in less than a year, so I found that a really great and creative platform. It was not something I thought would be embraced so quickly and I am grateful that it has been. I have gained a lot of fans and readers via my channel.

When it comes to editing, I guess, even at 42, I am an oldie in the writer stakes and do things a little old school, I don't use any medium beyond my word processing package, a pile of gorgeous hard cover leather bound journals that I carry around for when inspiration hits as well as a dozen or more pens.

What are your thoughts about ebooks vs. print books?

Before I make my argument here, I have to make a confession. I am a book sniffer and a bibliophile. At last count, my home library collection was well in excess of 10,000 books and that number is forever growing. I finish reading one book, I go and buy four more. My 'to read' pile is forever getting longer and I would not have it any other way, so I am a little biased when it comes to deciding between e-books and physical books. I do have a computer tablet that has the kindle program installed and I have purchases several books to read on it, as well as a few of the classics that are long out of copyright, but still, I personally prefer to read the physical book.

In saying that, I think both mediums are well received and I don't think they are competing with one another, but just offer the reader a choice. If anything encourages someone to pick up a book (or open a program) and read, then I am all for it. It's about getting books in front of readers, not whether one option is better than the other. I will admit that I do drop hints hoping I might one day get a kindle or comparative e-reader as a gift, but I think I may be a little too subtle with my hints.

What are your thoughts about self-publishing vs traditional publishing?

For a long time now, self-publishing has been a dirty word. Most competitions, literary agents, publishers and the like won't touch a self-published author. There is an 'us and them' mentality and words like 'real author' are tossed around when comparing self-published authors and traditionally published authors. I can personally see both sides of the argument and have experienced them both as I traditionally publish and self-publish.

The traditional publishing route can be tough to crack and getting a foot in the door is incredibly difficult to the point that it has become elitist. You have to be a best seller to get a publishing contract but you can't be a best seller without having a contract. I was lucky, almost a decade ago, a publishing house took a chance on me and published my first book. I was then asked by an international publishing company to write a book based on a crime story that I had featured on my website. From there, I have had many commissions to write many more. The traditional publishing route, once you are a part of it, is a great route as you get to focus on the most important part of an author's life and that is writing. You don't have to worry about finding editors, working on the artwork, creating book covers, writing press releases or any of the other fiddly bits that come with publishing a book. You get a publicist, who, if you're lucky like I have been, will get you some incredible interview opportunities that always translate into excellent book sales.

When it comes to self-publishing, you are essentially on your own to nut out every aspect of the book, from the writing to the artwork, cover design, editing and proofing. Unfortunately, many self-publishers do 'do-it-themselves' and this can often translate into a poor final product with poorly thought out storylines, unprofessional covers and terrible grammatical errors and it is those do-it-yourselfers who muddy the water and give self-publishing a bad name as they flood the market with poorly edited work, often en masse.

You can hire your own people to work on all of the steps to publishing, but it's an out of pocket expense that often does not translate in to sales. I have had so many self-publishing friends who have had problems with outsourcing the various steps to publication, from terrible book covers to shocking editing. That is not to say that everyone has problems as I have seen some incredible covers done by some very talented artists but if the artwork isn't good with a traditional publisher then they foot the bill and hire someone else, so that part of it comes down to financial burdens and risk on the self-publisher. So I must implore those on the self-publishing track to get recommendations for your cover artist, editor and proof-reader. There are many social media groups out there for writers, and most are extremely supportive. You will find the help you need and the services you require to make your manuscript great.

I think self-publishing is a fantastic route to take for those wanting to get their name out there, just do it the right way, find impartial people to read your story, ask for advice and take heed of what people tell you, get professional assistance, read up on ways to improve your craft. I had a friend from social media emailed me recently, she is starting out in writing and was reading another author's work—they had sent us all links to read his 'best seller' he boasted about his thousands of followers on the various social media platforms—she was concerned by the fact that his writing was terrible. She pointed out that it was poorly edited, with hundreds of typos and grammatical errors. I had a look myself, going to his link on Amazon. There I found dozens of 5 star reviews, claiming it to be the best book that the reviewer had ever read, but this was then counterbalanced by almost double the amount of reviews with 1 star, citing the terrible editing and proofing. This is an important lesson to learn when self-publishing. What reviews do think potential readers are going to care about? The gushing 5 star reviews—obviously written by bias friends or the honest reviews of strangers who will gladly point out the flaws? You can't take those reviews away, but you can ensure that they don't happen by making sure your book is polished. The more that self-publishers do this, the better the market will be and the more successful self-published authors will become. This is a market that has so much potential, if only every author took the time to make sure their work was of the highest standard.

How often do you write, and how do you find or make time to write?

How often do I write? Not often enough is always my answer. I do try and write every single day, but often life gets in the road, with full-time work, kids, university, household chores, shopping, social media, YouTube, TV etc . . . writing often gets pushed down as a lower priority. To counterbalance this and prevent it from becoming the norm, I like to make sure I always have a deadline, even if it is something I've set myself. I need to always have a project (or three) on the go, so I am inspired and motivated to write. A few times, I have become complacent and not done any writing for an extended period of time, or more to the point, not released the next book and I have had readers beg me to hurry up and finish 'the next book.' That is probably my greatest motivation to keep writing when I find my muse is snoozing on the job.

I often need to schedule writing time into my week, so I will let my family know that, for example, 'on Saturday morning I am going to set myself up on the deck and spend the day writing.' My family are fantastic moral support for my writing and they know when it's ok to interrupt and when it's not. If I am bashing away madly at the keyboard they know not to interrupt as I am 'in the zone' and it's best to leave me until I finish. If I am staring into space or holding my head in my hands then perhaps it's time to come and chat and help me reset. I also do an online writing session called 'Writing Race' run by the Australian Writer's Marketplace. Each Wednesday night a group of writers, from both novice and professional backgrounds, and together we chat online as well as bash out as much as we can in an hour. It is often a great time virtually surrounded by fellow authors and I often use it for free writing. The most I've ever written in that hour is 3,500 words, but often a good 1,000 words is achieved. You only compete against yourself, but it's a frantic hour of writing where I often find great inspiration. Several of my books and ongoing manuscripts have come from writing race ideas.

I think it is important to always have a pen and paper, tablet, something to write with. You never know when the muse might strike. As I mentioned earlier, I was at a swimming carnival when an entire storyline came to me out of nowhere. Had I not had a journal and pen with me, I may have lost the entire thing. You have no idea how much incidental writing you can fit into your day until you always carry the tools with you. I have even recorded ideas into my mobile phone when I have lacked writing materials. Which brings me to the point of always writing down ideas, never believe you will remember them later, you won't. I have a notepad full of paper napkins, sticky notes, torn off receipts, anything I had to use to write down an idea. From those ad-hoc notes, I have formed full stories, however I have many regrets about stories I had chosen to not write down, believing I'd remember it later.

Do you plan your whole book out in advance, or just let it flow? What does your writing process look like?

I plan books dependent on the subject. For my true crime work, it is often about choosing which cases I will write about, I choose a theme or type of crime and then work at it from there. In regards to my fiction work, each book has been different. For my Ritual series, I plot out the big picture stuff—the major story arcs the cover the entire series, then for each individual book I choose a type of ritualistic murder and then do as much research as I can before starting the manuscript. I have a vague idea of how the storyline will go, I usually decide how many victims there will be, what their names and demographics are, who the killer will be, how they will be caught and how we get to that point, then I just start writing. I have never written a book chronologically, that is, sequentially from Chapter 1. I will usually imagine a scene, often completely plotted out in my head and then I get it down on paper, it could be a bridging scene, the final death/arrest scene, how it links to another book, the big picture story arc, whatever comes to me, I write it. That chapter may never appear in the final book, but I write it down where I think it will fit in (this is where using style templates help with chapter numbers) and work with it in the storyline, often one chapter idea will lead to several others and so I get the ideas down under a chapter heading so I can revisit it later once I have thought it through.

The one storyline that came to me as a whole I thought would be the easiest to write but it fumbled along, and didn't quite work out as a novel so I tried it as a screenplay and it has come together well. That story I am writing chronologically as it is already completely plotted out, however writing something that is, in essence already written, albeit in my head, I am finding it rather mundane to write in comparison to writing in my usual frenetic style.

As you can see my writing processes differ from book to book and I think it is important to write however it feels comfortable, though some beg to differ, there are no hard or fast rules on how to write, just write, get it down on paper, your writing is guided by your own imagination, don't stop yourself from writing a scene that comes later in the story purely because you're not up to that part yet, you will lose incredible ideas if you prevent yourself from writing.

What's a typical working day like for you? When and where do you write?

My writing days often consist of fighting against procrastination and surfing the internet, both are the bane of every writer. It is so easy to be distracted by the world around you, but it is a skill to ignore it all and get on with your task at hand. My favorite place to write is the sunny deck outside my home. It has a massive 180-degree view and overlooks my yard and a massive area behind that contains walkways and sporting fields. I have the divine sounds of children playing, birds singing and people walking their dogs, I get to listen to the traffic beyond and the occasional busyness of my own little suburban street. I set myself up under the large umbrella that protects me and the computer from the sun and madly type away. My husband will bring me multiple cups of coffee whilst I continue to write. My children sometimes join me, on their own computers, writing their own stories or working on assignments.

I usually plan out what I want to achieve during the session, usually I set a minimum word count of around 5,000 words, writing up a certain scene, or perhaps starting something new. I will start out early in the morning and work hard at it, avoiding the internet as much as I can, and just get the ideas down into the draft, I never worry about typos, or grammatical errors, it's about getting as many of the ideas out of my head as possible. Sometime the original plan works, then sometimes I end up working on something completely different that flows easily. I never try to force anything or make it work, I'd rather let the ideas come. I keep a notebook beside me too, just in case another story idea comes to me that I need to save for later whilst working on the current project.

By the time lunchtime hits, my husband usually brings me a glass of wine to help me push further. I often write with a glass of wine (or two) beside my computer, I find it often calms me enough to help the creative juices flow. It has worked for many writers and I find it certainly works for me. I stop for breaks regularly to keep me fresh and rejuvenated, and to prevent the author slouch of leaning over the keyboard. If the weather doesn't allow me to sit outside, I will often curl up on my bed, surrounded by a dozen pillows—that are often covered in books and piles research and write on my laptop and still look out of my bedroom window and towards the fields beyond.

As a chronic insomniac I do some of my best work in the early hours of the morning. The house is silent, as is the world beyond my window and I enjoy using the ambience of darkness to work on a storyline that is not part of my current work in progress. I enjoy the quiet of the night and sometimes wake up only to write out an idea that has come to me during a dream. I think dreams are an important part of our imagination and I write many of them down to use in later storylines.

Do you ever get Writer's Block? If so, how do you deal with it?

I subscribe to the idea that there is no such thing as writer's block instead I believe a writer can have a problem when working on a current manuscript. For me, when this happens, I like to free write. Moving away from current projects and just writing anything that comes to me.

If I find that I am scared of a current work, where those doubts as a writer creep in and you question the quality of the work or the storyline, I will leave the project aside, open a new blank page and start writing. It doesn't have to go anywhere, it is about getting words on a page, having the ideas flow, until the muse wakes up and you find that you are able to go back to the 'real' project. Free writing for me is almost like therapy. I use it to get everything going, I might start by writing what is happening at that exact moment, the cat rubbing against my leg, the sounds of children playing outside, my response to a news story, it is almost like journaling but oftentimes it turns into a story that has gone on to be something bigger and better that the project that I was stuck on.

My novella, *The Cicadas Roar* is about two boys playing in a creek, yet the story began as a reflection on my childhood, playing at my grandparents' property. From those story beginnings, it became a what-if and then I was able to add sinister elements that ended up in the final story. I had started writing *the Cicadas Roar* when I found myself stuck on the ending to *Ritual: A Thousand Cuts,* I knew that trying to force something in *Ritual* was doing more harm than good, by moving away, I gave that story some distance, it allowed me to writing something different and new and so when I returned to *Ritual* I wrote with a fresh perspective and created a better storyline.

Do you read your own reviews? If so, how do you deal with bad reviews?

You must read reviews but you must do so with extreme caution, bad reviews can be debilitated to your artistic process, they can also destroy any confidence you have, but on the flipside they can be inspirational and give you the motivation to keep going. These days with the anonymity and immediacy of the internet it is very easy for someone to instantly give a good or bad review for a book, without ever considering how it will affect the author. Sometimes people forget that the author at the other end of their comments is real and the reviewer's words will either hurt or inspire the author. Some reviews are cruelly harsh, I once received a 1 start review for one of my books purely because the reader found 2 typos in a book that was over 85,000 words. That one hurt, and obviously even years later I still think about it, but honestly it is part and parcel of being a writer. You put your heart and soul into every word but there will still be people who will hate it. Remember that writing covers an infinite number of genres, we don't all like the same thing and so not everyone is going to like your story, but you just have to hope that if you've done everything well and that includes professional editing, cover artwork, and proofing then the bad reviews should be minimal.

Sometimes, reviews can actually be helpful even if they are negative. A reviewer might suggest having the book edited, or better cover art, or even an alternative storyline. Some reviews recommend changes to characters, claiming that they did not feel invested in the current characterizations. There are some really constructive reviewers out there that are even happy to have a look at your next work before it goes to print. You can gain some great insights from a bad review. Listen to your readers, you want them to keep coming back and if they give you a good suggestion on how that can be achieved, it is worthwhile listening.

My YouTube channel receives a lot of bad comments—not necessarily about me or my work, just that people like to troll and say awful things like "you should die." At first, I found it confronting. My heart hammered in my chest whenever I received new comments, I felt like I would vomit, it affected me quite badly. Reading awful comments like, "you should be raped,' was just so disgusting and uncalled for. I wanted to respond, I wanted to go tit-for-tat with the revolting keyboard warriors, instead I learnt that they are just moronic trolls with nothing better to do than post heinous comments on people's channels. I now just delete them, often flicking the bird at the screen as I do so, in a sign of my power over them. I don't give them air time, I don't reply, and I don't care about their revolting antics. Very few come back for seconds when they realize their comments have been deleted and no-one paid them any attention.

Other than reviews, do you hear from your readers very often? What kinds of things do they say?

Every so often someone will tag me in a photo or in on GoodReads, Facebook or Twitter, letting me know that they are reading one of my books. I find it strange to know when someone is reading my work, you always say a silent prayer, hoping that they love it. I often feel raw, exposed and terrified, it is bizarre, I want people to read my books but I am scared when they do, I think it comes down to the fact that we all just want to be adored.

With my true crime books, I get a lot of emails regarding similar cases to the ones I feature in my books. I often get requests to look at unsolved murders and create psychological profiles of possible killers. I can get dozens of requests a week, I used to work on every single one of them, but now I have to pick and choose as there are too many requests and only one of me. I do love hearing from readers and enjoy their comments, some just want to debrief after reading my work as it can get very dark at times and I am happy to talk people through their emotions and anything the books brought up for them.

Other comments I get are questions about new releases, what am I writing currently and I also receive a few requests for interviews. I do mentor many new writers, helping them with their own craft—which is one of the reasons I was happy to accept the offer to write for this book. I think it's important to share your knowledge and skills. If I can inspire one author to fight their self-doubts and strive to achieve their dreams, then I feel blessed to have been a part of their journey. I have helped several authors through to publication, gave honest advice regarding covers, storylines and characters and I think it's important to have this kind of relationship with other authors, both professional authors and new comers. I have my own mentors that guide me through my own publishing journey and I am grateful to them.

What are some ways in which you promote your books? What have you found most or least effective?

Every form of publicity is good for your book. With the release of each books I have done newspaper, radio and television interviews. Often it begins with a trickle, a small newspaper article and a radio interview, then the next call comes and the producer will say that they saw/heard me and would like to do an interview, the snowball affect usually lasts about 6–8 weeks after the release and I often do 3–4 interviews a week at the peak, sometimes they get me to write an article for them, others reproduce a chapter or snippet from my book.

The publicity trail is always the hardest part. I am not a naturally confident person—though some may beg to differ—I have terrible stage fright and so thinking about interviews terrifies me however I get through my interviews unscathed and I always get asked back when the next book is published. So that is a good thing.

Away from the professional publicity juggernaut, I publicize my books in my YouTube Videos, I also post links to new releases in the various Facebook groups I am in, as well as blog articles that then cross over to other social media boards. I also keep in contact with those that have interviewed me previously, just letting them know when the next book is coming out and give them my contact details should they want to interview me again. This professional relationship is important particularly with the larger audience platforms like national television programs.

In saying all of that, I don't feel that I am as successful as some authors are in their own publicity. I don't like to smother people with incessant self-promotion as I often find with some authors on social media. I do it only sporadically. I know that some create hype by posting advertisements continuously, but personally I don't like seeing the same thing over and over again, so I don't like to do that to others, possibly to my own detriment.

How easy or hard is it to make a living as an author?

I think my introduction proved that it's hard. I have released 16 books and still work full-time. I make money from writing, but not enough to pay home loans and school fees. Of course if I quit working full time and had more time to write, I might be able to earn enough to live. It is a vicious cycle and something I can't see me changing unless one of my books takes off and I can write full-time without having to also work.

Perhaps once my children are out of school and the house is paid off, I can 'retire' and spend the rest of my life completing those 50-odd unfinished manuscripts. It is certainly the plan and it will come to fruition one day, until then I will keep juggling all of my demands. I won't ever stop writing, I will always endeavor to make time for it, always writing down ideas and plotting out story ideas until my poor old brain gives up.

What advice would you give to someone aspiring to be an author?

I have peppered this entire Q&A with advice and tips for new authors, but I am glad to have a final platform to put it all together.

Jot down notes or write out fully formed ideas: Never let an idea slip through your fingers. That great storyline that popped into your head will not stay there for long. You need to write everything down.

Mix up your writing so you don't get stale working on one project: if your current project has come to a grinding halt, don't try and force it, work on something new, you will find once your creative juices are flowing that you will be able to return to your other project feeling refreshed and ready to attack it once more.

Set goals: From daily word counts, to pipeline dreams. Always set goals, challenge yourself, you have no idea where you writing will take you so reach for the stars.

Get something written each day and schedule time if you need to: Practice makes perfect and writing something each day helps hone your craft. Look back at your first piece of writing and look at something from today, we are always learning, never stop learning and never stop writing. If you think "I am too busy to write" then you need to schedule time in to get some writing done. It doesn't have to be a massive block of eight hours, half an hour here, an hour there will help you get into a routine.

There are no shortcuts: We all wish there were but there aren't any shortcuts to writing. You have to write the entire thing, you need to run through it multiple times, you need to be brave enough to delete massive slabs of writing if it just doesn't work. It takes time, it takes effort and most importantly it takes you to get it done.

Face your fears and put yourself out there: Writing is scary and writing is hard. No-one agonises over words like an author, but you cannot live in a safe zone. You need to push the boundaries of your skills and your ideas. Nothing ever comes from staying in your comfort zone.

"The first draft of anything is shit": Hemingway is apparently the author of this quote, it is something that all authors, particularly new authors, need to remember. Don't ever worry how that first draft looks. No-one will read it and no-one should read it. It is you telling yourself a story and then from there draft after draft you improve on it.

Write what you want to write, break the rules, make up your own rules: There are so many books on how to write a best seller, and many come with many rigid rules. I think this is detrimental to the artistic integrity of writing. Write what you want to write, don't let anyone tell you that you can't.

The editor is an author's best friend: Many writers fear editors, but it is imperative that you embrace them. They can help you shape your work. If you can find a good editor that will work with you and be a great platform of support for your work.

I thought I would end this with a few quotes that I keep on my desk to inspire me with my own work. I hope you find them as useful as I do:

*When your story is ready for rewrite, cut it to the bone. Get rid of every ounce of excess fat. This is going to hurt; revising a story down to the bare essentials is always a little like murdering children, but it must be done—*Stephen King

There is no such thing as good writing, only good rewriting— Robert Graves

*Be regular and orderly in your life, so that you may be violent and original in your work—*Gustave Flaubert

How can readers find out more about you?

Website: www.amandahoward.com.au

Facebook: www.facebook.com/amandahowardauthor/

Avril Sabine

Tell us about yourself and your books!

I'm an Australian author from Queensland and I write mostly young adult and children's speculative fiction. I've been writing since I was a young child and wanted to be a writer the moment I realized someone wrote the books I loved to read. I write in several genres including fantasy, urban fantasy, fairytales retold, romance, contemporaries, sci-fi, paranormal, thrillers, horror and western steampunk. Something most of my books have in common is that they're about strong characters or characters who find their strengths.

How long have you been writing, and how did you become involved in writing?

I've been writing nearly my entire life. When I first realized I wanted to be an author, I was so young I didn't know that's what those who wrote books were called. All I knew was I wanted to be the person who wrote the words in the books I loved to read. Even before that point I was mentally rewriting some of the books I read, creating the endings I preferred. At that stage I was mostly reading fairytales, which is what I was reading when I realized I wanted to be an author.

What are you working on at the moment?

I'm working on finalizing Realms Of The Fae 2: Marked By The Hunt which is due out March 2016, as well as doing some work on Demon Hunters 4: Premonition which will be published April 2016. I'm also organizing print editions for some of my books that are currently only available as ebooks while working on Rosie's Rangers 1: Justice, my western steampunk novel that will be available July 2016, as well as quite a few other projects. I always have several things on the go at once, alternating between them as I finish each stage. Some of the stories I'm currently working on won't be available until 2017. This isn't because it will take me that long to write each one, but because I set my manuscripts aside between each stage to gain some perspective before I work on the next stage.

Did you have any goals with writing, and if so, how well do you feel you've achieved them? What do you hope to achieve in the future?

I always have a plan for what I'm going to publish during the year as well as a fairly good idea of what will be coming out in the following year. This helps me keep track of what I need to work on and how long I have to finish it. I also have a whiteboard where I keep track of all my upcoming books and what stage they're at from first draft through to various edits, cover art and formatting. I plan to keep writing long into the future.

How long does it take you to write a book?

A first draft, on average, can take me anywhere from two to six weeks for a fifty to eighty-thousand-word story. Editing takes longer as the manuscript goes back and forth between myself and my editors. There are usually breaks between returning to each manuscript since I set them aside while working on other stories. The editing stage also depends on how many issues my editors find and whether they are large or small ones. Some stories also need more rounds of editing than others. There is no set time it takes to write a single book. In a year I tend to write at least twelve stories. A mixture of short stories, novellas and novels with the majority of them usually being novels.

What are the hardest parts of being an author for you?

There never seems to be enough hours in the day for all the stories I want to write. I have an extremely large file of ideas I've collected over the years and even if I never had another idea to add to them, and I continued to write a minimum of twelve stories a year, it would be impossible for me to turn every idea into a story. There are too many of them to manage that. Sometimes it's extremely difficult to choose which story to write next when I have so many ideas clamouring for my attention. Lack of time is definitely one of the hardest parts for me. I know many authors say editing is the hardest part, but I actually enjoy it since I learned how to edit. Some say first drafts are hard, but words tend to constantly flow for me. I also love dialogue, characters, settings, beginnings and endings. There is very little about writing that I don't love.

What do you enjoy most about being an author?

I love to tell stories. My head is always filled with characters demanding to have their stories told. I also love learning what will happen to each of my characters. Most times when I start a story I have no idea where it's going. Sometimes I have a vague idea of the ending, but no clear idea. It's fun to discover where a character is going and how they're getting there.

What books or authors have had the most influence on you as an author?

It was reading fairytales when I was a child, not yet old enough to go to school, that made me decide I wanted to be an author. I would have to say they've been my greatest influence since they were what helped me discover what I wanted to do. I've also continued to read them throughout my life, searching out both the original tales and their retellings.

What did you find most useful when you were learning to write and expanding your skills?

I found feedback the most useful when I was learning to write. Honest feedback that pointed out where I was going wrong and where I could improve. If you continue to make the same mistakes and no one points them out to you, then it's impossible to change them. Feedback was more valuable than any book I read on writing or that I read for enjoyment or understanding how other authors wrote them. It was also more valuable than talking to other writers about the techniques and craft of writing. But not all feedback is helpful. You need to seek feedback from those capable of not only providing constructive criticism, but who also have an understanding of story structure and the mechanics of writing. The first time I paid a reputable editor to look at one of my manuscripts I was amazed by how much I gained and learned. At the time it was money I struggled to scrape together, but it was worth every cent and my writing improved dramatically through understanding my strengths and weaknesses as a writer.

What author services do you pay for, as opposed to doing yourself? Things like cover design, formatting, editing, proofreading, etc.?

I don't design my covers or do all my own editing and I use Pressbooks templates to format my stories. I think it's important to leave the areas you're not skilled at to other people, rather than producing poor quality work. This is especially important as an independent author in a world where anyone can publish a story. If you expect readers to pay money for your work, you owe them the courtesy of publishing work of a professional standard. And even if you are an editor, you will still miss some of the problems in your own work. As the writer, you know what should be on the page and you know the background of the story and the characters. Some of these relevant details don't always make it to the page and can cause confusion for the reader. On the other hand, you don't want to overwhelm the reader with all the background information either.

What technology/services/programs do you use as an author? (email subscription services, Dragon software, editing software, etc.)

I have two laptops I use, one main one and the other for when I'm working between an edited word document of my manuscript and the original. I use Dragon Naturally Speaking and alternate between dictating and typing because I couldn't do either one continually with the amount of hours I spend working on my manuscripts. Dragon Naturally Speaking also allows me to do my housework while writing. Before I had the program, I often found myself dashing to the computer in the middle of different tasks, typing down the next line or two of the story I was currently working on. Now I dictate those sentences while I continue with whatever other task I'm working on. I also have a treadmill I regularly work at, setting my laptop up on a board on the handles as I can't sit for hours at a time. The other technology I use is the internet for research and Facebook as well as a website for keeping in touch with readers and keeping them up to date. I also have an email subscription service for those readers who prefer to receive my blog posts directly, hear news of what I'm working on before others do and be amongst some of the first to see covers of my upcoming books.

What are your thoughts about ebooks vs. print books?

I have both print and ebooks and love each equally for different reasons. I don't believe it has to be a one or the other choice. I tend to buy most of my books as ebooks and the ones I love and know I'll read again, I buy them in print too. Although I do tend to find it difficult to walk past a bookshop without wanting to go in and browse, often coming out with a book or two that I hadn't planned on buying. I have reached the stage where every new book I buy is a struggle to fit in my numerous and overcrowded bookcases. Ebook purchases are made with less concern about how I'll find space for them, so I tend to buy more of them.

What are your thoughts about self-publishing vs traditional publishing?

I chose to independently publish after receiving several offers from reputable traditional publishing houses, that wasn't in my best interests to sign and they weren't willing to negotiate the terms. I know there are positives and negatives to both, but at this point in time and with the offers I've received to date, being independently published suits me best. It is very much an individual choice and different styles of publishing will suit different types of people. There will also be some who will choose to be hybrid published. It is a question that has no single answer. What each writer wants from their publishing career can be different from that of other writers.

How often do you write, and how do you find or make time to write?

I make writing a priority. This often means I don't get a lot of sleep. Okay, I admit it, this means I rarely get much sleep. I write every day, or work on the edits my editors have sent me, sometimes writing as many as a hundred thousand words in a month. Words I'm happy with and that don't need to be deleted, only edited. I don't watch much television, I do read books though and I don't go out a lot. I prefer to spend time with my family when I'm not writing and often drag them along with me on some of my research expeditions.

Do you plan your whole book out in advance, or just let it flow? What does your writing process look like?

I don't outline. Sometimes I don't even know what the ending will be. Which is probably a big part of the reason why I manage to write so many words in a day. I want to find out what happens to the characters. I want to learn if they're all going to survive, if they'll reach their goals and how they'll achieve it. I'm like that with reading too. I can't put down a book that catches my attention and makes me want to know what will happen. It doesn't matter whether it's a book I'm writing or one I'm reading. And I don't start writing a book unless the initial idea captures my interest. For me it's more important to know what my characters want, what is stopping them from getting what they want and what they are willing to do and not do to attain their goal. Then I try and see if they can be pushed past their line in the sand.

What's a typical working day like for you? When and where do you write?

I have no typical workday. Sometimes I'll be wandering the house, dictating as I do the housework. Other times I'll be typing away on my laptop, a passenger in the car, often heading to a school for an author visit or to a workshop I'm running. Sometimes I'll be playing a computer game with the kids while I listen to Dragon Naturally Speaking read my manuscript back to me, making notes of things I notice needing to be fixed. Which usually involves me saying, "Watch my back for a minute." Then I stop Dragon from reading while I scribble my notes. Some days find us exploring places related to my stories like timber ship replicas, different towns, national parks and wetlands. There's also been hours spent at libraries and the national archives in the name of research. Not to mention the numerous phone calls to different places for strange details that I haven't been able to find online and long silences after I've asked my questions. I rarely have a typical day. The only typical part is that they usually involve writing or editing a lot of words and I don't manage to get a lot of sleep.

Do you ever get Writer's Block? If so, how do you deal with it?

I've never had writer's block, but then I've always chosen stories I'm fascinated by and want to find out what happens in the end. Writing for me is entertaining, even though it's a lot of hard work. It can keep me awake till all hours, invade my dreams with scenes for my stories and wake me up when I've barely gotten to sleep. There are also times when I feel completely drained and ready to collapse and then an idea strikes and I get my second wind, wired and ready to write for hours. I see stories everywhere I go, my mind is constantly filled with characters and my world is filled with words and books.

Do you read your own reviews? If so, how do you deal with bad reviews?

I rarely read my reviews. I actually tend to forget they exist. I think it's great that readers leave reviews to help other readers choose their next book, but if they want to make sure I read a particular review then they need to email me. And thankfully some of them do to tell me what they love about my books. I enjoy hearing from readers and knowing they've appreciated all the time I've spent on writing a particular story. I also know that not every book will suit every reader. Otherwise there'd be no need for so many different genres. Since I write in so many genres and have stories of varying lengths, I try to make it clear what genre each book is and give the word count so readers will know what to expect.

Other than reviews, do you hear from your readers very often? What kinds of things do they say?

I've had readers email me, write via snail mail or tell me in person how much they've enjoyed my books and what they'd loved to see me write next. Particularly which characters they want to hear more about. It's nice to know readers have enjoyed my books as much as I've enjoyed writing them. As a writer it's easy to become isolated from society since writing is such a solitary profession. It's nice to have those reminders that you do have connections with many other people, even if it's only through the pages of your books.

What are some ways in which you promote your books? What have you found most or least effective?

I've promoted my books in all the usual ways as well as some of the more unusual ones. The most effective would have to be when I've worn steampunk wings, from my upcoming novel Rosie's Rangers, to events. When people see the wings opening and closing it certainly catches their attention and has them asking questions about not only the wings, but also the book.

How easy or hard is it to make a living as an author?

It takes time to build a following and that length of time is different for every author. People also don't always realize how much work is involved in writing a book, even if you have editors, formatters and cover designers helping you. Nor is it something that if you do x, y and z you will reach your goal. As an author, the only thing you have complete control over is the quality of the books you write and how many you write each year.

What advice would you give to someone aspiring to be an author?

Read and write as much as possible. It might sound simple, but seeing how well written books are put together and studying how other authors keep you turning pages is a great way to learn. You also need to practice what you learn so writing regularly will help you improve. Getting feedback from a reputable and professional editor is also important so you can find the areas you need to work on and the skills you need to learn. And most importantly of all, if you want to be an author, don't give up. Persevere because dreams are meant to be lived.

How can readers find out more about you?

Website: www.avrilsabine.com/

Facebook: www.facebook.com/avril.sabine

C.L. Moore

Tell us about yourself and your books!

I work in the Spiritual industry and have been professionally reading Psychically for others from age 15. My visions and pre-cognitions are recorded as true and correct with a Detective in the NSW Police force from 2008 on. I am an Ordained Minister, a Teacher of Metaphysical subjects, Healer, Mystic, Candle Maker, Seamstress, a certified Dog Obedience Trainer and an Author of 3 Healing Systems, 23 publications and 7 Oracle card decks. My first Oracle card deck was featured in "That's Life" magazine Issue 13, 2014. Health and Harmony College has also published some of my work in their course 'Parapsychology' from 2010 on.

My books usually feature Paranormal content. They say write what you know. I definitely know weird, creepy and strange. History is my passion, so quite a lot of my books feature the past in some way, usually with a time travel element in them such as 'Rosalie' and 'The Treasure.' I also write Erotic Romance and my book 'Louisiana Heat' came 3rd in the Erotic category, Easychair Bookshop competition 2015.

How long have you been writing, and how did you become involved in writing?

As soon as I could write, I have been writing stories. The first time a teacher told me that he quite liked what I wrote, I was 8 years old and he featured it in a school paper. I won my first Literary award at age 10, blitzing the years above me for it. I won the Literary prize 2 years after as well. It came naturally, I couldn't contain the stories inside me, even then. Writing came as naturally to me as breathing.

What are you working on at the moment?

I always have several stories on the go and I write whichever one is speaking to me at the time. Currently, I am writing a western romance called 'All that Glitters,' and the 3rd book in my Guardians Trilogy called 'The Quest.'

Did you have any goals with writing, and if so, how well do you feel you've achieved them? What do you hope to achieve in the future?

I always strive to do better than my last book. Therefore, I feel that I will always need to keep achieving and completing that next book and the ones after it. My goals are to be as good as Stephen King and to hopefully have my books turned into movies.

How long does it take you to write a book?

I have written a book in 3 weeks, others take 6 months. 'The Treasure' took me approximately 2 years to write. Mainly due to the sheer scale of research I needed to do.

What are the hardest parts of being an author for you?

Honestly, I don't find anything hard about being an author. I absolutely love every minute of what I do.

What do you enjoy most about being an author?

I love the process of the characters coming alive and telling me their story. I love when I finish writing and can sit back and say, 'awesome, only another 20 to go.' The moment that I receive my completed and published book into my hands never gets old and is extremely satisfying.

What books or authors have had the most influence on you as an author?

There are so many great writers out there. My favorite author is Stephen King. I think his use of words and description is clever. Australian novelist, Judy Nunn, is also a favorite.

What did you find most useful when you were learning to write and expanding your skills?

Reading lots of books by a lot of different authors. Seeing how others described scenes, dialogue between people and how they could make you feel as though I was there in the story with the characters.

What author services do you pay for, as opposed to doing yourself? Things like cover design, formatting, editing, proofreading, etc.?

Editing, proofreading, some cover designs.

What technology/services/programs do you use as an author? (email subscription services, Dragon software, editing software, etc.)

I only use Word and Illustrator.

What are your thoughts about ebooks vs. print books?

Personally, I prefer print books. There is nothing that compares to holding a book in your hands and smelling the paper, ink and yes, sometimes dust!

What are your thoughts about self-publishing vs traditional publishing?

I have been with a publisher and they wanted to change my vision of the book, mainly creative differences regarding formatting and cover design. I didn't feel that I earned enough money for the amount of books sold. I stepped away from them and have been happy with how my books reflect my ideas and vision. I also receive greater royalty payments now I self-publish.

How often do you write, and how do you find or make time to write?

I write every day without fail. It may be only half an hour, but I make sure I get something down every day. On a productive day, I have written for 14 hours straight. I find I'm at my most creative in the wee small hours. If I'm on a roll, I just keep going and woe betide anyone who disturbs me. I'm usually so engrossed in what I'm doing that I don't actually hear people talking to me.

Do you plan your whole book out in advance, or just let it flow? What does your writing process look like?

I usually have an idea where I would like the book go, but I prefer it to be an organic process. If I am surprised at twists and turns in my books, then I'm sure my readers will be the same. I do, however, like to make sure that it all ties in and that there are no loose ends when it comes to a close.

What's a typical working day like for you? When and where do you write?

I usually write in the lounge room surrounded by all the noise. I find it hard to concentrate when it's dead quiet. Even early in the morning I have the radio or TV on for that background noise. I don't have a set routine; I write when the inspiration takes me. In saying that, I have tapped away on my phone note app when I've been in the doctor's, or on the train and waiting to pick up my grandchildren from school. I try and keep a small notebook in my bag as well.

Do you ever get Writer's Block? If so, how do you deal with it?

I don't usually suffer from the dreaded writer's block. If I find I'm not connecting to my work in progress, I go to another work in progress and work on that. I have plenty of them to always be busy. If one lot of characters aren't talking, then there is at least 20 more happy to chat.

Do you read your own reviews? If so, how do you deal with bad reviews?

Sometimes I do, other times I don't. I don't go looking for reviews, I usually stumble across them days after they have been made. They aren't something I worry about; I have other things occupying me. Quite often readers tell me what they think as many don't have Goodreads or Amazon and buy the books directly from me.

Other than reviews, do you hear from your readers very often? What kinds of things do they say?

Yes, I hear from readers quite often. They usually corner me when I'm out and tell me in a rather loud voice everything they love about my books. That in turn makes other people curious to see what is so great. I've sold quite a few books this way! The readers always love the twists and turns in my books. I have been berated for killing off favorite characters. Once I had a reader text me and say that they were quite angry with me because I killed off the character they loved. Usually though, people are very excited to tell me how much they loved reading my books and ask when the next one will be coming out.

What are some ways in which you promote your books? What have you found most or least effective?

As I do a lot of events Psychic reading, I always take my books and have them on my table. I have also had stalls at events selling them which has been very successful. People are always fascinated to meet a bona fide Author. At these events I have also been asked to speak about writing and being an Author. To be honest, I find selling and promoting my books like this is way more effective than Facebook promoting. Word of mouth is also very effective for me as I meet a lot of people at different events who sing my praises to their colleagues, friends and family.

How easy or hard is it to make a living as an author?

It is hard work. When I'm not writing, I'm promoting in one way or another.

What advice would you give to someone aspiring to be an author?

Write from the heart. Listen to your editor. Always strive to improve your craft.

How can readers find out more about you?

Website: www.authorclmoore.com

Facebook: www.facebook.com/AuthorCLMoore

Court LeRoy

Tell us about yourself and your books!

My name is Courtney LeRoy (I go by Court because I'm sick of people thinking I'm a chick).

Anywho, I'm a business major at Utah Valley University and plan on having a strong career in hospitality. I believe serving others is the best way to have a fulfilling life, so I'm pursing just that.

With that being said, I actually write books based on spirituality and poetry. I believe art is woven into everything we do and I incorporate these values even in the business world. Your art can be anything from building a car to painting a mural. All that is required is passion, intelligence, and love. Through these values you'll build a connection the same way Michelangelo did with the Sistine Chapel, in whatever medium you choose.

How long have you been writing, and how did you become involved in writing?

I've been writing since probably 2nd grade. When I was in 3rd grade I won 3 different essay/poetry contests and felt a divine connection with words.

This may sound weird, but I decided to write books because of screenwriters. I was a film major for 3 years and love working on a set. I also always found myself in the writing room constantly. I may not be the best writer but hopefully my love for the craft shines through my imperfections.

What are you working on at the moment?

Since I've self-published, I've had an amazing amount of people ask me how I did so. I love helping out others so I decided to write a very brief e-book that will not only walk you through the steps I personally use to publish books quickly and professionally, but also help with some common marketing mistakes. I will list the exact illustrators, editors, etc. I use. . . . no fooling around.

I want to make my e-book super condensed . . . like a 20 minute read.

I will also do a video for each chapter you can find on my website. I want to give the very best tools I know of to my friends, family, and random readers without any bullshit (sorry for cursing).

Did you have any goals with writing, and if so, how well do you feel you've achieved them? What do you hope to achieve in the future?

I would like to achieve a decent passive income from my writings.

In contrast to that last sentence, the most important thing to me is that I have readers who really connect with my writings. Even if I only have 4 people who love the words I put down, that'll be enough.

It's hard at this time to lay out my definition of success as far as writing because I'm still a full-time student with a full-time job. If you ask me after I graduate, I'd have a completely different response.

How long does it take you to write a book?

It depends on the content. If I'm writing a non-fiction book, then I write it extremely quick. I'm a very organized person who knows how to lay out ideas accurately and precise (according to my own standards). Granted, I'll still need my work edited a few times, but I can put everything on paper within a week . . . even longer pieces.

Fiction on the other hand can hang me up, which is probably a horrible writing habit. I need to find perfection on how to twist a metaphor or use an analogy for a situation and it can be maddening. The only honest I answer I can give to this question is indefinitely when it comes to fiction.

That's just for myself, if I didn't care so much about my fiction, I could write a book easily write the general outline within a month. I would then send it to an editor and take another 2 weeks to reprise.

What are the hardest parts of being an author for you?

Easily marketing.

I have creativity coming out my butt and there's a massive part of myself that doesn't care about monetary income. Because of this mindset, I often have no desire to market. This in turn makes me feel horrible if sales are down. I really need to be able to tackle marketing the same way a painter sees an empty canvas so it's more enjoyable.

What do you enjoy most about being an author?

When you love anything in life, you feel free and liberated when you're able to be yourself and find a connection with the world through some type of medium. This could be through your working or even just interacting with other human beings.

For me, words are my art. Being an author is like being a self-aware sunflower. Often I try to live to show the world there is still beauty to behold in our existence. However, I also love to be appreciated for the beauty I attempt to bring onto the world. When I find another who understands that concept which I try to capture through my writings, I feel complete and successful as an author.

What books or authors have had the most influence on you as an author?

For a business major this may sound random but philosophers have had the biggest impact on my writings. Specifically, Alan Watts.

I personally try to make my life both artistic and intelligent. I believe we live in a world broken into 2 realms: the business world and the perception world. Through this yin and yang, we have life as we know it.

The business world is very calculated, square, solid, mathematical and measureable. It is the reason we have a written language and how we continue to evolve as a whole.

The perception comes from the individual. Picture a wooden table. The business world has defined it as chestnut brown. However, my perception world tells me it's a dark brown which reminds me of my grandmother cooking Sunday meals for the family.

Both are true in their own right and only when we combine the two can we master art. It's the same for any medium. A painter must know how to properly mix his paint on his palette before he can illustrate his emotions on the canvas.

Alan Watt's has taught me how (or at least how to try) to do so through my writing.

Check out his book, The Book: On the Taboo Against Knowing Who You. It'll change your life.

What did you find most useful when you were learning to write and expanding your skills?

Udemy.com

I've always been decent with writing but learning to be an author is something completely different. You need advice from other authors who are in similar situations as yourself.

I'm a student with limited time and wanted to keep all the rights to my books. I was able to find courses aimed exactly at my situation easily on Udemy.com from other self-published authors who are passionate about helping others. It has been the greatest resource I could recommend. I also believe that the more you learn about your craft, the more you can accomplish. It's like walking into a war . . . you'd want the most ammunition as possible right?

What author services do you pay for, as opposed to doing yourself? Things like cover design, formatting, editing, proofreading, etc.?

I personally outsource for 2 things: My covers and editing.

I am horrible when it comes to anything that is visual. I have found that there are amazing cover artists for that will do a perfect job for $20. It's hard to logic out that I need to learn a new skill when I can find a master of multimedia at such a reasonable price.

The other is obvious. I have 2 different editors I pay and love. I believe writing is something that needs a few different eyes to make sure that it's not only grammatically correct, but that it flows and connects well. Any author can miss out on the basics, all authors need a backup. Hire a good editor (or two).

What technology/services/programs do you use as an author? (email subscription services, Dragon software, editing software, etc.)

This will be a short answer but I only use Wix.com and Word.

Wix.com is a platform to help me build my website and I love Word.

What are your thoughts about ebooks vs. print books?

I personally don't have a preference but sales wise, e-books are surpassing printed books. So that's something to take into consideration.

But I'm also not a book snob, I don't really care if my Kindle has that "new books smell."

What are your thoughts about self-publishing vs traditional publishing?

It just depends on what type of author you are and what your goals are.

Being a self-published author is really profitable and allows you to have all the freedom in the world. The crappy side of this is that you have to do everything yourself, which can be daunting.

If you do choose to go the traditional publishing route just do your research. There are a lot of new publishing company's out there that will ask for 60% of your sales and you'll only receive a few thousand sales through them. Not really worth it. But if you can get picked up by a major publisher, well then it's better to have a smaller piece of a million-dollar pie than the whole thing if it's only worth $10.

How often do you write, and how do you find or make time to write?

I feel like a lot of authors struggle to find time to write. I honestly never really have trouble finding time to write, I just write when I want to. The reason why this works for myself is because I love writing. It's really the only way for me to express myself at this time in my life. If my life feels a bit off, it's probably because I haven't done any writing as of late.

I usually write at least every other day (or work on formatting or ideas).

Do you plan your whole book out in advance, or just let it flow? What does your writing process look like?

I usually think out the whole book in my head for weeks before I begin to write. Once I get an idea of something I want to write about, my mind is possessed by it. Even at work or school, I'm still molding the idea and trying to make it perfect. Once I feel as though I have the concept sculpted in my mind, I begin to write and words flow incredibly smooth.

Even though I can push out a rough draft fairly quick, I do many self-edits before I actually pay for an editor. I find that my writings are massively improved after probably 2 or 3 self-edits.

What's a typical working day like for you? When and where do you write?

Healthy energy drinks, a white board, playing the same song on repeat, pen with pad, and my home desktop.

I never personally understood why people need to leave their house to write. I mean, I sort of get it (insert inappropriate joke about not being able to look at porn in a café) but I personally love my work station in my room.

Once I start writing I can't stop. Because of this, I have to be careful not to start late because last time I started at 11:00 P.M. I didn't stop until 5:00 A.M. I'm very off and on with my writing. Sometimes I won't write for a week but then my output will be a month's worth of work within one night.

Do you ever get Writer's Block? If so, how do you deal with it?

Sometimes I don't know the best way to say something but besides that, I honestly don't really get writers block. I think it's because I premeditate on my writing beforehand so much that I already know what's going to come out. I just sometimes struggle with *how* it should come out.

I also only write about things I love and care about. I'm not in a position in life where I feel obligated to write, so it's easy and fun for me, not work.

Do you read your own reviews? If so, how do you deal with bad reviews?

I generally only read the bad reviews so I can learn how to improve my work. If I have spare time I'll read my good reviews, but as long as someone enjoys my writing, I'm happy. I'm not really in this business for self-glorification (or really even money). My life is fulfilled through my work, not really what the world thinks about it.

However, usually negative reviews will give you feedback as to why they didn't like your work and you can use that information to better yourself, which is why I value negative reviews much more than positive ones.

Other than reviews, do you hear from your readers very often? What kinds of things do they say?

I have a lot of personal contact with people who read my stuff and usually they only say nice things. It's probably because they know me as a person and don't want to make me feel bad. Maybe my whole writing career is based off of my personality in real life . . .

I've also been teaching a lot of people how to self-publish a lot more lately than actually writing, and anytime you teach someone a new skill, they're always grateful. But yea, almost everyone is very happy and has good things to say.

What are some ways in which you promote your books? What have you found most or least effective?

The more time I spend learning how to be a successful author the more I can see the path I want to take.

I've found that I acquire new customers very easily by being very personal with them. The easiest way for this to happen is for me to teach them a new skill (usually for free, but that will be changing very soon).

I think no matter what you niche is, you should always be giving back. The great thing about giving back is that if you market it and do it correctly, you'll gain more than you give.

So that would be my advice, look within yourself and see what you can teach others and market it correctly.

How easy or hard is it to make a living as an author?

Being an author is a game of time in this day and age. Like anything else is life, you could hit the jackpot but you're most likely will need to grind your way to a comfortable place. However, it can be very lucrative and easy to have a passive income once done correctly.

What advice would you give to someone aspiring to be an author?

Learn about your new career as much as possible. You'll save so much money this way in the long run and seem professional among your peers. Learn how to format, edit, and self-publish. It's easy and you can even charge others when you teach them how to do it.

Only do things you love. When you work on something you love, it's easy. Make life easy.

Work around professionals in your field. You'll learn an amazing amount of information from them for free and have great contacts.

Make everything look professional. Even if you suck at writing, if you make it look professional, people will still buy it.

Then keep learning.

How can readers find out more about you?

Website: www.Poetrywithlove.com

Facebook: www.facebook.com/court.leroy

D.L. Richardson

Tell us about yourself and your books!

I started writing when my reading influences were Stephen King, Dean Koontz, and Anne Rice. So a few of my earlier works were horror, supernatural, psych thrillers. But, at the time, horror was the only genre and it was shelved in basements of bookstores so I wondered if I should write something else. And so I did for a while, I had some interest in women's fiction but it never got published. And then I decided to return to writing what I love to read. I also decided to write young adult fiction because a lot of my ideas weren't working as adult fiction. I'd write the opening chapter and then get stuck. The writing flowed when I changed the age of my characters, and *The Bird With The Broken Wing* got picked up by a small press publisher. I wrote two more YA novels, *Feedback* and *Little Red Gem.*

I try not to write the usual trope, I add as much realism as I can to my work so it rings true and connect with readers. My work also tends to feature redemption or second chances as the theme.

How long have you been writing, and how did you become involved in writing?

I wrote many first chapters about supernatural creatures until I finally completed my first horror novel in 1996. I showed it to two people who both enjoyed it, but it was horribly written and sat in a drawer for millions of years until a few years ago I turned it into a novella. I'm a nostalgic writer. I have kept every first chapter, partial or completed manuscript either in hard copy or digital copy. You never know when one of these can become an idea for something else. *Little Red Gem* was an idea from 10 years earlier that never felt ready to write until I turned it into a YA book. Writing isn't something I actively become involved in. I used to play in a band and I wrote all the lyrics. So obviously I like to express myself with words. I just wrote whatever came into my head. But I had no idea what to do afterward. Everything got printed out and shoved into a box until many years later when I joined the NSW Writers Centre and went to a few writing workshops, and I volunteered at a writer's convention and met other writers. Just being in the same room as a bunch of writers was like being in Heaven. It also made me realize that I had so much to learn.

What are you working on at the moment?

I'm working on a science-fiction novel about a future world where the world is divided in two halves of equal powers and an incident happens that risks the lives of millions of people living in one of the countries. It's about how far people will turn a blind eye in exchange for the perception of utopia, and how over regulation led to these population living under total control. And the cover up that happens to keep this perception of world peace in place. It's taken me a few years to write this. I worked on one character's side of the story first. Then I wrote another novel about players who get trapped in a virtual game. I returned to my sci-fi story and wrote the other character's story. Now I'm putting it together and adding in the science. Because it has no supernatural elements, I'm finding it harder to write. I can't just *make things up*. It's a rewarding challenge but I believe this will be the type of story that will linger in people's minds.

Did you have any goals with writing, and if so, how well do you feel you've achieved them? What do you hope to achieve in the future?

I've had dozens of goals over the years. A goal to get a short story published. A goal to write a novel. A goal to get a novel published. A goal to get another novel published. I set myself goals every year. Last year's goal was to conduct writing workshops and be a guest on a panel for Conflux, the speculative fiction convention based in Canberra, Australia. I achieved that goal and was listed on thirteen panels, but unfortunately I had to pull out after day one when my husband had a motorbike accident.

My goal for the next few years is to get a mainstream publisher and to write two novels a year.

How long does it take you to write a book?

It takes about twelve months to write a 105,000-word novel. It took two years each for the first few books. I'd like to say that the more you write the faster you get, but I went from working full time to work part time and I believe the more *time* you have the faster you get. Writing while working full time is a struggle. My goal is to get this time down to six months, so I can write two books a year. To do that I would need to be a full time writer, which currently I am not.

What are the hardest parts of being an author for you?

The hardest part at the moment is that I feel like I'm sitting in a canoe without an oar in a lake with no current and I'm using a tennis racket to pull myself to a river bank. Worse, I'm going to a river bank that is overcrowded and nothing I do is attracting anyone's attention. This stems from the sad fact that there are more writers than there are readers. I'm wracking my brain trying to come up with something else that I feel so passionate about that I could do. I'm sure other writers feel the same. We love what we do, but it's very difficult to get the attention of the readers. On the flip side, I think this determination to succeed makes me want to be a better writer.

What do you enjoy most about being an author?

While I love the writing process, and being able to work in my pajamas, what I love the most is the joy in people's voices or on their faces when they have read one of my books and loved it. Readers are waiting for my next book, and some who've read a snippet of my current book are dying to see it finished so they can read it. That is what I'm enjoying most at the moment.

What books or authors have had the most influence on you as an author?

When I started writing, my reading influences were Dean Koontz, Anne Rice, and Stephen king. They are the reason I write speculative fiction. They're the reason I watch X-Files and Star Trek. The love of speculative fiction no doubt sprung from my love of fairy tales as a child. The Brothers Grimm are awesome. I guess you could say that Jacob and Wilhelm Grimm influenced me to like Dean Koontz, Anne Rice, and Stephen King.

What did you find most useful when you were learning to write and expanding your skills?

I began writing before the internet so I relied on published books. I studied how great writers crafted their dialogue, their sentences, their descriptions, their chapter openings and closing. Then I joined a writers group and started taking a few courses. Writing courses are helpful because they conducted in an environment with other writers so you learn that you are not alone on this quest. The other thing I find most useful is that only other writers 'get' what you want to do. So if you're feeling as if nobody cares about your life's goal, it could be that you need to be amongst writers.

What author services do you pay for, as opposed to doing yourself? Things like cover design, formatting, editing, proofreading, etc.?

The only thing I've paid for what an appraisal by an agent, many years ago. She gave me a critique of a novel for $150 with the disclaimer that if she liked the book and went on to represent it then the money would be refunded. She didn't take it on but she did provide encouraging feedback and helpful critique. That book was not published, and I put it aside in a drawer and probably won't do anything with it because it was a women's fiction novel that I flirted with writing for a while. I am a whizz on computers and design so I don't need to pay anyone to format, I dabbled with book covers simply because I didn't like anything and if I was going to do it, I might as well do it all. And I've gotten much better at cover design. Bottom line, I'd pay someone to do something that I couldn't do myself or didn't like doing myself, and the great thing is that I love every aspect of writing.

What technology/services/programs do you use as an author? (email subscription services, Dragon software, editing software, etc.)

Rafflecopter for giveaways. Mail Chimp for newsletters. I use Microsoft Word for writing. Serif DrawPlus for cover artwork and promotional banners.

What are your thoughts about ebooks vs. print books?

I don't see a battle between the two mediums. It's like saying my microwave oven will replace my standard oven. Westerners are a bit spoiled for choice, we don't have just one of anything anymore. We tend to have both. A shower *and* a bath. A car *and* a bike. A digital camera *and* a sketchpad. A CD player *and* a iPod. So why not a Kindle *and* a shelf full of books. I enjoy a good story either way.

What are your thoughts about self-publishing vs traditional publishing?

My favorite quote on self-publishing is this: "The good thing about self-publishing is that anyone can do it. The bad thing about self-publishing is that anyone can do it." I've read rubbish that's been published by a major publisher and by a huge name author, and I've read rubbish via self-publishing channels. One major plus for traditional publishing is that they provide the writer with in-house editors, professional cover designers, and sometimes mass distribution. Provided the self-published author is serious about editing and cover design, then there's no reason they shouldn't do it. I was a hybrid for a while, two novels were with a publisher and one was self-published, but the publisher dropped all their young adult titles and so the rights reverted back to me. I was glad I'd had the experience editing and cover design to provide a benchmark for me to venture out on my own.

How often do you write, and how do you find or make time to write?

I write most days unless I'm struck with a migraine, the flu, or crashed my bicycle and cracked a rib. About once a month I'll give myself a day off, but I'm usually itching to get back into writing. As for making time to write, I'll write a few pages before work while sipping my coffee. I'll write a few pages after work. My deadline at night for writing is 9.30pm. On weekends I'll do chores around the house until lunch time, have lunch, then I'll spend the afternoon writing, before I stop for dinner. One thing I learned to accept was that I can't write a novel in one sitting. As long as you chip away it each day, it will get completed, but I'll give myself deadlines for first draft to be finished, then edits. Okay, the moral here is that you need to be somewhat self-disciplined or you won't find or make time to write.

Do you plan your whole book out in advance, or just let it flow? What does your writing process look like?

I am a plotter. I will always have an idea of where it's going, then I write brief chapter outlines noting what part of the back story I want added in, and then I fill in the blanks. I also write a 300-word summary so I know when I'm drifting off the plot line. On the days where I simply do not feel like writing, I will do research for the novel. All novels need research to add credibility to the story, and I make notes in books. First draft is just 'get it written down' with no fancy descriptions or dialogue. Then I'll do a range of edits to develop character arc, look at structure, look at voice, dialogue etc. Each morning while I walk the dog, I'm always mulling over the manuscript, so of course I come up with scenes or dialogue to add. These I make note of to add into the book later. Then I tick them off when I'm doing the edits to make sure I included them, if they're still worthy. I'll block out 3 days to do a final read over, usually at a nice quiet 'writer retreaty' place with limited internet access.

What's a typical working day like for you? When and where do you write?

I still work a part time job, but on my writing days, I do chores around the house, break for lunch, then I'll write usually from 1pm to 6pm. I write in my office. Yes, the internet is a huge distraction so sometimes I'll take the laptop (because I haven't been able to get the wireless function to connect properly) and I'll work on the laptop away from the computer. When I've done most of the edits I will take myself away someone quiet and tranquil for a few days to do the final read through. Then I'll get up at 8am and read over the manuscript till I fall asleep at night, and do this for a few days so I don't lose any part of the timeline. Sometimes I'll send the husband away to do the final read at home, but I usually find I get too distracted with Netflix or feel inclined to get out of the house and I tell myself to book a retreat next time.

Do you ever get Writer's Block? If so, how do you deal with it?

I have no problems coming up with ideas. Sometimes a story doesn't want to come out of my head, and I just push through until it does. Even if the first draft is dull and lifeless, keep writing because the magic happens in edits and sometimes the real beauty of the story isn't revealed until final round of edits. Other times I will change the age of the characters or the gender and this can work wonders in having all the pieces fall into place.

Do you read your own reviews? If so, how do you deal with bad reviews?

Yes, I read them. It's nice to get validation. It's especially nice to read a review where the person 'gets' what I'm trying to convey or connects with the character. But I will keep writing whether or not I get good reviews or bad reviews so they are not the stick by which I measure my success. As for bad reviews, the only way to deal with bad reviews is to *not* deal with bad reviews. Leave them alone. Accept that not everyone will like everything you write.

Other than reviews, do you hear from your readers very often?
What kinds of things do they say?

It doesn't happen daily or even weekly, but it does happen. One readers emailed me directly to tell me he loved *Poison In The Pond* because he could read it during his lunch break. People have posted messages on Facebook. One group of school girls sent me a photo of them holding up bookmarks I'd posted to them. Another reader posted a photo of my book covers on her Kindle. One teenager emailed me to say *The Bird With The Broken Wing* was her favourite book of all time. I loved reading that email. I've had one person ask that if I ever got to the UK could I stop by her son's school. I'd love to, but I don't see myself going to the UK anytime soon.

What are some ways in which you promote your books? What
have you found most or least effective?

What works for me: Facebook ads have been okay, but I boost posts or post ads mainly to get 'likes' rather than to sell books. Twitter is a good way to connect with readers. I have found that trying to sell books on social media is akin to committing virtual suicide, there are too many people shoving book covers in people's faces with "BUYME" plastered all over them. Readers are turning away from writers who do this. Blog tours work to promote books, though these are a lot of work because you write a lot of interviews and guest posts and there's no guarantee anyone is reading them. They do cost but the host site sources the blogs for you. I was surprised to open up an Google page I hadn't touched in ears to find out that the site had over 140,000 views and I'd done nothing to get these views. When you see that kind of statistic you have to wonder if promotion works. I've paid for ads on well respected review sites and these got a spike in sales. I send out newsletters to readers that I've gathered over the years. Giveaways via Rafflecopter seem to work. My author blog posts generate a decent number of views.

What didn't work for me: I've paid for blog ads and they got traffic but they were of little use when all you could do was slap a cover on the blog with a maximum of 25 characters to interest a reader. Any promotion where I just slap a cover on a site doesn't work. The number one rule for advertising is to give a reason to buy and a great cover amongst a sea of other great covers is not enough of a reason. Where I can add more text and talk to an audience is where I get a better response.

How easy or hard is it to make a living as an author?

Very hard.

What advice would you give to someone aspiring to be an author?

My number one piece of advice is to always remind yourself that nobody asked you to do this. Keep smiling and keep writing. That's all you can do. If you're not smiling, why do it?

How can readers find out more about you?

Website: www.dlrichardson.com

Facebook:

www.facebook.com/pages/D-L-Richardson/223019004391960

Dave Chesson

Tell us about yourself and your books!

I'm Dave Chesson, a father of three and husband to one . . . haha, yup. I'm still in the military so my online marketing and book publishing is done when the kids and family are sleeping.

I like Pina coladas, long walks in the rain and peanut butter. When I'm not corralling my three rambunctious children, I'm usually reading a sci-fi book, or working on my next project. Oh, and I'm definitely a movie nut.

My books are based on market needs. I'm not a fan of guessing whether or not my books will be of interest or succeed on Amazon, so I work hard to validate the idea before I even start writing. Because of this, I actually use a different pen name for each.

How long have you been writing, and how did you become involved in writing?

I've been writing online for over 3.5 years, but only got started in KDP publishing 2.5 years ago. When I started working online, I specialized in niche marketing and search engine optimization. After ranking lots of websites #1 on google for great search terms, I was disappointed to find that I wasn't making that much on just advertisement . . . I needed to sell my own product.

And that become my self-published books.

What are you working on at the moment?

I'm currently bottling up all that awesome niche research, kindle keyword search magic and bestselling idea generation magic into a set of software called Kindle Samurai.

Basically this bad boy will help authors to find bestselling topics and opportunities and help them validate their ideas before they begin the long process of publishing a book.

Did you have any goals with writing, and if so, how well do you feel you've achieved them? What do you hope to achieve in the future?

My goal is to create evergreen books. I don't want to spend time publishing something that makes money for only a couple of months but something that consistently brings in a steady income and always stays relevant.

How long does it take you to write a book?

Haha . . . too long. The idea validation process takes me a long time but thanks to Kindle Rocket, that won't be the case.

Once I have a validated idea that has a high chance of being a consistent bestseller, I immediate get to work conducting research . . . a LOT of research. In truth, I really take my time to put together the best book I can.

What are the hardest parts of being an author for you?

Writing . . . haha, I know, the definition of an author is someone who writes . . . go figure. But I'm not a natural or gifted writer—my high school English teacher could tell you that. In truth, my grasp of English grammar is poor and I struggle to be concise. This causes me to spend more time in writing and much more money in a good editor.

What do you enjoy most about being an author?

Seeing that something I wrote has been read by hundreds of thousands. That may sound like bragging, but it serious means a lot to know that people value and enjoy what you've created.

What books or authors have had the most influence on you as an author?

John C. Maxwell . . . not because his laws or management practice was excellent, but because he could take such boring information and weave incredible stories that make you enjoy every second of it. His style of storytelling in non-fiction is something I try to emulate in my books.

What did you find most useful when you were learning to write and expanding your skills?

Just to keep writing. I tried reading books and studying, however, I found that as I wrote more and more, I developed my own voice and crafted ways to express my thoughts better. Practice makes perfect, right?

What author services do you pay for, as opposed to doing yourself? Things like cover design, formatting, editing, proofreading, etc.?

I absolutely need a professional editor and proofreaders and I won't skimp on this either. However, I prefer to use a professional formatter because it's not my specialty and I don't enjoy it. I do make my own covers. I do this myself because I enjoy it and am very good at it.

What technology/services/programs do you use as an author? (email subscription services, Dragon software, editing software, etc.)

Over the past 4 years, I have spent over $15,000 in training, services, software and tools for my writing craft. About 80% of that was a complete waste. But that 20% has been really special.

I list the stuff that made the cut here:

www.kindlepreneur.com/top-tools-and-services-for-authors-writers-self-publishers/

What are your thoughts about ebooks vs. print books?

I personally love reading ebooks because I like to carry my Kindle with me wherever I go and whip it out when I have to wait in line or even go to the bathroom. However, if I need to study the material, then I totally prefer a print book. They are easier to mark up, and add sticky notes. I know ebooks can do this too, but I still prefer to study a print book over a ebook.

What are your thoughts about self-publishing vs traditional publishing?

Regardless as to whether or not you get published or are self-published, you'll need to know how to market yourself. Unless you are super famous or have the greatest book they have ever read, a publisher will not help you . . . they'll only demand from you and drop you if you don't come through. Might as well get a better percentage if you are going to have to do all the marketing yourself, right?

How often do you write, and how do you find or make time to write?

I write every morning between 4–6am. During that time, I will shut off email and social media so that they won't distract me.

Do you plan your whole book out in advance, or just let it flow? What does your writing process look like?

A mess . . . that's what it looks like. A wonderful structured mess. I plan out chapters and fill in the blanks with notes and thoughts, but in truth, only I see the structure in this. If you were to look over my shoulder as I wrote, you'd think I was crazy.

What's a typical working day like for you? When and where do you write?

I wake up at 3:30am, get my coffee, quickly check email and social media (only 30 min allowed), and then start writing for two hours. After that, I get ready and go to work. When I come back, I spend time with my family until the kids go to bed. Then it's my wife's decision of whether or not she wants to spend time with me or release me to get back to work on my writing.

Do you ever get Writer's Block? If so, how do you deal with it?

No, because I have lots of different projects that I can work on. If I sit down to write a book, but I have writers block for that subject, then I'll move on to something else. I'll do this until I get to writing.

Do you read your own reviews? If so, how do you deal with bad reviews?

I do because there are times where even the bad ones have some truth in them and are open invitations for you to improve upon yourself. However, many of these bad reviews are pointless, but you still should check them.

What are some ways in which you promote your books? What have you found most or least effective?

Email lists are crucial in today's market. The ones on top in Kindle are the ones who are in it for the long haul. They have built a following and a name in their industry. Basically they build off of each book's momentum and continue in an upward trajectory in success.

How easy or hard is it to make a living as an author?

Very hard. There are currently 4.5 million ebooks on Amazon right now. That's 4.5 million different competitors and they are all vying for the limited customers that Amazon has. This doesn't mean that you're doomed. It just means you need to be smarter about your book.

This isn't like the movie Field of Dreams. Just because you build it doesn't mean they will come. You need to work to market it.

What advice would you give to someone aspiring to be an author?

Two things:

1. Validate your book idea before you write it. Tailoring to a pre-existing and hungry market is WAY easier to be

successful than to try to create your own market that you think might exist.

2. The day you decide to write a book is the day you need to start marketing your book. Marketing is the hardest part and if done right, can be instrumental in your research and development of the book. Marketing, and writing of your book go hand-in-hand.

How can readers find out more about you?

Website: www.Kindlepreneur.com

Facebook: www.Facebook.com/kindlepreneur/

Derek Deopker

Tell us about yourself and your books!

I'm passionate about a range of topics including health and fitness, personal development, and entrepreneurship. Most of my books focus on the psychology of motivation for fitness with books like The Healthy Habit Revolution and Weight Loss Motivation Hacks. However, recently I've become more exclusively focused on personal development with my newest book Break Through Your BS.

In addition to these books, I love helping other self-published authors achieve success. I've created a few training courses and authored the book Why Authors Fail to give aspiring authors the insights I wish I had when I first started my self-publishing journey.

How long have you been writing, and how did you become involved in writing?

I started writing seriously back in 2012 with my blog ExcuseProof.com. However, it was more a means to an end of trying to make money online while talking about fitness. With consistent practice, I started to develop a talent for it. Now I consider it a labor of love.

What are you working on at the moment?

My business partner Ben Patwa and I are creating workshops and trainings to help entrepreneurs find their voice, write their books, and build a business sharing their expertise with the world.

Did you have any goals with writing, and if so, how well do you feel you've achieved them? What do you hope to achieve in the future?

Now that I've had seven books that have been bestsellers in their respective competitive categories on Amazon, my next goal is to publish a New York Times bestselling book.

How long does it take you to write a book?

I've written a book in as little as an afternoon when working from existing material. My newest book written from scratch though took about two and a half months. Generally, I have more ideas than I know what to do with, which is a quality problem to have because I started out with a lot of self-doubt and wondering, "What can I possibly write about?"

What are the hardest parts of being an author for you?

With regards to self-publishing, there are so many hats we need to wear unless one wants to outsource. While I have a passion for marketing, I find myself feeling overwhelmed with all the different channels such as social media platforms, blogging, and more to promote books. My focus in the upcoming year is to get more assistance in the marketing department so I can focus more exclusively on the writing and speaking side of things.

What do you enjoy most about being an author?

Making an impact. I love getting messages from people who tell me how my work has changed their way of thinking.

What books or authors have had the most influence on you as an author?

I read a lot of personal development, so authors like T. Harv Eker, Jack Canfield, and Eckhart Tolle are all influential.

What did you find most useful when you were learning to write and expanding your skills?

When I first got started, I would record videos and loosely transcribe what I said into a book. I never originally intended to be a writer. I believe starting out by transcribing my speaking may play some role in why my writing comes across as very conversational.

Learning copywriting and sales also helped me a lot with my writing because, as a non-fiction author, I not only have to sell my book but also my ideas.

What author services do you pay for, as opposed to doing yourself? Things like cover design, formatting, editing, proofreading, etc.?

I outsource cover design, editing, and proofreading. I use templates for formatting.

What technology/services/programs do you use as an author? (email subscription services, Dragon software, editing software, etc.)

For email, both Aweber (http://bit.ly/AweberFreeMonth) and Getresponse (http://bit.ly/GetResponseFreeTrials). I resisted using Leadpages for a while because I didn't want to pay monthly, but making the investment has been something I'm very satisfied with. The time it saves me makes it well worth it.

What are your thoughts about ebooks vs. print books?

I believe authors should definitely have both, and I personally still prefer to read print books.

What are your thoughts about self-publishing vs traditional publishing?

I love the freedom self-publishing gives me. I however would be very open to exploring traditional publishing if it makes sense for my business.

How often do you write, and how do you find or make time to write?

When working on a book, it's every day for several hours. However, on a day to day basis between books, it may only be a matter of a few minutes a day to journal some ideas and post on social media.

Do you plan your whole book out in advance, or just let it flow? What does your writing process look like?

The first bit of structure I work off of is a book title. This almost always comes first. Then I go into brainstorming without restrictions.

My early stage is extremely chaotic. For my last book, I had over 40,000 words worth of notes just from brainstorming over a couple weeks. There was no way I could even begin to organize them. However just getting my thoughts on paper was enough so that when I did start to outline my book, in the back of my mind I knew what the book would need.

After this free flow stage, I then gradually implement more structure, but still allow myself to be flexible to make changes as the book progresses.

What's a typical working day like for you? When and where do you write?

When working on a book, I do most of my writing in the mornings when I'm most creative and have had my coffee. I prefer to work in my home and never found myself as productive leaving my apartment.

Do you ever get Writer's Block? If so, how do you deal with it?

Not really. I have more ideas than I can possibly fit in a single book. However when analyzing my process, I'm also reading and being inspired by other things I see. The input of new information, such as reading a blog article, triggers my own thoughts and ideas on the topic or something related.

Do you read your own reviews? If so, how do you deal with bad reviews?

Yes, and I read them probably more than is productive. As far as "dealing" with the bad reviews, there's not much to do about them other than let them be. If it's something I feel *really* needs to be commented on, I may. In which case, I almost always start by saying, "Thank you for your feedback." Attacking the reviewer won't get far and often makes an author look defensive. Generally speaking though, I don't comment on any of my reviews.

Other than reviews, do you hear from your readers very often? What kinds of things do they say?

I usually hear from readers at least several times a week. I'm extremely grateful to hear them say how my books have changed their life. Sometimes they come to me with their struggles which I welcome. This both gives me an opportunity to help them as well as figure out problems that I can help solve in upcoming books or programs.

What are some ways in which you promote your books? What have you found most or least effective?

The two most effective ways I've found to promote a book are through ebook promotion websites and through an email list—either my own list or another's list.

How easy or hard is it to make a living as an author?

Hard and easy are subjective words. I would say it's challenging, but since I enjoy a challenge, it's not necessarily a bad thing. So even though it's "hard" at times to make money with books, if you have a willingness to do what's hard with enthusiasm, then what's hard becomes "easy."

What advice would you give to someone aspiring to be an author?

Have a reason that goes beyond you for being an author. If it's just about you, it's incredibly difficult to persevere. If you're doing it to help or teach others, then you'll have them think about to motivate you when challenges come up.

How can readers find out more about you?

Website: www.ebookbestsellersecrets.com

Facebook: www.facebook.com/derekdoepker

George Smolinski

Tell us about yourself and your books!

My personal journey with publishing began as a weekend project with my twin sons. At that time, back in 2013, they were seven years old and had a whole host of imaginary friends, all of whom were essentially large shapes. Think Edwin Abbott's "Flatland." I had heard somewhere that you could self-publish on Kindle, and I took the time to research the process while my boys drew up illustrations for the book. They dictated the stories, I wrote them up, and we published a trilogy of adventures, and even combined them in a paperback, "The Complete Adventures of The World's Friendliest Circle: Jubby Jubby Jow Jow."

I realized the potential of the platform, and then began to write my own books for Kindle, focusing on personal productivity at the outset. Books like "The Four Hour Workweek Toolbox" have been well-received, and I then decided to explore audiobooks as another way to reach readers. My wife is a professional actress, and as my success grew in publishing, I started Gutenberg Reloaded and hired her to work as a voice artist. Audio is a rapidly expanding platform, and we've now had over a dozen voice artists work with us to create over 200 audiobooks for our clients.

How long have you been writing, and how did you become involved in writing?

I've been writing for decades—I was a history major in college! Writing has always been a manner in which I'm comfortable expressing my thoughts. I'm definitely a person who likes to think about concepts and ideas and then present them in a logical, well thought out manner.

What are you working on at the moment?

Right now, I'm working with my friend and partner Jason P Jordan from Barnum Media Group to build the holy grail of audiobook production: A comprehensive guide that will give any author the ability to record their own audiobook! I've had so many people approach me for help with recording their own book (and people approach me with substandard audio that Audible has rejected), and there's something special about hearing an author record his or her own book. This will complement my recently-revised book "Recording Audiobooks" and provide even an audio newbie with the tools and concepts needed to successfully record their own audiobook.

Did you have any goals with writing, and if so, how well do you feel you've achieved them? What do you hope to achieve in the future?

My goal with writing has always been to help other people. By training I'm a physician and as such, that drive to help other people is an inborn trait. I help people every day as a doctor, but I can help so many more people by writing. I feel I meet this goal with every positive review I receive on Amazon! For the future, I hope to help authors reach more readers with my audiobook recording program. It's going to be amazing.

How long does it take you to write a book?

Forever! In all seriousness, my books are never done. I'm continually looking to provide updated, new information to my readers.

What are the hardest parts of being an author for you?

Proofreading. I absolutely hate it.

What do you enjoy most about being an author?

Getting a review on Amazon where a reader notes a particular portion of one of my books that has been helpful. It's incredibly rewarding and validates my purpose in writing.

What books or authors have had the most influence on you as an author?

The classics: Hemingway, Joyce, Orwell, Huxley, etc.

What did you find most useful when you were learning to write and expanding your skills?

A disinterested, trusted third party that could give me intelligent feedback about my writing. Nothing is better than having your writing criticized by someone who can give you that honest feedback.

What author services do you pay for, as opposed to doing yourself? Things like cover design, formatting, editing, proofreading, etc.?

I outsource everything, but it's easy since I own a publishing company!

What are your thoughts about ebooks vs. print books?

They're both fantastic. Personally, I love the smell of an old classic novel, but I also like the ability to be able to get a new book on my iPad while sitting on my couch.

Of course, audiobooks are really the next untapped medium for publishing, and I'm counting on that to be a large part of my publishing business. The research backs me up, as sales data from the U.S. and Canada indicates that audiobook downloads are growing at an incredible rate (26–28% per year) which is far outstripping the grown rate of eBooks (a "measly" 6–8% per year). In fact, the Audiobook Publishers Association 2015 press release noted that US audiobook publications **quadrupled** from 2010 to 2014 alone!

What are your thoughts about self-publishing vs traditional publishing?

Self-publishing is a classic example of disruptive innovation, as defined by Clayton Christiansen. Just as Wikipedia has trumped Encyclopedia Britannica and MP3's have killed cassettes, so will self-publishing spell the demise of traditional publishing. There will certainly be a role for traditional publishers in the future, but their role will be incredibly small compared to the market share they once enjoyed.

How often do you write, and how do you find or make time to write?

I try to write a bit every day, as I feel that writing is a skill set just like any other that degrades with disused. Finding time is tough, but even ten minutes can be useful to write even a few paragraphs.

Do you plan your whole book out in advance, or just let it flow? What does your writing process look like?

I've done both, either planning the whole book or just letting things flow. I think it's better to get everything out there and then start cutting during the editing process.

What's a typical working day like for you? When and where do you write?

I write in the evenings after work and after the kids are in bed. It's the only quiet time in our house!

Do you ever get Writer's Block? If so, how do you deal with it?

I can honestly say I've never had writer's block. Perhaps I'm just lucky!

Do you read your own reviews? If so, how do you deal with bad reviews?

Yes, I do read my own reviews, and I never let a bad review get me down. A bad review is an opportunity to improve my book if it's constructive criticism, and if it's an unwarranted bad review, I rely on Lincoln's wise words, "you can please some of the people all of the time and all of the people some of the time, but you can't please all of the people all of the time."

Other than reviews, do you hear from your readers very often? What kinds of things do they say?

I do have readers reach out via email or Facebook, and they often want more information about a particular part of my book.

What are some ways in which you promote your books? What have you found most or least effective?

I've had some success with Twitter, but a lot of my books serve as a reference and a lead generation tool for my publishing business. They provide a ton of value to readers, but they are most useful to me as a reference to which I can point people. As such, I place less stock in book promotion techniques.

How easy or hard is it to make a living as an author?

It's difficult, but just like with any other field, persistence and a bit of luck seems to be unifying traits of successful authors.

What advice would you give to someone aspiring to be an author?

"Write when drunk.

Edit when sober.

Marketing is the hangover"
　　　　—*Ashwin Sanghi*

How can readers find out more about you?

Website:　　www.gutenbergreloaded.com/

Facebook:　　www.facebook.com/GutenbergReloaded/

J. Stoute

Tell us about yourself and your books!

I'm from southwest Louisiana, I've always enjoyed writing and wrote several stories way back when, only to shelve them for all of time. It wasn't until 2014 that I decided to dive into writing to see where it takes me. My only goal is to write fiction, not aiming to stick to any one subject, I go where my stories take me. I enjoy getting feedback on the stories I write because it's the only way to know how an author is doing. When writing, I like to stay on point as much as possible such as, I'll tell you about a flower and sometimes I will describe it, other times I will leave the description to you and your imagination.

I was in the US Army for 8 years, I've been to Iraq twice in a civilian role, and I was president of two different motorcycle clubs. During one of my tours in Iraq, I was about 35 feet from a suicide bomber and took minor shrapnel in the process. I believe in living your life while you are able because, you never know when it's going to end.

I've been married for over 30 years and have 3 grown children, and 2 grandchildren.

I truly enjoy spending time alone. Time that allows for meaningful thought.

My titles include,

BloodLust — A Vampire Romance

Throttled Hearts — A MC Romance

Southern Complications—Surviving Abuse Romance

Kill List—A Social Thriller

A Partiot's Call—A Social Political Thriller

Deadly Recall—SciFi Thriller

Out of the Darkness Book One, Cause & Effect—Psychological Thriller

Out of the Darkness Book Two, No Redemption—Psychological Thriller

Saving Allison—Youth & Young Adult about a teen suicide.

Santa's Last Secret—My children's book written under the pen name A. Logan.

How long have you been writing, and how did you become involved in writing?

Since my teens, I have enjoyed writing. Back then it was more poems and songs. It wasn't until 1996 that I wrote my first two stories. One was a Christmas children's book and the second was a thriller. In '96, there was no such thing as self-publishing and these stories were shelved. It was in 2014 that I looked into self-publishing and realized that this would be a great way to enter the trade. In just over 12 months, I self-published 10 titles.

What are you working on at the moment?

I am currently working on two stories. The first is book two of BloodLust, a vampire romance and the second is another social-political thriller.

Did you have any goals with writing, and if so, how well do you feel you've achieved them? What do you hope to achieve in the future?

My only goal was to have a book published with my name on it (even if it was self-published). With 10 self-published books, one of which has just gone under a 5-year contract with a publisher, I would say that I have achieved my goals and more. As for the future, I hope to build more of a collection.

How long does it take you to write a book?

During 2015, I was able to complete a story in about a month. Since then, that time has gotten longer.

What are the hardest parts of being an author for you?

Marketing!!! It's tough out there and there is a lot of competition. For anyone with a small budget it's really hard to be seen.

What do you enjoy most about being an author?

Just knowing that I have been able to entertain someone, if only for a few hours.

What books or authors have had the most influence on you as an author?

As an author this will sound really bad but, no one has influenced me as an author because although I love to tell a story, I hate to read. I've been raked through the coals for that one!

What did you find most useful when you were learning to write and expanding your skills?

Working with editors and actually breaking down and reading what others have written. I never said that I didn't read, I do when I have to!

What author services do you pay for, as opposed to doing yourself? Things like cover design, formatting, editing, proofreading, etc.?

In the beginning, I tried to do it all and will be the first one to admit that my books were substandard. I now pay for editing, book covers, writing the blurbs, and sometimes promotion.

What technology/services/programs do you use as an author? (email subscription services, Dragon software, editing software, etc.)

I use MS Word for writing, Go Daddy email subscription Service, and Photoshop for images.

What are your thoughts about ebooks vs. print books?

I believe that both have their own place. I do well with print books when I am somewhere and can sign on site. Ebooks allow a much broader audience however, I'm but a small fish in a great big ocean.

What are your thoughts about self-publishing vs traditional publishing?

I think that self-publishing is great. If it wasn't for self-publishing, I wouldn't even have been asked to answer this questionnaire. I do believe that traditional carries much more weight; however, there are those that are doing very well in self-publishing.

How often do you write, and how do you find or make time to write?

Honestly, I'll go through moods when a story will just flow and I write every day. Other times, I avoid my computer like the plague. I'll just keep going over where I'm at and where I want to go with the story in my head and not write.

Do you plan your whole book out in advance, or just let it flow? What does your writing process look like?

I just let it flow. No outline and no idea draft. I just go with it and when I run out of story or get blocked, I stop and think it through until I get back on track.

What's a typical working day like for you? When and where do you write?

I do have a normal 8 hour a day job so my writing is limited to evenings and weekends. Most times I write while on my couch with the television on.

Do you ever get Writer's Block? If so, how do you deal with it?

YES!!! I simply stop for a while. This gives me time to reflect on what has been written already and then I'll tell myself, "Let's get some words out."

Do you read your own reviews? If so, how do you deal with bad reviews?

Oh YES, I read every one of them. For an example, my second book was Throttled Hearts and I read one review that I felt was brutal. It wasn't a one star but it was how it was written. I revisited the story and thought, *this is crap.* I went through the whole story to improve it then unlike the first run, I hired an editor. My first 4 books were done without an editor and I have been going back through each one and making them better. Back to the bad review of Throttled Hearts, once the book is completely refinished, I will offer the reviewer a chance for a re-read. All reviews matter.

Other than reviews, do you hear from your readers very often? What kinds of things do they say?

Not very often. I sometimes get comments on Facebook that amount to personal reviews.

What are some ways in which you promote your books? What have you found most or least effective?

I have tried a lot of social media advertisements which I have found to be almost useless. I have not found the perfect advertising platform that I can afford. I have tried many free promotions and totally disagree with that concept. It's almost like begging for someone to get your story and most people that download them actually don't read the book. My other point is, if I give away 500 books then that's 500 people who will never purchase that particular story.

How easy or hard is it to make a living as an author?

As stated before, I have a normal job that provides my living. At this point, writing is only a hobby. If it were my only income, I think I would be living in a box.

What advice would you give to someone aspiring to be an author?

Be prepared. Writing is the simple part. Everything after is what will hammer you, especially if you're on a shoe string budget. Marketing is the hardest part but DO follow your dreams.

How can readers find out more about you?

Website: www.jstoute.com

Facebook:

www.facebook.com/pages/J-Stoute/326594510865179

Jane Turner

Tell us about yourself and your books!

My main book is call "Thrive in Midlife." I wrote this when I hit a wall with menopause. I put myself through a wellness transformation program that I documented in my book for others to follow, as well as turning it into an online information program.

I've also written an eBook called "Mindset for Health" and another one called "Mindset for Authors."

The healing, transformation, and business boost that I got from the process of writing "Thrive in Midlife" led me to set up and run writing workshops which I love doing.

How long have you been writing, and how did you become involved in writing?

The first writing other than business reports and the like was in 2009 when I first thought of writing a book to boost my coaching business. I did numerous courses and got distracted in many ways until I synthesized everything and finally got my book written in 2014.

What are you working on at the moment?

I am working on a book with a similar structure to "Thrive in Midlife" (i.e. personal stories, case studies, and concrete strategies) to help people to get out of stress and enjoy life more.

Did you have any goals with writing, and if so, how well do you feel you've achieved them? What do you hope to achieve in the future?

The goal with "Thrive in Midlife" was to get publicity to drive people to my coaching business. I'm actually featured in the current issue of the Australian Women's Weekly (page 88 if you're interested) and have a chapter in a book called "Successful Women in Business," and another one in a book called "Success Uncovered." I also now write for a couple of online magazines as well ("Smart Healthy Women," and "Holistic Living Magazine"). So the publicity side of things is going pretty well and it adds credibility to the argument I attract people to my writing workshops with, i.e. that writing a book can open many doors. On that front I negotiated an important joint venture that I know being a published author had something to do with in terms of the deal that I struck.

The unintended consequence of writing the book was in the end more important than all of the above. I had to jump some hurdles and do some healing around owning my story, and now that I do there's no stopping me. I believe it's the person I've become that's what's really attracting people to my business, and I love the transformation I see my authors achieve during the process.

How long does it take you to write a book?

That the old 'how long is a price of string question'? I wrote "Thrive in Midlife" in about 4 weeks because it was content that I knew intimately and very little research needed to be done. To and fro between myself and the editor is not included in the 4 weeks of course.

What are the hardest parts of being an author for you?

If I didn't have another source of income, making money through books would be the hardest part. But to answer your question, the hardest part for me is in 'the middle.' I knock my ideas out and onto the page no problem, and structure my chapters and the whole book easily, but I suffer a bit of frustration and impatience around making the language flow well once I get my content back from being transcribed.

What do you enjoy most about being an author?

Not to sound shallow, but I love getting feedback. One woman who was dying of lung cancer let me know that she didn't want to finish my book because she found it comforting to have with her. I had no idea a book of mine would touch someone so deeply. She said that by sharing personal details like a history of binge eating disorder and body image issues was reassuring for her in terms of her own issues.

What books or authors have had the most influence on you as an author?

Brene Brown "Daring Greatly" is the answer to this question by a country mile.

What did you find most useful when you were learning to write and expanding your skills?

Learning to dot point my topics out and talking them into my iPod before sending it off to be transcribed was a game changer for me. This meant that I was not stemming the flow of the content by worrying about punctuation and such, and not slowed down by my typing skills.

What author services do you pay for, as opposed to doing yourself? Things like cover design, formatting, editing, proofreading, etc.?

I pay for all four of those services mentioned above.

What are your thoughts about ebooks vs. print books?

I love them both, but favor eBooks for cost reasons.

What are your thoughts about self-publishing vs traditional publishing?

I can't be bothered with traditional publishing, it all seems to hard.

How often do you write, and how do you find or make time to write?

It depends on where I am in the process.

Do you plan your whole book out in advance, or just let it flow? What does your writing process look like?

I see the whole thing in my mind and take it from there. I am a one chapter at a time person. As I said above, I dot point out my main points and talk my content out into an iPod to be transcribed. I then pull it all into shape in bursts of about an hour at a time.

What's a typical working day like for you? When and where do you write?

There's no typical working day per se. I coach and run workshops much more than I write. I have no special place for writing. Have laptop—will travel.

Do you ever get Writer's Block? Sometimes. If so, how do you deal with it?

I just walk away, change my state with meditation or a long walk (hopefully in the sunshine), and come back to it later.

Do you read your own reviews? If so, how do you deal with bad reviews?

No

Other than reviews, do you hear from your readers very often? What kinds of things do they say?

I actually don't hear from my readers often. The feedback I mentioned above is rare. I've had a bit of feedback about my book being easy to read, and that I have a good writing style.

What are some ways in which you promote your books? What have you found most or least effective?

I've really been focusing on the book writing workshops to be honest, and really slack about promoting the book.

What advice would you give to someone aspiring to be an author?

If it doesn't come easily to you, get some help. There are plenty of people like me out there.

How can readers find out more about you?

Website: www.writewithjane.com

Facebook:

www.facebook.com/people/Jane-Turner/100000419132221

K.S. Nikakis

Tell us about yourself and your books!

I grew up in the lovely town of Mansfield in NE Victoria. It has snow-capped mountains which are one of my favorite things in life; fantastic scenery, and a lake. I had horses as a youngster and spent a lot of time riding through these areas. I was chronically shy so being alone suited me. This landscape has remained a big influence and as a fantasy writer, I enjoy building new worlds.

I was clueless about a career and fell into secondary teaching, then followed with Teaching English as a Second Language, TAFE teaching and University lecturing. I am presently Head of Program of the Bachelor of Writing and Publishing at Melbourne Polytechnic. Working in education gave me the study bug and I have qualifications in ESL, Literacy, Professional Writing and Editing, as well as an M.Ed (Hons) and Ph.D.

My first three books (published by Allen and Unwin) are *The Kira Chronicles* trilogy. While I write fantasy, I've never written about elves, magic, wizards, medieval castles or complex political intrigue. I haven't written any dystopic stories or urban fantasy either. I'm interested in individual hero journeys of female heroes in particular. As a writer of Deep Fantasy, I want the story to say something meaningful about the big issues of life and death, hate and love, reconciliation and transcendence. *The Kira Chronicles* is about healing overcoming killing, but there are no easy answers in the story.

My fourth book is *Dragon tales,* published by Heidelberg Press. It is a reference book on dragons drawn from my studies. My M.Ed (Hons) looked at why people find dragons fascinating and the purposes dragons serve in narratives.

My fifth book is *The Emerald Serpent* which I published independently on Amazon in Oct 2015. It was a NaNoWriMo project in 2014. I've always been interested in the story of *St George and the Dragon* which can be interpreted as Christianity destroying Paganism (the dragon). I am interested in the dragon's viewpoint and how the female hero, a white-skinned, black-haired, emerald-eyed she-Eadar, must heal herself if the Eadar are to overcome the attacks of religious zealots.

My sixth book, *The Third Moon,* is under contract to Satalyte Publishing. It is also a NaNoWriMo project (from 2013.) It is the first book I've written from a male viewpoint, set in the far future, on another planet. The male hero is of indigenous Australian descent, who is plagued by inherited memories of his people's dispossession in the distant past—and then history repeats. I'm hoping the book will be out in 2016.

How long have you been writing, and how did you become involved in writing?

I began to write, out of the blue, when I was 38. I am now 60. English was always my favorite subject at school and I taught English, but it never occurred to me to write, or (gasp), attempt a book. It was something other people did. Then at 38, a switch flicked in my brain—suddenly. I think I was gestating stories for years and just needed a trigger. I've read something similar happened to the wonderful Sara Douglass.

What are you working on at the moment?

I'm writing a book called *Heart Hunter,* about a young Sceadu hunter (Fleet) who is given an impossible quest by the Sceadu's young female shaman (Siah). The shaman has married the man Fleet desires and as the shaman's rival, Fleet believes she is being sent to her death. Fleet's quest reveals the dual nature of words, of the shamanic and logical worldviews, and of the real nature of love — in all its forms.

I also have an angel series in process. Both *Heart Hunter* and the angel series were interrupted by my NaNoWriMo projects.

Did you have any goals with writing, and if so, how well do you feel you've achieved them? What do you hope to achieve in the future?

My goal was to get the first story I wrote (Book 2 of *The Kira Chronicles*) to come together as a satisfying story. I am a pantser, so I have no idea of what any story is when I start. I have to write it to find out. I wrote Books 2 and 3 of *The Kira Chronicles* and when I couldn't find a publisher, I wrote Book I. Like most writers, I was desperate for the stamp of approval from a commercial publisher. Having Allen and Unwin pick up the series was wonderful, but I now know how hit and miss this process can be. I'd had good feedback on the series from rejecting editors; I was lucky the editor at Allen and Unwin liked it enough to pick it up.

I am no longer desperate about publishers picking up my work — although I continue to pitch, and think it would be great. Thanks to Amazon and co. we can reach our readers through other means. My goals are now to write fabulous, meaningful, engaging and fresh Deep Fantasy stories. All writing is a struggle. You create something from nothing, no mean feat, and I am in full time work, with a long commute (I can spend over 3 hours in the car each day). My goal is to write all the stories presently in my head, and the ones I haven't thought of yet.

How long does it take you to write a book?

With my two NaNoWriMo projects, I wrote over the required 50,000 words in the month (and all but died in the process) and took another couple of months to get each of them to around 65,000 words. The rewrites and editing took another four to five months, so about eight months for each. I usually take a least a year to write a book of 100,000 words plus.

What are the hardest parts of being an author for you?

Getting quality time to write (not when I am exhausted) and getting words to obey me. I used to have a lot of self-doubt and feelings of failure too, but now I focus on enjoying writing the best story I can. You have no control over what is fashionable or what a publisher likes. You have to remember that above all else, you are a story-teller. This is an ancient and very respectable role to occupy in society.

What do you enjoy most about being an author?

I am never bored. There is always something to think of; always something exciting popping up in your head to surprise you; always something to do. I have no idea how other people exist without these other wonderful worlds.

What books or authors have had the most influence on you as an author?

I love Mary Stewart's *The Crystal Cave, The Hollow Hill, The Last Enchantment.* Her Arthurian Britain is brilliant with blood and dew. Her use of landscape was a revelation when I first read her. I've also read J.R.R. Tolkien's *The Lord of the Rings* about 30 times. The depth of this world creation is stunning as is the cultural depth of his characters.

What did you find most useful when you were learning to write and expanding your skills?

There's a lot of advice given to beginner writers. The most basic is not to give up. If you keep writing, keep honing, keep practicing you will get better. You must love the story you are writing. Story is everything. A good story told awkwardly will always trump a clichéd story delivered smoothly. It is really worth doing some writing courses too. The Diploma of Professional Writing and Editing is excellent but the Writers' Centers in all states offer great short courses. Writing is a craft; you have to learn it.

What author services do you pay for, as opposed to doing yourself? Things like cover design, formatting, editing, proofreading, etc.?

My son has a multimedia degree and I paid him to do the covers to *The Emerald Serpent* and *Heart Hunter* — he's a poor student again and needed the money. There were other reasons. I could have paid a stranger and had a slicker result (or with sites like Fiverr, a cheaper result) but I wanted to work with someone face to face, not remotely, and have someone very responsive to my ideas.

I've done all the editing. I work in the industry plus I learned a lot about editing from Allen and Unwin's excellent editors. The key is to leave at least 4 weeks between the second last and last edit. Even so, a professional editor would take the novels to the next level. Cost was a factor in doing my own editing but so was control. If you have no publishing contract then you might end up with editing you don't agree with and still have to find a publisher. Also, on Amazon, it is easy to upload another copy if you discover a glitch.

The book trailer was done by Dale Trott of Zero Cut Entertainment, a small company made up of former students of the degree I run. Dale was fantastic to work with. For those considering a book trailer, the original quote was $250. Stock images and music are used. I ended up suggesting $500 as Dale did a lot of hours of work and I was keen not to exploit a fellow creative. He was terrifically responsive to my ideas. Nothing was too much trouble and I am thrilled with the result.

What technology/services/programs do you use as an author? (email subscription services, Dragon software, editing software, etc.)

I just use Word. That's it. Lots of my students rave about Scrivener, but I can't be bothered learning it. I have notebooks and scrapbooks of pictures, and music which will help me get mood. As a pantser, I am pretty organic. I would rather just write.

What are your thoughts about ebooks vs. print books?

Given the choice, I would prefer to hand over my manuscript to a great company like Allen and Unwin and let them edit, design, produce, distribute, market and promote, but the reality is that it is really hard to get a contract with any large (or small publisher). Ebook platforms are a fantastic opportunity to get your work out there; just make sure you edit, edit, edit.

The two forms are not mutually exclusive. Successful ebook authors are not necessarily accepting contracts from commercial publishers, and many authors are using both systems. You have a lot of control over your ebook but you have to do everything yourself. I am not spending time on marketing until I have at least five books out. It is pointless using writing time promoting your ebook when you have no other works available. There is a lot of snobbery in the debate too, prompted by the rubbish that people can now publish. A good book will always be a good book no matter how it is published.

Even so, I have a lot of people, young and old, who are asking me when the print version of *The Emerald Serpent* will be available. They don't want an ebook.

What are your thoughts about self-publishing vs traditional publishing?

As per the previous question. Take pride in what you put out there. Do not launch anything you do not think is excellent. Give readers value for the time or money they have spent on your story. You are your brand.

How often do you write, and how do you find or make time to write?

I write most days after work for at least an hour and every weekend. I don't watch much TV and have to be dragged out for a social life. I often get stale. If you want to write, you have to sit down and do it. There is no other way. Some famous writers like Margo Lanagan wrote their fabulous stuff on public transport JK Rowling huddled in a café. Writing has to be incredibly important to you; not just a hobby.

Do you plan your whole book out in advance, or just let it flow? What does your writing process look like?

I am a pantser. *Heart Hunter* started with a single word: sceadu — the old form of the word shadow, which gave me a rain shadow, a shade (ghost), and the Jungian shadow. Bits of story come to me with music, or revelations while driving. It is like a giant puzzle I am solving over months or years. It bubbles along in the back of my mind and slowly I find the pieces and slot them into place. I used to worry it wouldn't work but I'm confident the story is out there now; I just have to find it.

Once I am writing, I loop back and edit as I go. With NaNoWriMo, you can't do any editing, there is no time. You just have to write like mad. I found this quite confronting but I got two fairly quick novels as a result. I dedicated *The Emerald Serpent* to one of our ex-students who ran NaNoWriMo and who forced me not to edit!

What's a typical working day like for you? When and where do you write?

Mon — Thurs: alarm goes off at 5:45 am; treadmill and weights; leave at 7:00 am; arrive at parking spot at 8:15 — 8:30; walk 10 mins: 8:45 — 5:45-6:00 at my desk or lecturing (I eat breakfast and lunch at my desk); home by 7:15; make dinner; desk for writing 8 — 8:15; be in bed by 10:30. I have a large study/gym where I write. Hmmm, reading this suggests I should get a life.

Fri — I have a research day at home. If I am not working on an academic paper I write from 8:00 am to about 6:00. 'Original Activity' (creative artefacts such as novels) are classed as research.

Weekend — will fit in about 8 hours of writing over the time. I live on 30 acres and there is a lot of mowing and poisoning to be done. I also do the housework, washing, ironing and mending. There are other family responsibilities too as my sibling lives interstate.

Do you ever get Writer's Block? If so, how do you deal with it?

I'm not sure I believe in writer's block. (A lot of people reading this now hate me!) Having said that, I was recently on a panel when a very well-known and successful writer said they had had writer's block for ten years. A lot of creative people have anxiety and depression and I'm guessing that being unable to write might be related to being anxious about writing *well*. I have no medical training; this is simply an observation of my students and my own state when I was depressed.

I am very well now but I do get tired and stale, and bored with what I'm writing, or lose confidence in it, but I can always write something! It might be crud, but there is always something to be said. Writing crud quite often will get you back on track. I think people freeze because their story/character is standing at some sort of crossroad and they don't know which road to take. Just move! (write!) There is a magic key called delete. The other thing to realize is that tapping on keys is the easy bit of writing. The rest is you thinking about the story all the time: sorting, mulling, sifting. You have to write *and* think.

When I am stale I play on Facebook, read a fav poem, look at the IKEA catalogue e.g. rest my brain. I also swear a lot. Have faith. You are the god of your own creation; it will go on!

Do you read your own reviews? If so, how do you deal with bad reviews?

I read all the reviews of *The Kira Chronicles* that I could find. Some were written by people who obviously hadn't read the books to the end, most were written by people who had. They were pretty positive, but you have to be grown-up enough to consider negative remarks. I consider all feedback as useful, but it is your right to ultimately reject it as rubbish. The rule is to never engage with someone who has just called your baby ugly!

The Emerald Serpent has had only two reviews by friends. I would love more. Reviews are seen as very important for ebooks. Overall, be grateful someone has: a) read your book b) taken the time to comment on it.

Other than reviews, do you hear from your readers very often?
What kinds of things do they say?

I mainly hear from people who have managed to read the first two in *The Kira Chronicles* but can't find Book 3, or read the first one and are desperate for the rest. They are saying nice things. I have copies of all three books so I usually send these out at cost price. The series is still on some online sites (although it shouldn't be as I got the rights back) and in libraries and second hand bookshops. I am intending to re-release it.

What are some ways in which you promote your books? What have you found most or least effective?

Commercial publishers do a lot of this for you but you need to be available for interviews and appearances. Regardless, it is usual to have a website, blog, twitter and Facebook accounts, and a presence on GoodReads. I have all these and don't use them enough.

I announce when I have something coming out, but don't repeat unless it is of use to the thread. I am uncomfortable with blatant self-promotion. I blog about writing in general; likewise with tweeting. I go to Conflux each year, and Contact16 in Brisbane this year will be my first NatCon. I go to GenreCon when it is on every second year. I have registered for WorldCon in Helsinki in 2017. I was a judge on the Aurealis Awards this year and entered for the first time. I go to the Small Press Network conference each year in Melbourne. I am involved in local library events when invited.

I am engaged in the writing community, so what I've written is on my bio, but I'm not overtly out there promoting. When I have more ebooks out, I will become more active. It is really a time v. return issue for me at present, especially as I am in paid employment.

How easy or hard is it to make a living as an author?

The stats say that you can't make a living as an author but you can as a communication professional. The degree I run, the Bachelor of Writing and Publishing, is designed to give students a broad set of skills across all forms of writing, and print and digital publishing. So students can work as journalists, copywriters and technical writers, editors and publishers as well as the more obvious choice of teaching. A lot of authors are now doing Ph.D's. A Ph.D is not an entry into academia however as universities have dozens of applicants with Ph.D's plus critically acclaimed novels plus 40+ research papers. Even getting sessional work is hard, and moving to ongoing employment rare. Also teaching looks easy from the outside but it eats up a lot of time and energy. As most authors will have to work at other jobs in parallel, try to qualify in an area that supports your writing career.

What advice would you give to someone aspiring to be an author?

Do it, but don't do it blindly. Not pursuing something very important to you has a terrible cost, but there is a cost to doing it too. If you want to have a degree as part of learning your craft, shop around for one that suits you. Have a brutal think about how you will live and what level of lifestyle you can tolerate. Are you okay renting? Not having holidays? Shopping at Savers? How important is security to you? How supportive is your present or likely partner? If writing is to be your only income, what networks do you have/can build to sell your work?

I know authors who are living well off their earnings, able to pace their books and have holidays. I know of others who seem to be on a treadmill of getting the next book out. I don't know any commercially successful authors who aren't secretly fearful their careers will come crashing down, then again, it is hard to think of any job that is secure.

I work in paid employment in an area related to my writing and that frees me up to not worry if my books sell or not.

How can readers find out more about you?

Website: www.ksnikakis.com

Facebook: www.facebook.com/ksnikakis (happy to have friends)

Ken Bluttman

Tell us about yourself and your books!

I am a person who dips his hand into many hats. I am a writer, also a web developer, a musician, a teacher, and have a knack for finances and numbers. I get involved with all sorts of entrepreneurial pursuits such as selling thing online, creating products or doing affiliate sales for products from others, and once in a while just stand up from the computer and realize— "there's a world out there!" —and then I got out for a walk.

On the personal side, married for25 years, have a 19-year-old son, and always have had an assortment of pets. Currently that's two cats, a lizard and a frog.

I have over 20 published books; several are out of print by now. They are primarily computer or technical books. My writing career has been through the traditional "have an agent, get signed with a publishing company" route. More to come following . . .

How long have you been writing, and how did you become involved in writing?

Always been writing, even as a kid. Then in my teens my focus was songwriting, including the lyrics of course. I started music college at age 17. I was a composition major, so perhaps I can stretch this and say writing music is part of my writing life! Later, in traditional college courses, such as Creative Writing, I always scored high. Guess I just had the talent to tell a good story.

Flash forward to me being employed as a programmer. It was 1999. I developed a cool method to accomplish something I had to do with the programming work. Back then there were many computer magazines, and I submitted a proposal to write an article about the technique I developed. All writers go around with the thought that getting rejections is part of the game, so I didn't expect to be accepted at first. Yet the magazine came right back to me with a simple question—"How fast could I get the article to us?"

A couple of months later my article was published. I received a copy in the mail. What an awesome day! Then I notice there was something placed in the magazine. A check for $300. I had not even thought I would get paid! And there it was—my first payment as a writer. Easy as pie.

A week or so after the magazine came out I got a phone call from some gentleman asking me if I would like to sign up with his literary agency. I had no idea my one article would lead to this. Turns out that (at the time) their agency was the largest in the world for representing technical authors. Sure, I signed up and to this day I am still writing books through this agency. They have landed me deals with many large publishers such as McGraw-Hill, Pearson, Wiley, and O'Reilly. If you are not familiar with these at least one you will know one—Wiley makes the Dummies books. I am a Dummies author.

Other projects I did through the agency were writing another 8 or so magazine articles, and some online articles for major companies such as IBM. I worked on the team that wrote the user manuals for Microsoft Office XP.

What are you working on at the moment?

At this point I am branching out into self-publishing on the Kindle and CreateSpace platforms. I did test the waters a bit a year ago with a bit of fiction and non-fiction, under pen names. I put it aside for the past several months as I had been tied up with a lot of work. Now though the balance of my time is shifting back in my favor and I expect to be putting out self-published fiction, most likely in the lucrative romance genre.

Did you have any goals with writing, and if so, how well do you feel you've achieved them? What do you hope to achieve in the future?

My original goal was to try to get a magazine article published! I have well surpassed that! At this point, the joy now is not completely the writing part of this, but the business side — how to max out on earnings. Self-publishing involves numerous details and as such the goal now is to grow a business.

How long does it take you to write a book?

Without distractions I could easily write 2000 or more words per day. I have never had "writer's block" or anything that slowed me down. The only caveat to that is with computer and technical books you often take a lot of screenshots and the publishers were very demanding about how to take them. Screenshots took as much time as the writing!

But let me throw in here the best advice for any writing endeavor — create an outline! When you work from an outline you have in essence already created your book, and the writing is essentially filling in the blanks. So even if it takes you a few days to work out the outline (and that would include characters, plot, etc, for fiction), then the actually writing becomes an effort of filling in the blanks.

This is what has helped me not have any problems with output. There is no guesswork as I write. I am following the outline.

What are the hardest parts of being an author for you?

I tend to help people too much. The point for me personally here is that most of my books have been instructional — essentially helping other programmers and web developers. However each time I had a book published I would be contacted by my readers for more assistance. I used to respond to everyone.

After a while that became impossible. Now I sadly ignore most requests for help. It' not a good feeling.

What do you enjoy most about being an author?

Being creative!

What books or authors have had the most influence on you as an author?

When it comes to the technical side — none. I seem to be a leader in what I do with programming and web development so there are no real sources that I look up to. At best I associate with some peers.

Fiction however — wow, I have a long list! I read many classics and love books like those from Russian masters (Dostoevsky, Tolstoy, etc). Other classis authors I love are Herman Melville (Moby Dick, Bartleby the Scrivener), George Orwell, and Franz Kafka. I like a lot of modern thrillers such as books from Michael Crichton. I am a science fiction buff and poured though many books from many masters. Ray Bradbury was a literary hero of mine. I did stumble upon an author over the past year that blew me away, and is self-published — Edward W. Robertson. His "Breakers" series — such great characters!

What did you find most useful when you were learning to write and expanding your skills?

Just write, and then write some more. Try out new techniques. Create scenarios and write them out. For example, write a 1000-word story about two people who can't stand each other but are stuck in an elevator and have to work together to get out. Or write a story from the perspective of the antagonist who in his/her view is doing the right thing and can't understand why others don't see that.

Stretch past your comfort zone. Never written a western? Read a couple and then try writing one.

What author services do you pay for, as opposed to doing yourself? Things like cover design, formatting, editing, proofreading, etc.?

All. I have written so much in my life that the thrill of accomplishment and having books out is old hat now. So it's now about growing a writing business, and that means outsourcing as much as possible, even some writing (ghostwriters).

What technology/services/programs do you use as an author? (email subscription services, Dragon software, editing software, etc.)

I just write in Microsoft Word. Going through publishers I've worked with many of the top editors in the field. I've learned many tricks from them, which has led me to be able to now do most if not all of my own editing.

What are your thoughts about ebooks vs. print books?

Both formats have a place. The advantage of ebooks is you can quickly update your book and republish it. On the other hand there are issues with how much you can earn as the rules seem to change all the time. For those starting out I'd suggest get a few ebooks out. It provides a lot of experience that is useful before having printed books created.

What are your thoughts about self-publishing vs traditional publishing?

I am a very successful traditionally published author and my advice is to self-publish.

When writing my books it could take months—not from my efforts but from the processes that are in place with traditional publishing. With self-publishing you could decide today to have a book out next week.

How often do you write, and how do you find or make time to write?

I write when I am working on a writing project. Time makes itself available. Wake up early, skip a TV show, have a quick meal. Do what you need to do to make time to write.

For those less along in the writing game it is a good idea to set a schedule, perhaps at least 30 minutes per day. Whatever works best. You do want your time at writing to be productive.

Do you plan your whole book out in advance, or just let it flow? What does your writing process look like?

As much as possible is planned out in advance.

What's a typical working day like for you? When and where do you write?

I have a home office. Simple setup—a long table with three computers on it. I switch which computer I am using based on what I am working on. I know that sounds strange, but here is why. Some writing I do is for blogs. So I might be writing on one computer and viewing the blog on a different computer as I update the post. It's just my style.

Do you ever get Writer's Block? If so, how do you deal with it?

I have never had that. However, I do find it useful to take breaks to get a fresh perspective.

Do you read your own reviews? If so, how do you deal with bad reviews?

I read some reviews. More to the point I just take a quick gaze at the rating. As long as the rating is good enough that to me is pertinent. I've learned a long time ago that reviews can be all over the place. Someone gave me a bad review because their copy of my book got ruined while in transit to them. I had nothing to do with that, but I get the bad review. It happens.

To this day I am holding an email I received about 12 years ago from a student in China. She told me my book helped her pass the computer course she was taking, and she was able to graduate. That email is worth a thousand good reviews in my heart.

Other than reviews, do you hear from your readers very often? What kinds of things do they say?

I hear from people around the world. They usually want some programming help but I just can't devote the time anymore. One funny thing that happened is I got a "thank you" email from someone in Sweden. Then within the next week I got three more, all from Sweden. Turned out some people got together and formed a study group—and were using one of my books as their guide! Wow!

What are some ways in which you promote your books? What have you found most or least effective?

I don't promote. The publishers do that—or they don't. I don't really know. I do of course know that my books sell. I receive royalty statements and royalty payments. Once I get going with self-publishing I will promote heavily. I believe you have to be proactive to get noticed, so I will advertise, send to lists, and do whatever other steps are good. Letting a book sit and hoping for the best is not a good approach.

How easy or hard is it to make a living as an author?

This is such a subjective question. We all are at a different place in life and our expenses are different. A single person can easily make a great living with their efforts going into self-publishing and perhaps blogging.

Throw in a family to provide for and the situation changes. But I will say this—brush up on your marketing and business skills. If you can write, and can market your writing—you can make a living. Being a good at it can make you a great living!

You must learn to deliver what an audience wants which may not be what you personally prefer. Keep looking at your writing as a business and takes the steps a business would to be profitable. The opportunities have never been better.

What advice would you give to someone aspiring to be an author?

The default answer to this question is always the same — write! And then write some more. The more you write the better you will become. And study techniques, but then apply them. All the knowledge in the world is nothing if you don't use it.

Don't be afraid to make mistakes, and don't be critical of yourself. The journey of 1000 miles begins with the first step.

How can readers find out more about you?

Website: www.kenbluttman.com

Maggie James

Tell us about yourself and your books!

I'm a British author currently living in Bristol. I write psychological suspense novels, being lucky enough to do so full-time.

I wrote my first novel, entitled His Kidnapper's Shoes, whilst travelling in Bolivia. An impending birthday inspired me, along with a healthy dose of annoyance at having procrastinated for so long in writing a book. His Kidnapper's Shoes was published in both paperback and e-book format in 2013, followed by three more novels and a novella. I've also written a book for would-be authors, entitled Write Your Novel! From Getting Started to First Draft. I'm now working on my sixth fiction title, Burning Obsession.

Before turning my hand to writing, I worked mainly as an accountant, with a diversion into practicing as a nutritional therapist. Diet and health remain high on my list of interests, along with travel. Accountancy does not, but then it never did. When not writing, going to the gym, doing yoga or travelling, I can be found seeking new four-legged friends to pet; animals are a lifelong love!

How long have you been writing, and how did you become involved in writing?

I was always writing as a child, never doubting I'd grow up to be a novelist. Things rarely turn out as planned, however! As a young woman, I lacked confidence, persuading myself I required more life experience to complete a novel. Moreover, the enormity of the task daunted me; how could I ever string together 80,000 words into a readable story?

Instead, I ended up an accountant but the urge to write persisted. It nagged at me, demanding answers as to when I planned to get off my butt and achieve my dream. Then work went sour, leading to an epiphany for me. Time to become an author! With that intention, I left accountancy to travel for a year, planning to write my novel whilst away.

A few months into my trip, frustrated by the fact I still hadn't written anything, I had my second epiphany. Shamed by the prolific output of another author as I browsed her website, I ran out of excuses; something had to change, and fast. My fiftieth birthday was in sight; the thought of reaching such a milestone date without having written a novel was unbearable. Finally, I was ready.

My plan of action involved travelling to Bolivia to hole up in a town I'd heard was beautiful and not leave until I'd finished my novel. The next morning I booked myself on a bus to La Paz, fought off altitude sickness after arriving and then travelled to Sucre. In this gorgeous colonial-style city things fell into place at last. I wrote every day between the end of December 2010 and February 2011 until I completed the first draft of His Kidnapper's Shoes. What a thrill! I cried with joy after I wrote the last words. I'll never forget the emotion of that moment.

What are you working on at the moment?

I'm editing my sixth fiction title, Burning Obsession, involving a serial arsonist. As he targets Bristol, the body of Ellie Golden is discovered in a burned-out house. The teenager's distraught relatives descend into accusations; before long a family member is arrested on suspicion of her murder, shattering relationships already worn thin. Only Lori, Ellie's sister, believes the police have the wrong man. Whilst coping with her grief, she struggles to support her mother Louise, for whom Ellie was to have been a living kidney donor. Meanwhile, more fires blaze across the city.

Who is burning Bristol, and why are the fires moving ever closer to the Goldens?

Did you have any goals with writing, and if so, how well do you feel you've achieved them? What do you hope to achieve in the future?

My ambitions for my career are limitless; I'll take it as far as I can go! His Kidnapper's Shoes was published in 2013, and I'm pleased with what I've achieved since then; three more novels, a non-fiction book on writing, and my free novella, Blackwater Lake. I've also set up my website and got to grips with marketing. In the future, I aim to build my readership and email subscribers, and connect better with my audience. It's easy for authors to hide behind their keyboards, but I enjoy forging personal connections.

What else? I'm working on getting my titles into audiobook format; Write Your Novel and Blackwater Lake should be ready by early April or even before. The rest will follow over the course of 2016. I'd also love to get them translated into foreign languages, starting with Spanish.

How long does it take you to write a book?

The first draft takes me about two months although I can finish in six weeks if I push myself. In practice, I burn out that way, so I prefer to pace my writing. The longest part, for me, is the revision/editing process. My first attempt is rough, as I suspect is the case for many novelists, which means I take ages to polish it into something readable. At least two to three months are needed before I release it to my wonderful team of beta readers.

What are the hardest parts of being an author for you?

I don't come from a marketing background, so I've had to learn how to promote my books; I still consider myself very much a beginner at it. In our fast-moving world, the goalposts are always shifting! In common with many authors, part of me simply wants to write, nothing else, but the marketing side is essential and can't be ignored. To circumvent this, I'm considering using a virtual assistant in the future.

What do you enjoy most about being an author?

The sheer pleasure of writing; I love painting pictures with words. I'm lucky enough to be doing the one thing I've always dreamed of as a full-time profession — how wonderful is that?

What else do I enjoy? Connecting with other authors is a delight; they offer support in a career known for its isolation. The help I've received has been invaluable; I try to return the favor when possible.

What books or authors have had the most influence on you as an author?

Every fiction title I've ever read has influenced me. I learn something from each novel, whether it's good, bad or indifferent. Since becoming a writer, I've found it hard to switch off my internal critic when reading, though! In my head, I'm often thinking 'Wow, he described that well' or, 'Hmm, I don't like the way she wrote that.' When I'm wearing my reader's hat, it's annoying, but as an author it means I'm continuing to absorb new things.

Names? I admire Stephen King immensely. In my view, he's a master wordsmith, and his prolific output is awe-inspiring. For writers, his semi-autobiographical work 'On Writing' is a great read.

What did you find most useful when you were learning to write and expanding your skills?

The most useful piece of advice I've ever received was not to ignore any gut feelings that something in my writing needs tweaking. I'm not talking about howling mistakes, but those parts that are OK, and yet seem a tad off. Many times I can't identify what's wrong at first, let alone how to fix the issue. It would be easy to disregard my intuition and say 'stuff it!' but I don't. If a passage doesn't sit well with me, chances are it won't for my readers; time spent solving the problem is well worthwhile.

What author services do you pay for, as opposed to doing yourself? Things like cover design, formatting, editing, proofreading, etc.?

Definitely cover design. I'd love to produce my own covers but lack the patience and the artistic skill. Believe me, I tried! My efforts were laughable, however, so I turned the job over to Donna, my lovely graphic designer. She's a joy to work with and I've been delighted with what she's done. An eye-catching cover is essential, I think. I used a pre-made one for Blackwater Lake, however, which worked well.

Everything else I do myself. Scrivener, my wonderful writing software, seamlessly formats my books for kindle and other e-reader devices. As for editing, contrary to the standard advice, I do my own. Amongst my beta readers are individuals with a keen eye for typos; they've been great in finding any I've missed. I've heard too many tales of woe from authors who've paid a lot of money for editing services with poor results. Besides, nobody can know my story, the message I'm trying to convey, as well as I do.

What technology/services/programs do you use as an author? (email subscription services, Dragon software, editing software, etc.)

For email, I prefer Mailchimp; besides being easy to use, it's free for up to 2,000 subscribers. I have Dragon on my computer but I prefer to write my novels via a keyboard, despite being the world's worst typist, a constant source of frustration for me! Something about using my fingers fuels my creativity in a way speaking aloud doesn't.

For writing software, I'm madly in love with Scrivener. Microsoft Word, although good, doesn't satisfy my inner geek. I tried other programs such as yWriter and Write It Now, both excellent, but something drew me towards Scrivener. Although I hated it at first, something eventually clicked; I can't imagine using anything else now. Features I adore include the split screen facility, the ability to store my research within the program and being able to compile straight to kindle format, In addition, it's incredibly versatile.

For editing software, I'm a fan of Pro Writing Aid, great for spotting when I've used words close together or too often. As for my website and blog, Weebly is wonderful. Simple, inexpensive, and it does everything I require.

Other stuff? I use Microsoft OneNote to capture plot ideas, my writing goals, links to my books, checklists for my blog, etc.—it's invaluable! Trackerbox documents my historical sales figures whereas Book Report keeps tabs on my current ones. Finally, Klok records my time. Often it reveals too much messing around on social media sites and not enough writing!

What are your thoughts about ebooks vs. print books?

There's room for both. I envisage print books being around for a while yet. Long term, I'm not so sure; the world is turning digital, with all the advantages technology offers, and we've come too far to retreat. Besides, I'm a keen traveler, loving the fact I can pack hundreds of books onto my Nook and enjoy them on my trips. For curling up for a good read, however, nothing beats the sensual experience of a print edition, especially if it's new. The smell and texture of a virgin novel are wonderful! So I'll continue to buy both, including hardbacks.

What are your thoughts about self-publishing vs traditional publishing?

Self-publishing holds all the aces for authors, in my opinion. I'm not sure why anyone would consider the traditional route, but occasionally I run into people who still believe self-publishing to be second best. For many authors, however, it is very much their first choice. The higher royalties, monthly payments and full control over one's writing career are huge benefits, ones impossible to ignore.

How often do you write, and how do you find or make time to write?

Despite the oft-quoted advice, I don't write every day. I need my weekends free to decompress; however much I love my job, my creative juices require regular breaks. As for finding the time, I'm incredibly fortunate to be a full-time novelist.

Do you plan your whole book out in advance, or just let it flow? What does your writing process look like?

I'm a planner, up to the stage when I can't plot anymore and I itch to get writing. It's only by plunging into the story I know whether my outline works; often what I've envisaged as a chapter only requires a scene, or vice versa. I write in the mornings, keeping the afternoons for marketing work. Despite being a night owl, I'm more creative first thing, so I structure my time accordingly.

What's a typical working day like for you? When and where do you write?

I write for 3-4 hours in the mornings. That time will sometimes be occupied by editing and revision, which I class as part of the writing process. It's all moving my book forward to the finished product. Afternoons are reserved for blogging, tracking my sales and marketing. I keep standard office hours, preferring the discipline that approach offers, and I maintain a timesheet to keep me accountable. As for where I write, I'm lucky in having a dedicated office at home.

Do you ever get Writer's Block? If so, how do you deal with it?

I don't, and I suspect that's true for most authors who plan. If you've prepared a structured outline, it's hard to plead writer's block, as you always have a guideline to follow. I went through a stage of mini burn-out, however, after I published The Second Captive. The month before publication was hectic as I was keen to complete the novel before flying off to Asia. Afterwards I struggled to plot anything worthwhile; as hard as I tried, I couldn't weave a story out of the ideas I liked. In addition, my laptop failed whilst I was in Thailand, which I now consider a good thing as it forced me to take a break. My burn-out led to my non-fiction book, 'Write Your Novel! From Getting Started to First Draft.' I'd intended to publish a confidence-inspiring book for would-be novelists for a while, and writing something other than fiction helped get me back on track.

Do you read your own reviews? If so, how do you deal with bad reviews?

I rarely read my reviews, good or bad. Another novelist once quipped to me, 'that way madness lies,' and I agree. Reviews are written for other readers, not authors, and my days are better spent writing. I've heard of authors who have agonized for weeks over a scathing review, which wastes valuabletime. Even worse, a few have attacked people who have posted bad reviews—that's not the sort of publicity an author wants to attract!

It's impossible to escape criticism. Even the classics attract their share of word warriors on Amazon. A one-star review I read of 'Pride and Prejudice' slammed it as 'clap-trap from start to finish'! People are entitled to their opinion, and if that includes disliking an author's books, then fine.

Other than reviews, do you hear from your readers very often? What kinds of things do they say?

Yes, I'm often contacted by my readers, either via email or social media, and it's wonderful. Here's a recent message I received on Facebook from a complete stranger: 'I have just read your book Black Water Lake—brilliant, I couldn't put it down. I've ordered another three of your books and can't wait to get started.'

Such comments are becoming more frequent, which delights me. One of my aims is to connect better with my audience; I invite everyone who signs up for my newsletter to email me about the books they enjoy.

What are some ways in which you promote your books? What have you found most or least effective?

I use promotional services such as BookBub, Book Hippo, etc., along with Fiverr gigs. I've found them great when combined with a 99c/p deal on Kindle Countdown. Less successful have been Facebook adverts although I'm still testing the waters. An author friend of mine has found them very effective, and Mark Dawson's incredible achievement in this area is inspiring. I'll keep trying!

I prefer to keep everything online. An author friend has achieved a lot of sales through appearances at book fairs, etc., and I've tried such methods without success. My belief is that my time is better spent reaching a global audience rather than a local one.

How easy or hard is it to make a living as an author?

I'd say it depends on your mind-set. If you believe making a living as an author is hard, most likely that will be your experience. If, however, you decide to go for it, do everything you can to succeed and don't get deterred, your odds of success are good. Of course, it depends on how much money you require to make a living, how good your books are and whether you promote them well.

What advice would you give to someone aspiring to be an author?

Don't delay, start today. (Wow, I'm a poet as well!) I loathe clichés, but life is too short to ignore your dreams. Novelists have never had it so good, so why wait?

It's important to be as business-like as possible. Make your story as good as possible, get it professionally edited if need be, and splash out on a striking cover. Then give it your best shot! Stay positive—it makes a huge difference.

How can readers find out more about you?

Website: www.maggiejamesfiction.com

Facebook: www.facebook.com/MJamesFiction/

Mark Messic

Tell us about yourself and your books!

My name is Mark Messick and I'm 16 years-old. I've been writing constantly since the age of 10. I published my first book back in January of 2013 and have been working my butt off ever since, experimenting with all sorts of marketing techniques.

I'm now at the point where I'm making a pretty steady full-time income ($4k/month) from my books, and couldn't be more happy.

Also, just a couple of days ago I launched my very own Kindle training course for authors: www.booksalesdoctor.com

How long have you been writing, and how did you become involved in writing?

I've been writing since the age of 10, which is when I dropped out of public school to start homeschool. I became terribly bored, and at first writing was just a way to entertain myself. But I quickly discovered that I had a burning passion for writing, and would stop at nothing until I was a full-time, bestselling author.

What are you working on at the moment?

Well, right now most of my time is going towards my author training course, Book Sales Doctor.

But I'm also working on a book on the side, which I'm hoping to launch in the next 30–60 days. It's tentatively titled "*Shut Up,*

Brain: How To Be Adventurous, Torch the Rules, and Live Life To the Fullest."

Did you have any goals with writing, and if so, how well do you feel you've achieved them? What do you hope to achieve in the future?

Even when I was 10 years-old my goal was always to become a bestselling author. I think I've pretty well achieved that goal by now. ;-)

In the future I hope to turn my writing into more of a full-fledged business with multiple backend products, maybe a coaching package . . . the whole works.

How long does it take you to write a book?

I'm typically a pretty fast writer. I average 2,500 words per hour. (And that's just typing. I don't use any speech-to-text software or anything.) I wrote my book *Live the Life You Want* in 24 hours. And I think I also wrote another one of my books (*The Stupidly Simple Happiness Formula*) in 24 hours as well, as part of a 24 hour writing challenge.

But if we don't count those books, I'd say I average 2–3 weeks per book. Maybe an entire month if I'm also working on another project (website, backend product, etc.) at the same time.

What are the hardest parts of being an author for you?

I honestly don't know if I can answer this question. I've loved every single second of my author journey, back from when I was 10 years old and opened up Microsoft Word for the first time . . . all the way until now, 6 and a half years later.

What do you enjoy most about being an author?

Getting positive feedback from readers. Hands down, that's the best part. When I hear from a reader that I brightened their day or put a smile on their face or changed their outlook on life . . . oh man. It's the most amazing thing ever.

What books or authors have had the most influence on you as an author?

James Altucher, for sure. He's such an inspiring person, and not only has he changed my writing career, but also my entire life. He's one of the best nonfiction writers I've ever encountered, and I love every sentence that he's ever written.

As a writer, you can learn so much just by reading his stuff and observing how he does what he does.

Definitely check out his book *Choose Yourself*. It's amazing.

What did you find most useful when you were learning to write and expanding your skills?

Hmmm. I'd say a big thing that you can do to improve your writing is to surround yourself with good books in your niche. Completely immerse yourself in your subject, whatever it may be.

They say you're the average of the 5 people you hang around most, right? Well, I think that your writing is also the average of the 5 authors that you read most.

Read what you want to write, you know?

What author services do you pay for, as opposed to doing yourself? Things like cover design, formatting, editing, proofreading, etc.?

I use Archangel Ink for all of my outsourcing needs. Cover design, editing, audiobooks, even book description writing. They offer everything you could ever possibly need as an author.

What technology/services/programs do you use as an author? (email subscription services, Dragon software, editing software, etc.)

I use Active Campaign for my email list, and Microsoft Word for all writing/formatting needs. Nothing fancy.

What are your thoughts about ebooks vs. print books?

I recommend that most authors put most of their focus on ebooks, because they're easier to market and sell. There's nothing wrong with getting a paperback version done (I've got paperbacks of a lot of my books) but they won't sell very well, unless you do something special to promote them.

What are your thoughts about self-publishing vs traditional publishing?

I think self-publishing is a much more feasible and effective method of publishing for most authors. And, in a lot of cases, I think you can be more successful with self-publishing than traditional publishing. Would I ever consider traditionally publishing a book? Sure. Maybe. But for right now self-publishing is working really well for me, and I see no reason to do anything different.

How often do you write, and how do you find or make time to write?

Unless I'm working on another project (like the author training course I just put together) I write every day. That's the only way to put out as many books as I do.

RE how I find time to write . . . one thing that's worked really well for me is to look for little 5 minute pockets of time throughout the day. Even though 5 minutes isn't very long, I'm often surprised at how much I can get done in such a short time. It's not unusual for me to crank out 250 words during one of these little 5 minute bursts.

And if you can string together enough of these 5-minute writing bursts a day . . . you can easily add a couple thousand words a day to your WIP.

Do you plan your whole book out in advance, or just let it flow? What does your writing process look like?

I'm a very heavy outliner. I usually write a 1,000-word outline for every 10,000 words that will be in the final book. It's not rare for me to write a 3,000 – 4,000-word outline, which will turn into a 30,000 – 40,000-word book.

What's a typical working day like for you? When and where do you write?

I'll typically write for 1–2 hours in the mid-morning, and then work on marketing, email, blogging, etc. for another hour after that. Then I've got the rest of the day free to work on school, hobbies, and just whatever.

Do you ever get Writer's Block? If so, how do you deal with it?

Sometimes I'll think I have Writers Block, but once I actually plant my butt in front of my desk and start writing, it's not actually that bad. The key is just to get started.

I've got a quote from Louis L'Amour hanging above my desk to remind of this:

"Start writing, no matter what. The water does not flow until the faucet is turned on."

Do you read your own reviews? If so, how do you deal with bad reviews?

Yeah, I read my reviews. There's a lot to learn from both positive and negative reviews. Positive reviews let me know what I'm doing right, the things I need to keep doing. Negative reviews let me know what I can do to improve my writing and make my next book better.

Well, sometimes.

Other times negative reviews are just complete crap and don't help me at all. In those cases I just let it go and never worry about those reviews ever again. I don't comment or anything. I just forget about it. It's not worth stressing about.

Other than reviews, do you hear from your readers very often? What kinds of things do they say?

Yeah, that's one thing that actually really surprised me. I get a TON of emails and FB Friend Requests from readers.

And, most of the time, if someone took the effort to reach out to me they have nothing but positive things to say about my books.

Although, one time I got an email from a crazy lady, which was hilarious. She started out talking about my most recent book (*Stupid On Purpose*) but then started telling me her entire life story. Everything from lessons her father taught her as a kid, to the one time she nailed a frog to a log and dissected it in her backyard. And then she kept sending me pictures of swords of knives that she owns.

Fun stuff. ;-)

What are some ways in which you promote your books? What have you found most or least effective?

I've got three promotion strategies that I love in particular:

Guest blogging. This is a great way to tap into the audience of an authority in your niche, and send a ton of traffic to your book or email list or whatever. I typically get AT LEAST 100 email subscribers from every guest post I publish.

Podcast interviews. This is pretty much the same as the first one, but instead of writing guest posts you record interviews for podcasts in your niche. I've found this to be just as effective as guest blogging. I can expect 100ish subscribers for every interview I do. Although one time James Altucher asked me to be on his podcast and I ended up getting 500 email subscribers from that. That was a good day. :)

Traffic Tsunami. You know all of those $0.99 Kindle promo sites? Well, most of them don't have enough traffic to really affect your book sales, at least not on their own. But what happens when you get 5, 10 . . . heck, *50* of those sites to promote your book on the same day? Let's just say the results are pretty dang amazing. I talk about this technique A LOT more extensively in my training course for authors.

How easy or hard is it to make a living as an author?

It's pretty easy once you know what you're doing and you have a good system in place. Unfortunately, finding the right system can be pretty hard. It took me about 2 years before I had my first successful month on Kindle.

There's so much marketing advice out there, but most of it is complete crap.

The important thing to remember is that it is possible. Heck, if I'm 16 years-old and making a full-time income on Kindle, imagine what you could do. Like I said, it's not that hard once you have the right system.

So, what is the right system?

Well, I don't think there's a one-size-fits-all answer to that question. Every niche, every book, and every author is different. Different marketing strategies work better in some situations, and not as well in others.

However, I think there are 3 core types of marketing strategies that tend to work for *most* authors. Short term, long-term, and hybrid. I hate to keep plugging my course, but I *do* discuss how to use all 3 of these strategies quite extensively.

What advice would you give to someone aspiring to be an author?

Don't give up.

My first month I made $1.05. It would have been easy for me to give up after that. But I didn't. And I still ended up working my butt off for 2 more years before experiencing any sort of success. It would've been easy to give up at any point during that time. But I didn't. And *that's* why I'm successful.

And you can be just as successful as me, if not more. You just have to persevere, keep pushing forward, and never give up.

If you give up before you give yourself a chance . . . you'll never be successful, and that would positively suck.

How can readers find out more about you?

Website: www.booksalesdoctor.com

Facebook: www.facebook.com/mlmauthor

Michal Stawicki

Tell us about yourself and your books!

I live in Poland, Europe. I've been married for over 15 years and am the father of two boys and one girl. I work full time in the IT industry, and recently, I've become an author. My passions are transparency, integrity and progress.

I write personal development books based on my personal experience. Their topics are scattered all over the place—from helping your kid improving his grades, to fitness, speed reading, time management to personal philosophy and perseverance. I simply map my personal development journey and count on inspiring others to follow my path.

My books are not abstract. I avoid going mystical as much as possible. I don't believe that pure theory is what we need in order to change our lives; the Internet age has proven this quite clearly. My writing shows that I am a relatable, ordinary guy and not some ivory tower guru.

How long have you been writing, and how did you become involved in writing?

I published my first eBook on Amazon on 26th of May 2013. I started writing it on 8th of April the same year.

Up to 33 I was an average guy with average aspirations and ambitions. My life was OK, but I felt I lived below my potential. In August 2012 out of boredom I had read *"The Slight Edge"* by

Jeff Olson. I had not read a single personal development book in 16 years prior.

For the first time I've heard that success and failures do not depend on personal talents or luck, but on doing small things persistently over time.

I couldn't get rid of that book's message from my mind. About a month later I finally decided to give it a try. I wrote several goals, came up with several disciplines and started absorbing personal development materials *en masse.*

In November 2012 I wrote my personal mission statement. It was verbose, over 1300 words, my life was a mess and I had a lot to improve. One sentence in my mission statement was: *"I'm becoming a writer."* Up to that time in my life I wrote only a handful poems to the drawer, a short story from Role Playing Game session with my friends and my master thesis. But the soul searching done during the process of creation personal mission statement revealed that I want to be a writer.

I had no clue what was involved in that.

At the beginning I thought about writing fiction in Polish, my native language. I wrote a couple short stories, published one of them on the forum of big magazine and fellow writers were nice to point out the whole load of shortcomings in my writing. I realized that it will take me years to develop my writing skills.

At the same time, I kept a daily blog in English. I shared with my friends an abbreviated version of personal mission statement creation process and one of my friends encouraged me to write an eBook about this.

Thus, I started writing that first book in English. I played with the thought of making big bucks out of it, but frankly, I didn't expect much. I was hooked when during the first free promo at the book launch my book was downloaded over 450 times. People were willing to read what I had written! That was the amazing feeling. It only progressed when, after the promo, people started buying the book. They were willing to spend their hard earned money on my work!

The rest is history.

What are you working on at the moment?

I'm in the middle of publishing my *Six Simple Steps to Success* series. Three volumes are published, 4 more wait in the processing queue.

In this series I teach a few simple, tangible skills that I discovered are common among successful people, like taking care of their health, knowing themselves or networking. I believe that if you master all of the six areas and do what successful people do, there will be no way but to succeed.

Did you have any goals with writing, and if so, how well do you feel you've achieved them? What do you hope to achieve in the future?

I never had goals. I had dreams. I wanted to be a millionaire selling my books. Well, this definitely didn't happen. On the other hand several of my books sold over 1,000 copies, my writing has really influenced lives of my readers and I earned the first substantial sum of money outside my day job.

Almost 1.5 years after writing my personal mission statement I finally changed the sentence *"I'm becoming a writer"* into *"I'm a writer."* Back then I've just published my first bestseller and earned half of my salary in royalties.

In the future I want to achieve more: more value provided to my readers and more lives changed. I know that number of copies sold and royalties will follow. That's my experience.

How long does it take you to write a book?

My books are short, the longest one is less than 35,000 words. The writing part is easy for me. I can write such a book in a month.

Publishing is another thing. It takes me about three months to process the book through all the phases, since brainstorming the content till putting the book on the digital shelves. Editing, proofreading and marketing are much less enjoyable for me and I tend to drag them.

What are the hardest parts of being an author for you?

Doing it part-time. My past choices (mortgage and so on) chained me to my day job. I cannot quit it before making six figures. I'm forced to take care of my writing business while living my life. It's grueling, not to mention that my day job is so much less satisfactory than my readers' success stories.

What do you enjoy most about being an author?

Making the difference in the lives of others. I'm an introvert and I also have this burning desire of helping people. Those two things are hard to marry, but writing allows me to do exactly that.

What is more, I can do it on the large scale. Tens of thousands people had already read my books. The age of digital communication made the connection between author and readers not only possible, but even easy. I've been contacted by dozens of my readers saying that they got better results in weight loss, parenting or in sticking to their goals for a long time. That's my real reward.

What books or authors have had the most influence on you as an author?

It's really hard to say. I've read thousands of books in my life and they all contributed to my writing a bit. My ghostwriter friend claims that the two basic writer's skills are reading and writing. I attribute to my reading habit a lot of my style. My readers complimented my writing hundreds times and this comes off like a surprise. I should suck at writing with no practice and no skills. I don't, because I had read and have read a lot.

I use Craig Ballantyne's outlining method. He is a Canadian millionaire who made his fortune in the fitness industry and writing is for him just a tiny part of business. I especially like the way he incorporates questions into the outlining process. The writing is much easier when you simply answer the questions.

The way I structure my whole publishing venture I learned from Steve Scott. Writing shorter books, diving into the topic deeply and succinctly is what works well for me.

The only book I used for learning "the craft" was *"On Writing Well"* by William Zinsser and I didn't even finish it. Nonetheless, it made a profound impact on how I approach writing and I'm glad I picked it before I had written my first book.

What did you find most useful when you were learning to write and expanding your skills?

Practice, practice and practice. I "learned" on the way, I don't have time for studying. Day job, family, church community and my own personal development progress leaves no leeway for study. However, I wrote over a million words since I decided to become a writer at the end of 2012.

As I said, I have the foundation of reading thousands of books and some dose of talent, too. It's not just a pep talk either. It's not that I delude myself. My first book is among those that sold over 1,000 copies.

Practice really makes a master. My ghostwriter friend picked my books when I had seven of them and she told me that she clearly saw my improvement over the time. The same are saying my readers who have been following me over the years.

What author services do you pay for, as opposed to doing yourself? Things like cover design, formatting, editing, proofreading, etc.?

I do just a few things. First and foremost, I write. I used my friends' input in one book and had basically written the whole other book—"99 Perseverance Success Stories"—by my co-author. Those are my only two adventures with outsourcing the writing part.

I do my own formatting, mostly because I'm a Scrooge. I can do it myself during the process of reviewing editor's corrections.

I also do my own market research, keyword research, and write my book descriptions.

All the rest: a cover design, editing, proofreading, whatever else, just name it, I outsource.

In the past I had cooperated with Archangel Ink and they did everything except writing for me. I still use their superb editing and proofreading services. They are not the cheapest, but worth it. I have done my last few books with the same team and I just love to work with them.

My covers are done by Jyotsna's team at HappySelfPublishing.com.

What technology/services/programs do you use as an author? (email subscription services, Dragon software, editing software, etc.)

I use Scrivener for writing the first draft of my books. I found a simple Word documents much easier to process through multiple revisions with editors and proofreaders. I also use Word for a spellcheck. I try to give my editors as clean copies as possible, so they can focus on the flow, not on typos.

I use Aweber for email subscription service. They are certainly not perfect, but I did my learning curve with them and have no intention to repeat the process with a different provider.

What are your thoughts about ebooks vs. print books?

I have different opinions, depending on what angle we consider this duel.

As a reader I love print books. I almost don't read them anymore, my eBook vs. print ratio is about 10:1, but I still love the feel and smell of print books. Unfortunately, I lead a very active lifestyle and managing the stock of paperbacks is just too much for me. I read over 100 books a year and most of them I store on my Kindle.

As an author I prefer eBooks. They make something like 95% of my income and formatting for eBooks is significantly easier. Practically it's no work at all. Preparing a manuscript for a print format is altogether different matter. I value print versions, because the profit margin is higher and most of the time I can access totally different audience with them.

What are your thoughts about self-publishing vs traditional publishing?

Nowadays, the Big Five deal has only two advantages:

- they pay a hefty advance; it's very handy for an author to receive money at the beginning and avoid the necessity of waiting for revenues for months or years, and:
- they have superior traditional distribution channels.

But publishers pay authors too little, thereby holding them back. Yeah, I know, "the hefty advances." But just a small group of top authors receive those. The rest receive advances that are smaller by an order of magnitude. And the Big Five pay their authors a royalty that is usually only 7 to 15 percent. That's robbery!

I earn about 60% of the retail price of my books, which is about 50% more than the huge authors earn (picture King, Grisham, and Rowling here).

I can now earn almost five times more than a traditionally published author on a less-than-beneficial contract. Publishers starve the authors giving in theory the access to distribution channels, but with no real marketing effort behind.

Self-publishing is superior to traditional publishing in every aspect. It's better both for authors and readers. The only party which suffers in the effect of self-publishing revolution are big corporations calling themselves publishers.

How often do you write, and how do you find or make time to write?

I write every day. My goal is to produce 1,000 words a day and I miss this amount only a few days in a month. Writing those 1,000 takes me about an hour. I've already hinted how busy I am and this is not an easy feat to meet this goal each day.

But writers write.

This activity is not optional. I may not eat, not sleep, but I have to write. With that attitude I haven't missed a single day since 23rd of September 2013. You always make time for the things that matter.

Do you plan your whole book out in advance, or just let it flow? What does your writing process look like?

Starting from the beginning: idea capture.

My "system" is very feeble, when the idea comes, I try to put it on paper ASAP. Not the whole work, but the idea of course. Be prepared, like the boy scout says. I carry with me all the time sticky notes and a pen. Some great ideas were preserved that way.

Brainstorming

When I am not inspired and the flow of words is reluctant (and that's the norm; if you will wait for inspiration, you could have starved) I always start from brainstorming session. I simply dump on paper everything that comes to my mind in regard of particular subject. I know that none of it will be ever seen by anybody, so the internal critic has no chances to intervene. It beats the writer's block quite efficiently. If you spend half of your "writing" time staring at the blank page, you are not going to be a very productive writer.

It happens quite a lot that my final piece contains the whole sentences from my brainstorming sessions. That's another advantage.

Outline

Next, I outline my writing. In case of smaller pieces, like a blog post or article below 1,000 words I usually skip this phase, my brainstorming session gives it a structure in a by-the-way matter. In case of books I found this step priceless. More important than the actual outlining process is how it affects (improves!) your writing.

First of all it gives your message or story the structure. I wrote my first few books without outline and fortunately for my readers they were short. Without an outline I:

- ramble
- write slower, because I stop all the time thinking what to write next
- jump from topic to topic

- introduce on a whim new sections which don't fit very well the overall message
- forget about important points

and commit other writing atrocities.

By outlining your work you avoid most of those mistakes, meaning that your writing is better.

Writing

Having an outline, I follow it and write every day till the book is finished.

Editing

Editing is a quite important part of writing. Here comes the lesson: most writers suck at editing their work. And that's fine. Repeat 10 times aloud: *"I suck at editing and that's fine!"* There are some rare individuals who are able to produce excellent, almost print-ready work from their first draft. They are to be admired, not emulated. It's a talent, like an absolute pitch.

The worst thing you can do for your writing is editing WHILE writing. It's a big, fat NO! Nothing improved more my style, my speed and the flow of my content than ignoring this itch to correct a random typo or go back and insert a comma.

When writing, concentrate on putting the words out of your head and on the paper. You can chisel them later . . . but only if they will appear on paper in the first place. Hence, write and don't pay attention to your mistakes when you create the content.

What's a typical working day like for you? When and where do you write?

I wake up early morning 4–5 am, sleep deprived as usual. I do my morning ritual which has very little to do with any work and much with motivation and maintenance of my physical, mental and spiritual wellbeing.

I work for about an hour and I'm off to my day job. I commute almost 1.5 hours in one way. I spend about 50 minutes on a train and usual I use this leg of my commute as a writing session, producing from 600 to 1,000 words. Sometimes I am able to smuggle my stuff between the tasks I do for my employer. Sometimes I have so much work and overtime that I barely find time for my writing, family and personal development at all.

If I haven't produced 1,000 words I usually write on a train back home as well. Everything else—marketing, interacting with readers via email and social media, supervising the publishing process (editing, covers, etc.)—is done in a hectic manner when I found a spare minute and have access to the computer.

I try to habitualize the most important parts of my business like pre-editing my texts (a clean draft, remember?) and cultivating my email list. Those tasks are on my daily habits list with other activities important to me, like my personal and spiritual development.

Sometimes I'm too exhausted and I sleep on a trains. Then I write whenever and wherever I can: at the office during working hours, at home between household chores or when everybody else finally are asleep.

Do you ever get Writer's Block? If so, how do you deal with it?

I don't. I don't ever get pink unicorn or fire-breathing dragon too.

Writing is not an option, it's a must.

I have one secret weapon when I feel resistance. I simply write something else. I have dozens unfinished writing projects. I have no writing schedule, so I can freely switch from writing a non-fiction eBook to novel or blog post or Quora answer . . .

Do you read your own reviews? If so, how do you deal with bad reviews?

Yes, every single one of them. There are no bad reviews. There are only bad reviewers :-;

Frankly, there are only two types of negative reviews:

- opinions—these I shrug off
- feedback—those I try to apply to my writing

One of my books was trashed in ratings on Goodreads. I asked the readers who gave me one star reviews about their opinion and a few of them, independently, said that it was too verbose and poorly edited. I edited the book once again, cutting out 10% of the content and I haven't heard complaints about that book again.

Other than reviews, do you hear from your readers very often? What kinds of things do they say?

I encourage my readers to sign up to my email list. I sent them updates about my future books and some personal development tips. From time to time I have the real avalanche of interactions, like this week when I asked for volunteers to beta-read my next book.

Apart from email list I think I don't have a single week without an email from my readers. Those are usually two kinds of messages — they either ask for advice (all in all I write how-to personal development books) or they thank me for the difference my books and articles made in their live. I love those success stories the most.

What are some ways in which you promote your books? What have you found most or least effective?

There is very little promotion I do for my books. With my multiple obligations I chose to focus on writing, not marketing. The only real promotion I do nowadays is stacking the promos from book promo sites at the beginning of a book launch.

I tried to revive my older books by using Countdown Deals and free promos in the past, but it was never worth the hustle. I prefer to spend time with my family or to write the next book than organizing the promotions.

And within less than three years of my author career I noticed that free promotions give less and less return. You need to put a lot of effort to take the free promotion off the ground to get the same results as in 2013.

In the past I took part in a few online book events and the results were awesome. Unfortunately, I had to organize them myself and again, even the good results didn't justify the massive amount of work that needed to be put in organizing the event.

A few months ago I started to be active on Quora and this platform serves me well in promoting my books. The eBooks sales results weren't directly affected very much, but I gained some traction in paperback sales and eBooks sales outside of Amazon. Before Quora those revenue streams were about 3% of my business, now they are more like 10%.

Also, the traffic to my blog doubled and I'm finally getting some email subscribers from it. I consider Quora my long term promotion strategy that will build awareness about my brand among Quora readers via multiple points of exposure to my books titles.

How easy or hard is it to make a living as an author?

It's very easy in my opinion. I do it part time, maybe 15 hours a week and in 2015 my revenues reached half of my IT consultant salary. The income was about half of it, because I reinvest a lot, but here is the picture: I've been writing, in a foreign language, for less than three years and I earned half of my salary. I studied 10 years and have been working in IT for 12 years to achieve my current salary level. Almost every author I know who is writing full time makes decent money.

It doesn't change the fact that this is a highly competitive occupation. There are millions and millions books out there and at least hundreds of thousand people who wrote them and want the attention of readers too.

I think it's worth it nonetheless. Writing is the most fulfilling thing I've done in my whole life.

What advice would you give to someone aspiring to be an author?

Writers write. Write every day.

The days of publishers are the thing of the past. Forget about getting an agent and a book deal. It will be time for that (and only for vanity reasons) when you become a successful self-published author.

Remember who your boss is. They are your readers not literary critics, Amazon or your neighbor telling you that you cannot make a living writing. Always take good care of your readers. We live in the interconnected world, take advantage of that and connect with them. Your "boss" will tell you what "he" expects from your books which will spare you a lot of second guessing and dead ends.

A self-published author is an authorpreneur. Writing talent is not enough to make a career. You need rudimentary skills in moving in the online world. You need your own platform—a blog, podcast or video channel—and you need to build your email list from day one (or preferably months before publishing the first book).

Educate yourself in social media, email marketing and publishing. You don't have to be an expert, but you need the basic level knowledge to recognize if someone wants to rob you or offers a decent service for a fair price.

Don't start a writing career to make a lot of bucks. At the beginning you will spend more than you earn. In the first eight months I earned something like forty bucks.

Yes, you can make a lot of money exploiting the system. I know a few Kindle Gold Rushers who are making thousands every month. One of them told me that he will quit this activity as soon as he will build a business "he could stand behind." None of those Kindle Gold Rushers are worth calling an author and they don't add value to the lives of their readers. That's a bad karma waiting to bite them back in their asses.

Prepare for the long haul. I will write for the rest of my life. I recommend you the same approach to your author career.

How can readers find out more about you?

Website: www.expandbeyondyourself.com/

Mitch Goth

Tell us about yourself and your books!

Originally from Wisconsin, I'm currently living in Ohio where I'm studying for a degree in literature from Antioch College. Along with my writing, I'm an avid paranormal investigator with almost seven years experience now. My books, surprisingly, are not horror. They're not far off though, mostly sticking in the thriller genre. I've strayed from that genre a few times, but it has mostly stayed in the thriller/suspense. Right now I'm expanding a little. Just started writing my first paranormal horror novel, and it's a great experience!

How long have you been writing, and how did you become involved in writing?

I've been a writer for pretty much all my life, coming up with stories whenever I had a chance to daydream since grade school. It wasn't until high school that I started actually writing them down. During my freshman year, I wrote my first novel-length manuscript. A year later I wrote another. I started self-publishing in 2013 with a series of crime thrillers. Since then, most everything I have written has been novel or novella-length and landed online in the self-published world.

What are you working on at the moment?

Right now I'm working on my first paranormal horror novel, with the working title *Over the Ha-Ha Walls*. After a long time trying to figure out how to put my personal paranormal experiences into a piece of fiction, I think I finally figured it out. I'm about 20,000 words into it and it's going very well. It's nice to diversify genres sometimes. I would suggest every writer give it a try at some point.

Did you have any goals with writing, and if so, how well do you feel you've achieved them? What do you hope to achieve in the future?

When I first started, I had all sorts of writing goals. At first, all I wanted was to successfully publish a book, and that was almost twenty books ago now. Now my goal is to just let writing keep taking me in the direction I'm going now. Self-publishing has been growing and developing as a legitimate publishing medium for years now, and I'm excited to see where it'll be, and where I'll be, five, ten, twenty years down the road. I have no defined goals for the future besides keeping on writing. If a writer never quits, they'll get where they want to go.

How long does it take you to write a book?

That depends on what I'm trying to do with the story. Some of my shorter novellas or novels take only a month or two to write. More recently I've been writer longer books (80–100k words) and that has taken longer. The books I have most recently completed took about three and a half months. I try to write as much as I can everyday, often doing 1,000 — 3,000 words per day.

What are the hardest parts of being an author for you?

The hardest part is everything that comes after the actual writing. Editing is a long, hard process, but one I need to do. Formatting the book for paperback and ebooks is often a hassle. Everything needs to be perfect if you want it to come out right. There's so much technical stuff added into the creative process when it comes to writing for publication. All of that is the hardest thing, mostly because it takes me away from the actual writing.

What do you enjoy most about being an author?

The writing. I started doing this because I like telling stories, seeing where it goes, creating characters and worlds and seeing what happens to them. It's the best experience in the world.

What books or authors have had the most influence on you as an author?

When I was younger I read a lot of Stephen King. His work was part of the reason I got interested in the paranormal to begin with. In terms of my own writing, I get my inspirations from a lot of different writers. Classic writers like Kate Chopin and F. Scott Fitzgerald inspire me to write. I think that maybe if I keep working I'll be as good at it as them someday.

What did you find most useful when you were learning to write and expanding your skills?

Above all, the most useful thing I did when learning to write (aside from writing) was observing the world around me like a writer. I overhear conversations all around me and hone in my ability at making realistic dialogue by analyzing and listing to how people actually talk. I look at things around me and think about how I would describe them in a book. I take in my environment and consider it as a narrative setting. The way to better writing is to go out and live, experience the world and everything in it like it is part of a book where you're the main character.

What author services do you pay for, as opposed to doing yourself? Things like cover design, formatting, editing, proofreading, etc.?

I pay for very little. I get a cover designer who is a close friend to do that work for a lot less than the costs of the average designer-for-hire out there. In terms of editing, I have a group of beta-readers that I depend on and use the ProWritingAid software, which is only a few dollars for a year subscription and it's very useful when it comes to early rounds of editing. Formatting, even though it's a headache, is something I do myself. I like to be a self-contained cottage industry whenever I can.

What technology/services/programs do you use as an author? (email subscription services, Dragon software, editing software, etc.)

For marketing I often use Ereader News Today for select promotions. I use ProWritingAid for my editing. To help reach my readers and fans, I use MailChimp for news on new releases and promotions happening.

What are your thoughts about ebooks vs. print books?

They co-exist quite nicely. A lot of people thought that ebooks would be the death of print, but that's like saying cars would replace bicycles or escalators would replace stairs. Things can exist together, and do often. Books are no different. I like the feeling of actually turning pages and holding a book in front of me, but I often opt for ebooks because they're cheaper and I can get them right away.

What are your thoughts about self-publishing vs traditional publishing?

The traditional publishing industry is, well, an industry. It'll do what it wants to do, it'll send people down the river when it feels like it, it'll promote the same old same old because that's what sells. It's a business first, and that rubs a lot of people the wrong way. It's a lot like the music industry in many ways. The industry wants you to think that what is on the front stands in bookstores and promoted on sponsored social media posts is all there is. But, just like in the music industry, there's so much great stuff beneath the surface in the form of independent artists. You just have to dig to find it, and know the difference between what's good and what's bad in that realm. The industry wants to tell you that you're not smart enough to tell the difference yourself, that they need to be the gatekeepers because people can't be their own gatekeepers. They want to dictate what's good for the reader and what the reader wants, but the reader is an individual.

Many people who aren't big readers aren't because they can't find a book they like, because it doesn't fit into the industry cookie cutter. Once indie publishing gets more out there in the world, more people will find interest in reading, because more unique, niche-genre stories will find audiences that the industry will swear doesn't exist. Independent publishing (self-publishing) is, in some way or another, the future. It's much bigger than it used to be, and will keep growing. Whether it will unseat the industry as the leading seller has yet to be seen, but it provides readers and writers both with a special, never before seen place to read and be read without industry restriction. It is true artistic freedom for the writer and freedom of choice for the reader. It'll be around, and growing, for a long time.

How often do you write, and how do you find or make time to write?

I try to write every day, but that doesn't happen sometimes. I run on a college student schedule, which changes in terms of classes and jobs every three months. So my writing times and writing frequency changes based on that. More often than not, I'm able to fit writing into my daily (or near daily) schedule because I prioritize it over most everything. If my college work gets in the way, I don't do that work until my writing is done. That strategy has caused some minor conflict in the past, but I'm doing what I love and powering forward in my writing career. Writing most likely won't always be able to be my top priority, but I'm hell bent on keeping it that way while it still can be.

Do you plan your whole book out in advance, or just let it flow? What does your writing process look like?

I am definitely an outliner through and through. Before I write the book I plan the whole plot out. An outline of mine often ends up anywhere between 20 and 40 thousand words. I find that's the only way I can keep my story straight, my characters well developed, and my story free of plot holes. Although that's not to say my story and my characters can't surprise me. I leave enough things able to shift and change freely with the story that it doesn't come out too rigid or lifeless due to outlining. I have found my perfect center when it comes to medium, a mix between intense planning and freedom for my story. If you plan too much, the final product will clearly follow a formula and become less interesting, but if you go by the seat of your pants you risk digressing or shifting the story in a weird direction and lose track of it (if you're anything like me, that is). I commend those who can just let it flow, they can hold their creativity and story in place a lot better than me. Without my outlining, my stories would be far more "out there" and, well, crazy beyond traditional crazy story standards.

What's a typical working day like for you? When and where do you write?

Well, my writing times change when my school and work schedules do. As of right now, I find time to write shortly after lunch for a few hours. The last three months of last year I was a night writer, the three month period before that I was a late afternoon/evening writer. Time is never much of a factor for me, as long as it isn't too early in the morning or late at night, my mind just isn't straight enough to do it then. The "where" of it has always stayed constant. I write in my own room, alone. I can't have anyone in the room and it has to be a constant writing space. I can't write in one place one day and then switch to somewhere else the next. I'm a nester, and I'm very protective of my nest once I build it.

Do you ever get Writer's Block? If so, how do you deal with it?

I have yet to get writer's block in the normal sense of the term. My mind is always on creative mode and always creating new ideas, and that's actually my problems. I come up with too many ideas too quickly, and struggle to pick one and dedicate myself to it, which can put a pause on my writing process. But, sooner or later, I always get back on track and keep those unused ideas in my mind to grow and change so hopefully I can use them later. For instance, the paranormal horror novel I'm working on now is a shift from a story I tried to write two and a half years ago. I went with another story back then and let this one sit in its cocoon and come out better than I ever could have made it then. Writer's block has never been a problem, but a crowded mind has kept me stalled temporarily. But, I will always prefer too many ideas than none at all.

Do you read your own reviews? If so, how do you deal with bad reviews?

I always read the reviews I get, good or bad. With the good ones, it's nice to get an extra boost of motivation to keep going, that someone out there liked what I wrote enough to write a five-star review.

With the bad ones, I take it in stride and stand by them. They hurt, but that's part of the process. If you can't handle hurt and rejection as a writer, you won't go too far. You could write the perfect novel, and still only 99% of people will like it, if that. There will be bad reviews for everything you write and put out to the world, that's a fact. You've just got to deal with it. Take it further even, like I do, stand by them. A great artist will stand by their failures and shortcomings as confidently as they do their accomplishments. Not only do they ground you and remind you that you're not perfect, they'll remind you that you'll always have work to do, always have growing to do as a writer, as an artist. Your work is never finished.

Other than reviews, do you hear from your readers very often? What kinds of things do they say?

It's not often I hear from readers outside of reviews, but it's always a great experience when I do. I find that there aren't many people in the world that will harbor enough hate for a work to seek out the writer when they don't like it, but there are many who will do all they can to let the writer know, personally, just how much they loved it. I have gotten a few emails from people saying that they loved the first book in a series and can't wait for the next or, in one case, that one of my books actually changed their lives. I never thought I would get a piece of fan mail like that, but even though it was a few years ago now it still motivates me to continue. If one person has already felt something that deeply for my work, I can't wait to see what people will think ten years from now. When I started publishing,

I said if I can impact one person in some way with what I write it would be worth it. So far, it has been very worth it, but I'm not done yet. There's more people I can reach, more I can entertain, more I can impact in any way. I'm far from done.

What are some ways in which you promote your books? What have you found most or least effective?

I promote my books using both my own platform as well as promotional services. The promotional services do well for short bursts, but aren't much for residual sales. They work well for a few days at a time, but if you want longevity you need to build yourself a platform. That can be done in a variety of ways. A good way to collect long term readers and buyers is a mailing list, which can be done easily with MailChimp. It's usually a long process to collect enough people with that list to build a strong, stable reader base. I'm not even there yet. Platforms need a lot of work, but the bigger they get the better you look to publishers and agents, if that's your end goal anyway. I'm also a big user of social media as a marketing tool. I find my Facebook page a great way to reach new people, as I'm always getting a good stream of new 'likes' and growing my reach for every post and every promotional link I send out there. With that, Facebook is an easy way for fans to connect with writers. Sometimes, emailing an author intimidates people a lot more than a simple Facebook message or wall post. It's an informal, yet powerful way to get to know the people who read your work.

How easy or hard is it to make a living as an author?

It's rough. I'm nowhere close to it, not many are. Many people think book writing is some kind of gold ticket to fat royalty checks and advances from major publishers. That couldn't be any more false. Self-publishing needs work, and lots of it, if you're going to make a living off it. I hope to make a living of it one day, but I'm years off from that, unless one of my releases is a wild runaway success (fingers crossed!). And in the traditional publishing world it is just as hard. These days, advances aren't huge for first time authors, or even for many contract extensions. The industry isn't what it used to be. Even if you do get a solid advance, you'd do well to invest that right back into your book marketing, because the companies aren't doing much of that anymore, and if your book flops they'll drop you and you're back at square one. There is no easy way to make a living as an author, but that shouldn't be the only goal to it. If you started writing with your only goal to make lots of money and live off it, you got into it for the wrong reasons. Yeah, getting money for what you write is amazing, and the more that comes in the better. Like I said, I hope to make a life off it someday down the road. But that's not what it's all about for me. It's about the writing, telling a story, and giving it to people who want to read it.

What advice would you give to someone aspiring to be an author?

Practice before you do anything. I know you might think your first manuscript is great stuff, but let it sit. Write more manuscripts, hold back on them. Go back to the first, see all the ways you can improve it based on what you learned from all the others you wrote. Practice before you reach out into the publishing world. And never lose track about why you started writing in the first place. There have been plenty of times where I saw low, or no, sales for a while and wondered what I was even doing. I got rejection letter after rejection letter from publishers and agents, and I thought maybe I would have better chances being a doctor or a jeweler, something normal like that. Then I remembered I was writing for years before sales and query letters even became a thing in my life. That's not why I started, that's not why I kept at it. I keep at it because it's my passion. I couldn't stop if I wanted to. All that other stuff is secondary as long as you remember why you started doing it. If your base is strong, you'll never fall.

How can readers find out more about you?

Website: www.mitchgoth.blogspot.com

Facebook: www.facebook.com/MitchellGothAuthor

Monique McDonnell

Tell us about yourself and your books!

I am an Australian author who writes contemporary women's fiction including chick lit and romance. I have written all my life especially as a child when I loved to write short stories and poetry. At University I studied Creative Writing as part of my Communication degree. Afterwards I was busy working in public relations I didn't write for pleasure for quite a few years although I wrote many media releases, brochures and newsletters. (And I still do in my day-job!)

When I began to write again I noticed a trend—writing dark unhappy stories made me unhappy. So I made a decision to write a novel with a happy ending and I have been writing happy stories ever since.

I a member of the writing group The Writer's Dozen and our anthology Better Than Chocolate raised over $10,000 for the charity Room to Read and helped build a library in South East Asia. I am also a member of the Romance Writers of Australia.

Since 2013 have written and published five stand-alone romantic comedies and Any Way You Slice It, Any Way You Dream It and Any Way You Fight it the first books in the new six book Upper Crust Series.

I live on Sydney's Northern Beaches with my husband and daughter.

How long have you been writing, and how did you become involved in writing?

I've been writing since I was a kid. My mother has notebooks full of my angst-ridden poetry. I did a minor in Creative Writing at University but it was a soul-sucking experience and I stopped for a few years after that. I began writing in earnest about 10 years ago. I signed up for a course called The Year of the Novel at the NSW Writer's Centre and the objective was to write the first draft of your novel in that year. I did that and I've been writing consistently ever since.

What are you working on at the moment?

At the moment I'm half way through publishing a series of romantic comedies — The Upper Crust Series. It's a six book series and I've already published the first three books with the second three due out in the first half of 2016.

Did you have any goals with writing, and if so, how well do you feel you've achieved them? What do you hope to achieve in the future?

I love a goal. Working alone as an author, if I didn't have goals I would have given up years ago. My goals have changed over the years. First it was to finish a novel. Then I wanted to see if I could write a second novel. I wanted to be brave and put my books out and try to get published. I didn't achieve my goal of traditional publication so I changed my goals. Once I decided to be an indie author I wanted to develop strong branding for my books and build my bookshelf up. This year my goal is to publish three novels in my series, two novellas and a standalone novel. Who knows what will next?

How long does it take you to write a book?

That's a tough question. I can do a good draft in a couple of months if I'm on a roll. The writing and rewriting is slower for me than that. Of course some books are easier than others and sometimes I put project aside and come back to it. The more I write the faster I get because some things are innate for me now that definitely weren't at the start.

What are the hardest parts of being an author for you?

For me the hardest part of the writing is editing, I'm just not that excited by it, but it's part of the process so I have to just do it. In terms of being an author the constant promoting is the hardest part. The online landscape changes so quickly that just when you think you have it sorted it shifts again. Keeping on top of it is exhausting.

What do you enjoy most about being an author?

I love the writing of the first draft. For me diving into a new world and making friends with new characters is pure bliss.

What books or authors have had the most influence on you as an author?

As a child I was a voracious reader (I guess nothing has changed) but Little Women was my favorite book and I wanted to be like Jo. Even though I write nothing at all like him Pat Conroy's novels really stuck with me. In my genre I've been inspired by Meg Cabot and Janet Evanovich who write fun stories you don't want to put down.

What did you find most useful when you were learning to write and expanding your skills?

I'm in a writing group at the NSW Writer's Centre and that has been invaluable from me. I've been in that group for ten years now and without it I would have given up years ago. I'm also a member of the Romance Writers of Australia. I attend their conference every year and that has also provided me with both great information and resources but also an expanded network of writers I can lean on for support.

What author services do you pay for, as opposed to doing yourself? Things like cover design, formatting, editing, proofreading, etc.?

I pay for cover design, editing, proofreading and formatting (Although I plan to learn how to format myself this year so that I can update the back-matter of my books easily.)

What technology/services/programs do you use as an author? (email subscription services, Dragon software, editing software, etc.)

Technology is not really my bag but I've had to learn to embrace it. I have a website and blog hosted on Weebly, I use Mailchimp for email subscription, and I write in Scrivener, I use both Tweetdeck and Hootsuite to manage my social media posts. I've used some services on Fiverr.com to help me get things done at a pinch as well. I tried using Grammarly but it ate my book and ruined about 2 months of my life in doing so, therefore I will never use it again.

What are your thoughts about ebooks vs. print books?

As an indie author I love ebooks. The truth is even I'm an Australian writer most of my sales are in the US and those lovely people like ebooks. I do have print copies of my books but there just aren't that many avenues for me to sell them. I do a local signing or two every year and my friends and relatives prefer print so I get print books done but for me ebooks are easier and more practical.

What are your thoughts about self-publishing vs traditional publishing?

If someone offered me a traditional paperback publishing deal, I'd be thrilled. I think most writers want that if they're honest. I still want to see my book at the airport, thank you very much. Now that I've said that I don't think I would be getting any more sales with a traditional publisher selling only ebooks of my books (a couple of the big romance publishers would be exceptions but not one of the smaller ones). I check my sales against my peers so I know where they're at and where I'm at. I've pitched to agents and publishers who have basically told me as much. Are my sales amazing? No. Would they do anything much more than I'm doing? No. I look at their covers and they're using the same stock photos I use. I use the same editors. It would save me the cost of an edit and cover but it would cost me lots of knowledge and control.

How often do you write, and how do you find or make time to write?

I try and write every day. I'm lucky because at the moment I'm self-employed so I can work my writing time around my job.

Do you plan your whole book out in advance, or just let it flow? What does your writing process look like?

I'm a bit of a mix of planner and plotter. I usually get an idea for the book and it's usually a premise about the main character. So I start at the beginning and go from there. Sometimes I get a third of the way in and do a plot map for the whole book then. Other times I write the first draft and then make a list of scenes per chapter to see where the gaps are and if the book is balanced or unbalanced.

What's a typical working day like for you? When and where do you write?

I read a great book last year that explained that we need to work out our most productive times of day and I have found that very useful. I already knew I was definitely not a morning person but I examined my habits more clearly than that. As I said before I work from home so I can often balance my time to my advantage. I tend to do administration and simple tasks first up while the caffeine kicks in, both for my writing and my job. If I have to do creative tasks for work, I do those between ten and twelve noon and then go back to admin for a while and then I write between two and four. If I don't have to be creative I write first and do it in two blocks. I try and spend at least two hours a day writing (I don't mean editing and blog posts when I say writing I mean new scenes). I write usually on my dining room table but sometimes in cafes, at the library, in the car if that's how it has to be.

Do you ever get Writer's Block? If so, how do you deal with it?

I certainly do. After I had a novel sit at a publishing house for 9 months (during which time they gave me lots of reason to hope) only to be rejected I didn't write for a year. I was crushed by the process more than the rejection itself. Now days I have a daily writing practice. In 2015 I started a Facebook group #1000wordsaday where authors encourage each other to reach that goal and beyond daily. Seen as the group was my idea I now feel like I have to show up and that means I tend to write through my blocks, even if what I write is rubbish.

Do you read your own reviews? If so, how do you deal with bad reviews?

I really don't read them much anymore except to acknowledge them. I love them, and I appreciate them, and I absolutely wish I had more but somewhere along the line I've learned to switch off that paranoia. The truth is some people think a 3-star review is very generous and other people think that's scathing so it's way too easy to turn yourself inside out. If someone takes the time to leave a review good or bad I guess that means your book has touched them in some way.

Other than reviews, do you hear from your readers very often? What kinds of things do they say?

I hear from readers via Facebook messaging and email. Sometimes they ask when the next book will be out or they just write to say they enjoyed a book.

What are some ways in which you promote your books? What have you found most or least effective?

I do free days for my books every now and then although free is certainly not what it was a few years back. (My first free days for a book I had 30,000 downloads with no Bookbub). I use some of the smaller book promo sites but I tend not to pay much to promote free days. I seem to get pretty solid results anyway. I don't think book tours are all that useful unless you do a review tour. Nor do I think getting a service to Tweet about your book, unless it is a new release, helps. I do price pulsing and that can be helpful especially around release day. I'm on Twitter and Facebook and I think that helps some. I quite like Facebook parties because they're a good way to engage with readers and capture new readers. Similarly, I've done some blog hops that have helped me find new readers.

How easy or hard is it to make a living as an author?

Oh, it is hard, there's no question about that. I'm definitely not making one yet. I enjoy writing and telling stories and I hope that one day that translates into me making a living from it.

What advice would you give to someone aspiring to be an author?

I have several pieces of advice. First, write the book you want to write, but write it. Second, be careful who you share it with; you don't want people crushing your spirit because they don't know how to give constructive criticism. Third, even constructive criticism is hard to take as a writer but don't dismiss it out of hand, sit with it and see if it resonates with you. Fourth, keep in mind that ultimately it's your story so you don't have to take that advice if you don't want to, only if it feels right.

How can readers find out more about you?

Website: www.moniquemcdonellauthor.com

Facebook: www.facebook.com/MoniqueMcDonellAuthor/

O.N. Stefan

Tell us about yourself and your books!

I have two thrillers published and am writing a third due to be released later this year.

How long have you been writing, and how did you become involved in writing?

I've been writing for many years. I got involved when a friend asked me if I'd like to join a Saturday morning writing group to make up numbers. I was hooked from then on.

What are you working on at the moment?

My latest thriller 'Guns and Roses' is the second book in my Amanda Blake series. The first one is titled The Deadly Caress. I plan to release this thriller in the latter half of 2016.

Did you have any goals with writing, and if so, how well do you feel you've achieved them? What do you hope to achieve in the future?

My goals are to get better and better writing stories that people enjoy. I hope to hit the best sellers lists worldwide. Although, I haven't embarked on translations of my existing thrillers as yet.

How long does it take you to write a book?

It can take anywhere from six to ten months to complete a book. This includes many drafts and a couple rounds of editing and proofreading.

What are the hardest parts of being an author for you?

I find editing the biggest challenge as being so close to a story makes it difficult to spot all the typing mistakes and holes.

What do you enjoy most about being an author?

I love making up stories and sharing them with others.

What books or authors have had the most influence on you as an author?

I enjoy such a variety of stories it's hard to pick. I guess I would have to include Lee Child, Jodi Picoult, Sue Grafton, Terry Brooks, Patricia Cornwell, H.G. Wells, P.D. James, Stieg Larsson, Tim Winton, Alice Sebold and William Shakespeare.

What did you find most useful when you were learning to write and expanding your skills?

Writing conferences and courses have been immensely helpful. I always go with an open mind hoping to take away one new skill. Also, I find writing blogs on the web a mine of useful information.

What author services do you pay for, as opposed to doing yourself? Things like cover design, formatting, editing, proofreading, etc.?

I always hire an editor, proofreader and cover designer. I don't think it helps an author's profile to save on paying someone to do these tasks. If the reader has a poor reading experience due to bad editing or proofreading, then they are very unlikely to buy your next book.

A cover is your first selling point, and if you are not versed in cover design and creative software then leave it to someone who is as an amateurish cover conveys to the reader that the contents of said book are substandard as well. This is especially so on Amazon Kindle where one click can lead your potential buy to another book.

You can find someone who will do a very nice cover on Fiverr.com for you. That leaves you time to concentrate on writing. For my second thriller I had two covers made because the first one didn't have the right feel and the feedback on it from my Facebook friends was negative. I found another cover designer and she created a great cover for me.

So far, I have been doing the formatting myself. It's not a job I particularly enjoy doing but I have some knowledge of software and it gives me the opportunity to pick up an error in my story that I had missed previously.

What technology/services/programs do you use as an author? (email subscription services, Dragon software, editing software, etc.)

I don't write in a notebook first like some authors. I type my stories directly into the computer in Microsoft Word as I find this quick and easy. I'm a fast typist and I can keep up with my thoughts, usually. Word has options to let you know misspelt words, passive phrases and the like. I use these apps but don't rely on them entirely as it's not fail safe. Also, I use Microsoft Inspiration for mapping my characters as far as attributes, speech preferences as in swear words, where they went to school, their likes and dislikes, what motivates them and so on. It's a simple inexpensive program where I pull balloons onto the screen and connect people that are related in some way be it as friends or sisters and click on the balloons to open the notes on each person where I include their characteristics.

Not so long ago you had to convert your Word file into another program before you could upload it to Kindle. This is no longer the case and you can upload your Word file directly to Kindle. Just ensure that you check all formatting is consistent throughout your book.

What are your thoughts about ebooks vs. print books?

I believe there is a place for both ebooks and print books. There is something to be said for being able to download a book and start reading it right away. You can have thousands of books downloaded on your IPad or kindle to take with you on holidays. I usually start reading one book and if I'm not enjoying it, I move on to the next. Print books are lovely to hold and I love going into a book store and browsing. The only drawback with ebooks versus print is that if you want to go back to a certain spot to check this or that, it's far easier to do that with a print book. I equally enjoy print books and ebooks.

What are your thoughts about self-publishing vs traditional publishing?

Self-publishing has opened up a new world for authors that would never have been picked up by traditional publishers or authors that didn't get a good deal with the traditional publishers. I don't believe Fifty Shades of Grey would ever have been offered a contract by a traditional publisher had it not sold millions of copies as an ebook first.

Publishing houses are playing catch up with where online book retailing is going. It the same old analogy of not being able to turn around an elephant quickly enough. I don't know where it will end but there are new publishers cropping up all of the time and the nimble will get there and the slow to change will not. Years ago, the traditional publishers dictated the terms to an author but that is in flux now as the landscape has changed forever. Without authors and readers, publishers would not have a business.

How often do you write, and how do you find or make time to write?

I snatch moments to write whenever I can. I've written in cafes, pubs and with grandchildren running around me.

Do you plan your whole book out in advance, or just let it flow? What does your writing process look like?

I do like to plot out the story line but I don't always stick to it. The characters sometimes dictate where the story should go. As long as the ending fits within my plan, I go along with where the characters lead me.

What's a typical working day like for you? When and where do you write?

I don't have a typical writing day as I write where ever I can. I take my laptop when I go on short holidays but not when I go overseas as that's too cumbersome and I wouldn't get enough time to write. I do like to get 1000 words down, however, I have produced 10,000 words in a day at times. Other times I'm lucky to produce 300 words. So it does vary.

Do you ever get Writer's Block? If so, how do you deal with it?

I can't say I get writer's block. I prefer to think of it as the scene I want to write hasn't matured in my head. I find if I can't write a scene, I let it simmer in my thoughts for a couple of days and then have another go.

Do you read your own reviews? If so, how do you deal with bad reviews?

I always read my reviews and am delighted if a reader has enjoyed my story. Bad reviews can make me feel like I should give up at first, but I manage to push through this and keep writing. If it's a constructive review, then I keep this in mind as something to tone down or improve in my next book.

Other than reviews, do you hear from your readers very often? What kinds of things do they say?

When I hear from readers, it's usually to say that they have enjoyed my book. Some have asked how I come up with the ideas for the story they have read.

What are some ways in which you promote your books? What have you found most or least effective?

I have a Twitter page and a Facebook promotional page. I find these to help with sales. Also, I have used paid promotions with Facebook which have only gotten my name in front of an audience but not generated any sales. Twitter promotions do result in sales but the percentages are very low. I have never offered either of my thrillers on a free promotion as I believe the people who download a free book usually are only downloading it because it's free and never intend to pay. These customers may not even read the book which doesn't help the author at all. They rarely leave reviews either.

In conclusion, I use free advertising as much as I can and carefully target paid advertising from various promotion companies.

How easy or hard is it to make a living as an author?

As an author, if you want to make a living, then you'd better be writing another Fifty Shades of Grey. Though this market is fast getting saturated as well. Another way is to write non-fiction on how to make money or better marketing for authors as there is a dearth of writers wanting to market their book and not knowing how to attack this.

If you write fiction, then you need to be in it for the long haul and write more books to get a following. It's rare for a first book to make it big but you might just be that author.

What advice would you give to someone aspiring to be an author?

Write about anything and everything. Just write. Then decide what genre you most enjoy and write in that genre. That doesn't mean you can't change. I thought I wanted to write contemporary romance but after a few years, I shelved that and moved on to thrillers. Nothing is wasted for a writer, and I used the writing skills I'd developed earlier in my thrillers. I have tried my hand at fantasy and after my next thriller will move back into this genre, as it felt quite liberating to make up worlds.

I will write the third book in my fantasy trilogy before I go back to the first and ready it publication.

How can readers find out more about you?

Website: www.onstefan.weebly.com/

Facebook:

www.facebook.com/ON-Stefan-543137822419408/

Paul Brodie

Tell us about yourself and your books!

I started writing my first book in July 2015. It was called Eat Less and Move More and documented my struggle and success with weight loss. During that same time I wrote my second book, Motivation 101, which is based on one of my motivational seminars. I launched Eat Less and Move More in August and Motivation 101 in October. Motivation 101 became an Amazon bestseller and I was thrilled with the momentum.

In November I launched my third book, Positivity Attracts. The book is based on another of my motivational seminars and it was my biggest success yet and was my second bestseller. With my fourth book I wanted to share how I started in book publishing with writing and launching my own books and created Book Publishing for Beginners. The book was launched in January and I am really pleased with the results of the launch. It also created a lot of opportunities with fellow authors who were looking for coaching and I am able to help them with creating and launching their books.

How long have you been writing, and how did you become involved in writing?

I started to write last July. Writing was always a goal of mine and I decided to just do it and get started. I had wanted to write Eat Less and Move More for a couple of years and was thrilled to get started and I cranked out the book in three days.

What are you working on at the moment?

Currently working on my fifth book, The Pursuit of Happiness. It is based on another of my motivational seminars and focuses on ten ways to improve your happiness.

Did you have any goals with writing, and if so, how well do you feel you've achieved them? What do you hope to achieve in the future?

I feel that I am on pace currently with the goals that I want to achieve. Starting out I knew there would be a learning curve and that it would take a few months to get income coming in and I was prepared for that. My goal is to enjoy writing but to also run it as a business. I want to continue to write four books per year and have books lined up to write through the middle of 2018 currently. My goal was to write books based on my life and also with the motivational seminars that I give.

How long does it take you to write a book?

It depends on the book. I wrote Eat Less and Move More in three days, Motivation 101 was written in a week, Positivity Attracts was written in a day, and Book Publishing for Beginners took me a month. Every book is different.

What are the hardest parts of being an author for you?

The wealth of information that is out there can be daunting at times. There are many moving parts in book publishing and writing the book is only one part. You have the book cover to get designed, the book description and sales copy to help sell your book, and the biggest part being the marketing because without marketing no one will be able to find your book. There are other factors including wanting to build your e mail list and learning about landing pages and funnels. It can be quite intimidating at first but it gets much better over time.

What do you enjoy most about being an author?

I enjoy the creative process of writing the books. As a self-published author you have full creative control and I like being the master of my own destiny and only having myself to answer to.

What books or authors have had the most influence on you as an author?

Tao of Jeet Kung Do by Bruce Lee was a great influence as he wrote in the book about how we must conquer our own self and our fears to be successful. Tuesday's With Morrie by Mitch Albom was also a great influence as I have had several grandfather type teacher mentors in my life who are no longer with us.

What did you find most useful when you were learning to write and expanding your skills?

With writing my goal is to have a conversational tone and to simply explain complex ideas and strategies in a simple, accessible way that readers can implement immediately. I am self-taught when it comes to writing. With expanding my skills, I read a lot of books and if I see a great quote or concept then I like to add it to my toolbox.

What author services do you pay for, as opposed to doing yourself? Things like cover design, formatting, editing, proofreading, etc.?

I have a fantastic editor who has edited all of my books. Also have an incredible book cover designer and someone who converts my manuscript to MOBI for the Kindle editions of my books. I record my own audiobooks and also convert the paperback version myself.

What technology/services/programs do you use as an author? (email subscription services, Dragon software, editing software, etc.)

I use Microsoft Word to write my books and adobe to convert to PDF. With building my subscriber list I use mailchimp and lead pages for my landing page for offers to my readership.

What are your thoughts about ebooks vs. print books?

Both editions are great. I like to read both ebooks and paperback. Ebooks are great when traveling as they can all be stored on my iPad to save space.

What are your thoughts about self-publishing vs traditional publishing?

I love self-publishing because you have full creative control. With traditional publishing you have more constraints and less control over the finished product of your book. Both avenues are great options but for me I prefer to be able to have control over all aspects from the content, book cover, and marketing of the books.

How often do you write, and how do you find or make time to write?

In my career I am a Special Education Teacher so it can be a challenge at times to write. I typically find time at the weekends. During the week I have a lot going on with teaching during the day and with BrodieEDU at night with the business aspects of my company and coaching fellow authors.

Do you plan your whole book out in advance, or just let it flow? What does your writing process look like?

I let it flow. What I have found with my process is that I can be pretty prolific once the inspiration hits. My style is definitely not traditional as I do not budget time out of my day to write for an hour or two. That method works well for many authors but I prefer to let it flow when the time is right.

What's a typical working day like for you? When and where do you write?

I will typically write on the weekends and will start in the morning and will not stop writing for many hours. Again, my writing style is to start when the inspiration hits. I typically write while relaxing on my living room couch.

Do you ever get Writer's Block? If so, how do you deal with it?

I have not had a major case of writers block yet but I am sure that might become a challenge down the line. The main thing I do is always enter any notes or ideas into my iPhone for my books and reference those ideas when I am writing the books.

Do you read your own reviews? If so, how do you deal with bad reviews?

I do read my own reviews. Most of my reviews are great but you will always get a few 1 star reviews. You have to focus on the positive and all of the love that your readers give you. You can only focus on the positive and not on the negative and as an author you definitely develop a thicker skin after you write several books.

Other than reviews, do you hear from your readers very often? What kinds of things do they say?

I do get e mails and Facebook messages from readers with how much they enjoy reading my books and how the books have helped them. My goal is to always focus on the positive with readers and it is a great feeling to get those positive messages from readers.

What are some ways in which you promote your books? What have you found most or least effective?

I use several paid promotions including Buck Books, Reading Deals, Robin Reads, and Books Butterfly. Those promotions help drive readers to my book and also generate a lot of sales. I do that for the first week and then Amazon typically takes over as the books are considered hot new releases. I used to post in book groups on Facebook but never really noticed a great return on investment. With the recent Facebook crackdown on posts in those groups I decided to leave all of those groups.

How easy or hard is it to make a living as an author?

It takes time to make a living as an author. I read recently that only 10 percent of all authors make over $10,000 in their first year. Fortunately, I am on pace to be in that top ten percent. The main thing is that you must run it as a business. My goal is to utilize as many revenue streams as possible from having Kindle, paperback, and audiobook editions of my books for each launch and to focus on the back end with having coaching clients, book signings, and public speaking opportunities from the books. You must maximize all revenue streams if you want to make a full time living as an author.

What advice would you give to someone aspiring to be an author?

Do not quit your job yet. Embrace the grind of working two jobs because that is how it will feel. You must have a game plan as you will most likely not make a small fortune from publishing your first book. There are always exceptions to the rule but I have learned that the successful authors are the ones who publish a new book every 3-4 months and build on that momentum. Consistency and being prolific are the keys to becoming a successful author.

How can readers find out more about you?

Website: www.BrodieEDU.com

Facebook: www.facebook.com/paulgbrodieauthor/

Phyllis H. Moore

Tell us about yourself and your books!

Hello! I am Phyllis H. Moore a retired social worker. I have reinvented myself twice since my retirement in 2004. My first reinvention was to own and operate a bed and breakfast with my husband for seven years. You never know people until you sleep with them. That was an experience. After selling the B & B, we moved to a cabin in the country and I began to write three years ago.

How long have you been writing, and how did you become involved in writing?

I have been writing for three years. I thought I might like it because I like to tell stories. I entered a zone when I sat down to write and I enjoy it.

What are you working on at the moment?

I am working on compiling some short stories into an anthology. They are eerie stories of hauntings. I am also working to get a new book ready for editing and designing covers for two books I hope to publish later in the spring. I am actively marketing four novels I have published to Amazon Kindle and CreateSpace and Draft2Digital.

Did you have any goals with writing, and if so, how well do you feel you've achieved them? What do you hope to achieve in the future?

I had no idea what I was getting into. I like writing, so I feel accomplished because I have written masses of content. People enjoy reading what I write, they say. That is gratifying. I want to improve my writing and become more proficient at designing covers and formatting.

How long does it take you to write a book?

I have no idea. I do not pay attention to time when I am writing. I have the luxury of not worrying about time.

What are the hardest parts of being an author for you?

Formatting and cover design. I'm working on it. I don't like marketing, but once I do it, it's not so bad.

What do you enjoy most about being an author?

Writing!

What books or authors have had the most influence on you as an author?

Robert Owen Butler, *From Where We Dream*, is the best book on writing I have read. I also like Stephen King's, *On Writing*. I have read Butler's book three times. He is a Pulitzer Prize winning author and I had a chance to meet with him privately at an author's workshop last year. I have read his book three times and often go back to it. For pleasure I like to read Southern Gothic female authors, Fannie Flagg, Harper Lee, Rebecca Wells, Kathryn Stockett.

What did you find most useful when you were learning to write and expanding your skills?

Webinars, Beth Hayden, Jon Morrow, Derek Murphy, Ashton Cartwright. I went to an Algonkian Writer's Conference. That was where I met Robert Owen Butler. Fantastic small group of writers. That was my favorite experience.

What author services do you pay for, as opposed to doing yourself? Things like cover design, formatting, editing, proofreading, etc.?

Book covers I have done with Fiverr, I'm trying an editor. I have done my own with the four novels currently published. I have done my own formatting, but it's not great. I'm still working on it.

What technology/services/programs do you use as an author? (email subscription services, Dragon software, editing software, etc.)

This is my weakness. I'm challenged in this area. I learned to type on a Remington with a manual return and have to make myself not put two spaces after a period at the end of a sentence. I blog and send newsletters from the web site I designed on WIX. I couldn't figure out WORD PRESS. Maybe I'll learn more. This is not my favorite thing to do.

What are your thoughts about ebooks vs. print books?

Personally, I enjoy ebooks, but there are many people my age who do not have ereaders, so many of my readers want print books.

What are your thoughts about self-publishing vs traditional publishing?

I attempted the traditional publishing route, but I decided to venture into self-publishing and I am glad I did. I don't have time to wait on all the people involved in traditional publishing.

How often do you write, and how do you find or make time to write?

I write every day. I have no other demands on my time, so I have no trouble finding time to write.

Do you plan your whole book out in advance, or just let it flow? What does your writing process look like?

I do not outline. I wrote my first novel in a type of free flow, then rewrote several times. That is my preference and it has worked for all my books.

What's a typical working day like for you? When and where do you write?

I write in the living area of my small cabin. I have it to myself because my husband disappears to his office at 6 a.m. I write with no other distractions, no music, no TV, just me on a couch or chair with my laptop.

Do you ever get Writer's Block? If so, how do you deal with it?

Never.

Do you read your own reviews? If so, how do you deal with bad reviews?

Yes, I read them several times. I mostly have five star reviews, which doesn't seem honest. Three stars seems honest, there are better writers and worse. I know I need reviews.

Other than reviews, do you hear from your readers very often? What kinds of things do they say?

I prefer talking to readers. I get to meet them at book signings and I enjoy hearing what they have to say. I also get comments on my web site.

What are some ways in which you promote your books? What have you found most or least effective?

Facebook Ads, Pinterest, Indie Promotion Sites, Fiverr promotions. The most productive have been articles in my local papers.

How easy or hard is it to make a living as an author?

I could never depend on writing to make a living. Luckily I do not have to rely on writing to pay my bills.

What advice would you give to someone aspiring to be an author?

Write! Write! Write On!

How can readers find out more about you?

Website: www.phyllishmoore.com

Facebook: www.facebook.com/phyllishmooreAuthor/

R.J. Vickers

Tell us about yourself and your books!

I have always been a writer and a traveler; though I grew up in Colorado, I'm now lucky enough to live with my husband in beautiful New Zealand. Fantasy has long been a passion of mine, and the majority of my novels fall into that category. However, I've been branching out lately and writing a series of travel books that combine my love of the outdoors with my fondness for photography.

This past year, I published *The Natural Order,* the first book in a Young Adult fantasy series; a prequel to *The Natural Order;* and *College Can Wait!,* a gap-year guidebook for reluctant students.

How long have you been writing, and how did you become involved in writing?

I've been writing since the age of seven. At one point, when I was just about to start high school, I had a flash of inspiration — the only career that I truly wanted was that of an author. It had taken me a while to figure that out, but it was pretty obvious by that point. I devoted much of my free time to writing, and had already started my first novel by the age of thirteen. I couldn't imagine myself doing anything else.

What are you working on at the moment?

Several projects! I'm working on the second book in the Natural Order series (Young Adult fantasy), titled *Rogue Magic,* as well as an epic fantasy novel, *Fall of Lostport*. And on the nonfiction front, I'm working on an adventure travel guide to New Zealand's South Island, where I've been fortunate enough to live for the past two years.

Did you have any goals with writing, and if so, how well do you feel you've achieved them? What do you hope to achieve in the future?

My ultimate goal is to make a full-time career of writing. I have hundreds of books in my head that I hope to write someday, and I can imagine nothing I would enjoy more. A few years ago, it would have been very difficult to make a living as a writer, unless you fell in the top 2% of authors that got marketing support from the Big 5 publishers. But now, with the boom of ebook and independent publishing, it's easier than ever to earn a living writing. You just have to consistently produce high-quality books and connect with your readers. I'm now well on my way to setting up a proper career as an author, which is fantastic.

How long does it take you to write a book?

Anywhere from a month to two years! I love writing books during National Novel Writing Month (NaNoWriMo), where you're challenged to write 50,000 words in the month of November, but I usually save my easier projects for then. The more intensive projects (mostly epic fantasy novels) take several years to complete. Of course, that's not counting the months or years of editing that follow . . .

What are the hardest parts of being an author for you?

Two things:

The first is sitting down and getting the writing done! I now have a home office I work from, which makes it much easier to focus and write a solid amount very day, but before this I had to escape the house if I wanted to accomplish everything. I find my most inspired writing sessions happen while I'm tucked away in the corner of some cozy café.

The second is dealing with the initial round of feedback on my writing. I have two fantastic beta readers who read every first draft I've ever written; I find I can't pinpoint any issues in the manuscript without their guidance. But I've just received feedback on two novels from both of them, and I have a LOT of revision ahead of me. More than I expected. They're very insightful, of course, but sometimes constructive criticism hurts.

What do you enjoy most about being an author?

I love devoting my time to my passion! I enjoy the entire process — writing, revising, and marketing — so any time I'm working on a book, it's a fun challenge. It's incredibly satisfying to finish a book, and even more so to hear that people love what I've written.

What books or authors have had the most influence on you as an author?

In recent years, I've been hugely influenced by *The Name of the Wind,* by Patrick Rothfuss. The language is stunning, the world rich, and the characters complex. And I have to mention JK Rowling as well — I am always blown away by her characterization. Even with over 200 characters in the Harry Potter series, each one manages to remain both three-dimensional and memorable.

What did you find most useful when you were learning to write and expanding your skills?

NaNoWriMo was huge for me. I used the annual challenge as a way to play around with genres I usually wouldn't touch, which allowed me to grow as a writer and also to improve my use of language. Some of the books I wrote taught me to use rapid pacing to drive the plot, while others gave me the chance to deeply explore the internal lives of my characters. In fact, in an early draft of *The Natural Order,* you can see exactly where I put aside the book to write a NaNoWriMo book. The language improves VASTLY from the pre-NaNo section to the post-NaNo section.

What author services do you pay for, as opposed to doing yourself? Things like cover design, formatting, editing, proofreading, etc.?

I'm a trained copyeditor, so I do most of the proofreading and copyediting myself, though I always have a friend read over the final manuscript to catch any typos that escaped me. I also do the formatting, though it's a complete pain. As far as cover design is concerned, I have done both—outsourced the work and tried it myself. I thought I was decent at cover designing, but after getting my fantasy series covers updated with the help of a professional cover designer, I think I'll stick with the professionals from here on.

What technology/services/programs do you use as an author? (email subscription services, Dragon software, editing software, etc.)

I'm a bit traditional in that I still write with Microsoft Word—I might transition to Scribner at some point, but I hate learning new programs.

I use Mailchimp for my newsletter, and I find it to be a very straightforward, easy-to-manage program. I've designed my website with Wix; though most people recommend Wordpress, I found the setup restrictive and too technically complex. With Wix, you can move and fiddle with and change elements as much as you want, and it's a very intuitive way of working with page design that gives me a great deal of creative freedom.

What are your thoughts about ebooks vs. print books?

As a reader, I hate reading ebooks! I enjoy reading nonfiction ebooks, especially ones related to ebook publishing, but reading fiction off a screen just feels like a chore. I don't think I'll ever convert to reading ebooks.

As an author, though, I think the ebook revolution is fantastic. With print books, you're confined to a three-month trial period at a bookstore with your book's spine facing out. Heaven help you if your last name starts with an end-of-alphabet letter (mine is Vickers); no one ever bends down to look at the bottom shelf unless they're looking for an author they know. Once the trial period is up, your books are returned (and most likely destroyed, if you're with a traditional publisher) and your book's life is over. With ebook (and print-on-demand) publishing, books have a much greater chance of success and longevity. That's a huge bonus for authors.

What are your thoughts about self-publishing vs traditional publishing?

Until very recently, I was 100% behind traditional publishing. There are too many bad-quality self-published books floating around, cluttering up the self-published market, and readers have no way (apart from reviews) of knowing if they've chosen something worth reading.

However, the tables are turning. Traditional publishers — especially the Big 5 — lack the flexibility necessary to compete in today's market. Traditionally published authors can't play around with pricing to see what works best, or discount a book for a major promotion, or set the first book in the series as permanently free to hook readers. And traditionally published authors don't have real-time feedback on their sales, so they don't know which of their marketing efforts are paying off. Self-published authors, on the other hand, can play with their platforms as much as they like to make them competitive. They can hone in on strategies that work, and maximize their visibility with clever pricing and promotion strategies. Today, traditional publishing is losing its hold on the book market. Independent publishing is increasingly becoming the best way to go.

How often do you write, and how do you find or make time to write?

I try to write a little bit every day, though that obviously doesn't happen all the time. Morning is my most productive writing time, so I block off the time between breakfast and lunch for zero-distraction writing. I can usually write 2,000 or 3,000 words in that time, either focused on one project or split between two. I don't turn on the internet until noon, and I retreat to my office with a cup of coffee, where I know I won't be disturbed.

When I was busier, especially when I was working full-time at my day job, I had to escape to a café on weekends to get any work done.

Do you plan your whole book out in advance, or just let it flow? What does your writing process look like?

It depends on the book. I wrote one book that was planned to the chapter before I started writing, and while the end product was a very solid, well-written book, I lost a lot of the joy in the writing process.

Usually I start a book with a general idea of the overarching plot, and I write a few chapters before realizing I've run out of everything I had originally planned. Then I have a frantic brainstorm session (often involving several long walks for inspiration) where I fit together the rest of the plot and sketch out a vague outline of the remainder of the book. I often diverge from the outline, but it's reassuring to have a direction mapped out.

What's a typical working day like for you? When and where do you write?

In the morning, between breakfast and lunch, I devote two or three hours to internet-free, distraction-free writing. I get most of my work done that way. After lunch, I go for a walk to clear my head, and then spend the afternoon marketing, updating my website, and interacting with my readers. If I have a deadline looming, I often spend the evening writing a bit more.

Do you ever get Writer's Block? If so, how do you deal with it?

Of course! And as for dealing with it, that depends on the cause of the block. If I have no idea where the plot is going, or I've reached an unsolvable knot, I go for a long walk and puzzle out what to do next. That almost always works wonders.

If I'm just stuck because I don't feel like writing or I feel like my writing is awful, I can always get back into the swing of things by doing a two-hour session at a café.

Do you read your own reviews? If so, how do you deal with bad reviews?

I do, and it's either incredibly encouraging or incredibly depressing. When I get bad reviews, I usually overthink them and obsess about fixing whatever the reviewer didn't like. Some of the negative reviews bring up good points, and I keep them in mind for future books, and others I realize have more to do with the reviewer than with my work. After receiving my first one-star review, I looked at the reviewer's history and realized they gave almost every book they read (including *The Hunger Games!*) one or two stars. It's all about keeping things in perspective.

Other than reviews, do you hear from your readers very often? What kinds of things do they say?

I often hear from readers anxious to read the next book in the Natural Order series—it's coming out in June this year, so hopefully they'll enjoy it! I also like to keep my readers in the loop by asking for their feedback on new covers and sights to include in my travel books, and it's always fun to hear their thoughts.

What are some ways in which you promote your books? What have you found most or least effective?

I've tried practically everything. With the print edition of *The Natural Order*, I hosted a book launch party, which was fun but didn't attract many attendees I didn't already know. I also went on a book tour around the South Island, which led to quite a few bookstore sales though less reader engagement than I'd hoped for. I've enjoyed speaking at schools and other events, and that seems to be the best way to connect with readers.

As far as ebooks go, a lot of my promotion strategies have to do with gathering an email list of readers and scheduling strategic promotions that send my books high in the Amazon rankings. One recent strategy that has proved surprisingly successful is putting up a permanently free prequel for the Natural Order series, which draws readers in and entices them to buy the first book in the series.

How easy or hard is it to make a living as an author?

With low-risk ebook publishing leading book sales these days, it's easier than ever to make a living as an author. The only requirement is a time investment. The more high-quality books you publish, the more chances you have for readers to stumble across your work. Once you have ten or fifteen books out, you gain a steady readership that goes on to buy your other books, thereby driving sales of your entire list. I've only published three books so far, but I'm aiming to publish at least five more this year, and even with just three out there, I've seen a huge increase in sales. When I promote one book, I often see a boost in sales for the others, which is excellent.

What advice would you give to someone aspiring to be an author?

Keep reading and writing! The best way to learn to write well is to read voraciously, and the best way to improve your writing is to keep writing. I've written 12 novels now, as well as two shorter books, and most of them will never see the light of day. But without writing those "practice" novels first, I wouldn't be half the writer I am today.

How can readers find out more about you?

Website: www.rjvickers.com

Facebook: www.facebook.com/rjvickersauthor/

Renae Kaye

Tell us about yourself and your books!

My name is Renae Kaye, and I'm a suburban housewife with two small children. I'm a voracious reader, and have consumed romance ever since I was old enough to get my hands on it.

About four years ago I stumbled into the world of MM (or M/M). For those who don't know, MM is basically gay romance. The MM designation is given to show it is a male-on-male scenario, as is FF (female-on-female or lesbian romance) and MF (male-female or heterosexual romance). This terminology can be used to describe many other pairings such as MMM, MMF and so on. The same story tropes exist as an MF romance (i.e. there must be a happy ending, no rape or incest, cheating is frowned upon, etc.) and I often describe my genre to people as "Mills and Boon with two guys." Of course it is a lot more than that to me, and there are many differences, but it's a parallel people can easily grasp.

As with MF, there are a lot of sub-categories of MM: erotica, BDSM, fantasy, historical, paranormal, sci-fi, YA, NA, western, mystery, etc. My writing falls into contemporary with a side-dish of humor.

I am very new to the writing game, as I have no formal training at all. In 2013, I hit a rut where I couldn't find the type of book I wanted to read. Cheesed-off with the latest offering from a previously adored author and unenthused with the books out there, I decided to write my own story. The story was to be for my own reading only, but my best friend wanted to read it too . . . and loved it! At her urging I sent it to a publisher for consideration. I picked my favorite publisher—American-based publisher Dreamspinner Press—as I heard that they gave constructive feedback with their refusals. (Please note, I never expected a contract from them. I simply was looking for feedback!) At that stage they were accepting MM manuscripts only, although now they have many other imprints too. To my absolute astonishment, they accepted it.

My first novel, *Loving Jay,* was published in April 2014 and went on to win several debut author awards, plus a third place for humor. Since then, I have also published *The Blinding Light* which was a #1 best-seller on Amazon, *The Shearing Gun, Safe in His Arms, Shawn's Law* and *You Are the Reason.* As well as novels, I have a number of short stories out as standalone or as a part of anthologies.

My novels are available in eBook, print and audio format, and various titles are being translated into Italian, French and even Korean. Most of my work is published through a traditional publisher, but I have also self-published.

I now write primarily in the MM genre, but occasionally write words on MF novels. I'm looking at collecting together a number of MF manuscripts before publishing them under a different pen-name.

Being from Western Australia, I love basing my stories in Perth. Several stories occur in the rural areas of WA—Dumbleyung and Margaret River have been locations so far published—and I have plans for more settings within my state. I think of it as introducing the world to my country.

I first started writing when I had two children at home. They are now in primary school, and I've settled into writing as a career. I'm not quite full-time yet, as a household and family keep me very busy, but I look forward to writing (hopefully) for many, many years to come.

How long have you been writing, and how did you become involved in writing?

I've been a prolific reader forever. I've always thought about writing, and as a child I made up many stories. However, my family and teachers all steered me away from literature and arts. I was gifted in math, and was told to pursue that as a career.

It wasn't until I was a stay-at-home mother with two small children that the thought of writing professionally crossed my mind. I wondered if I could earn a small income by selling a combination of articles, short stories, longer stories and whatever I could get my hands on. The first step was to *attempt* to write a story.

It took me three months to write my first novel, and the first submission I ever sent to a publisher was accepted. That was back in 2013.

Looking back on my life, I was always scribbling down stories as a child and teen, but had been discouraged from taking it further from negative comments from the adults around me. My first story was supposed to just be for me.

After my first story was accepted, I was pushed in the deep end of being a writer. I had no idea what I was doing, and it was only through social media (Facebook especially) that I found other authors and they guided me. I'm still learning, and I think that any author who thinks they have nothing more to learn needs to give up the profession.

What are you working on at the moment?

Like any good author, I'm across a myriad of projects at one time. In order to earn a living as an author, you must not simply concentrate on a single book and expect to hit the jackpot.

I've just finished proofing my next release, my release after that is in submission phase with my publisher, and the release after that needs about three days work on it and that can go into submission as well.

I have two stories—one a novella, one a novel—that I'm serious about finishing soon, I'm researching another novel, and I'm plotting out a series of four novellas I'm going to try.

I'm also working on finishing off another manuscript that is for a new pen name of mine.

Half of my time is devoted to promotion. I blog on two separate sites each week, and I'm also working on promoting the new French translation of my novel. Soon the next audio, and the next Italian translation will be out, and I have to book promotion for my next release.

No rest for the wicked.

Did you have any goals with writing, and if so, how well do you feel you've achieved them? What do you hope to achieve in the future?

My goal was always to earn an income from writing. If I could earn money from writing, I wouldn't have to return to the workforce part-time once the kids were in school.

Writing is a great profession for a hands-on mother. I'm able to drop responsibility and be there for the kids when they need me. If they're sick, I don't need to call in sick to my employer. If they have assembly or a school sports day, I can be there. I can take them to school, and pick them up every day.

On that front I have achieved my goal. I'm earning an income. I'm building an audience.

For the future I hope to continue this. My husband and I have agreed to a "minimum income" I must earn per year in order to stay home and write instead of finding employment.

The hardest thing for an author is the infrequent and unstable income. While self-publishing will give you a monthly pay check, my publisher only pays quarterly. And it's not a guaranteed amount. It takes a lot to wrap your head around. Your effort and expenses all come before you press that "publish" button. The lag time for editing and payments means that I usually don't get paid until 14–18 months after I finished writing the novel.

The payoff, however, is that the book continues to pay without any (or much) effort on your behalf. With luck, the books that I've written will continue to provide me with an income for the next 5–20 years.

How long does it take you to write a book?

A book for me is around 60,000 — 80,000 words. Without any extra distractions, I will write a book in 6–8 weeks (that's draft it and self-edit to a point you're happy to submit it to a publisher or beta reader.) However, you always have distractions. As a published author, you have numerous rounds of edits which take up a lot of time, with lull periods between. When releasing a new novel you have a lot of promotion that draws you away from writing too.

If I get a spare week, I can pop out a short story in 3–4 days.

My aim is for at least three novels and one short story published per year.

What are the hardest parts of being an author for you?

Edits. Bad reviews. Uncertainty. Keeping up with social media and trends.

Edits are hard. No matter how you logically tell yourself that the editor is trying to *help* you, you will in some way feel that it's a personal slight when they tell you you've written it wrong. With each edit, I try to improve on my craft, but I will always get it wrong somewhere. Things that sound perfectly fine to me can come out garbled to someone else. This all needs to be fixed up. Not only are edits hard on the ego, but they're hard work to push through and consider each sentence in a 200+ page novel.

Bad reviews can make you angry or destroy you. They are taking your "baby" and picking it apart. I don't mind a review that can legitimately poke holes in a manuscript, but the reviews where the reader hates the whole book because they don't like feminine guys, or thinks that they could've written a better ending, make you want to reach through the computer and strangle people. Unfortunately bad reviews care part-and-parcel of being an author.

Uncertainty is a big part of being an author, and unfortunately I'm not a gambling person. You never know how your next release is going to go. You never know if people will love or hate your stuff. You never know how much money you are going to earn. You never know if someone is going to have the exact same plot as you. You never know if someone is going to use the same cover model as you did. You can learn to hedge your bets, but uncertainty is a big part of authoring.

And lastly, social media is a big must for authors in my type of genre. Other genres may get away with not having it, but for me, most of my promo is done using social media. Readers like to have the personal contact with an author that social media provides. Having a "real" person on the other end of Facebook is a wonderful advertising tool for your book. You can show pictures of your real life, or not (people are successfully anonymous at times). You can drop titbits about your next publication. You can build a following. Authors who only use Facebook once a week, or use it only for promoting their covers, can find they struggle to engage readers. Readers want the personal touch. And your best promoting tool are readers who recommend you to other readers.

As an author, unless you are writing fantasy or historical, you also need to keep up with world trends. Characters who mention world events, use their mobile phones to date, love Uber rides and are on the latest vegan diet will resound with your readers. If you're fifty, and you're writing about an eighteen-year-old, you're going to have to know the language. That is the sign of a good writer.

What do you enjoy most about being an author?

Making people laugh and entertaining them. Really. This is what writing is about. It's about telling a story that will make them smile, make them feel and make them want to turn the next page. It's knowing that they're caught up in the world that you've created and fallen in love with the characters that seem so real to you.

The best part is when you get emails, comments and reviews from readers that say something like, "I almost peed my pants," or "People were giving me strange looks on the bus," or "I stayed up to 3am to finish it. I couldn't put it down."

I also feel a lot of satisfaction in the messages I get that say, "Thank you for writing about Alzheimer's in this way. Sometimes I forget to see the amusing side of my mother's illness," or "Thank you for writing sensitively about your character being a rape victim. This is exactly how I feel."

What books or authors have had the most influence on you as an author?

I think every book touches you in some way. The pacing and rhythms of story-telling sink into your subconsciousness if you read a lot of books.

Authors who have influenced me the most? Susan Elizabeth Phillips — I love her style and the humor in her book, and the way that her stories are just not about the two people falling in love, but weaves the stories of their friends and family around them. Julia Quinn — she just makes you fall in love with falling in love. Nalini Singh — a master wordsmith and story teller with an imagination that is extraordinary. Marie Sexton — the first MM author I ever read, and caused me to fall in love with the genre. NR Walker — the Australian MM author that made me believe that if she could do it, maybe a mummy-from-Perth could have a chance at publishing too.

What did you find most useful when you were learning to write and expanding your skills?

Objectivity. As I said previously, I have no formal writing qualifications, so I never attended a school or did a course to learn how to write. I rely on myself a lot. I will write something, then put it aside for a while and then come back to it. When I reread, I read as the audience, picking up on things I don't like and then fixing it.

I don't believe in finishing writing the books and sending it off to the editor immediately. I like it to percolate a while. If it still makes sense in a month's time, then it should work with your audience.

What author services do you pay for, as opposed to doing yourself? Things like cover design, formatting, editing, proofreading, etc.?

Going through a publisher means that they handle all of that, but the author's input can be crucial. With cover design, I need to guide the cover artist to what is suitable for the story, but at the same time allow them to do *their* job. As an Australian author going through an American publisher and sometimes getting a European cover artist, it's vital that I watch out they don't put anything on the cover that doesn't look like an Australian background.

My publisher works nicely *with* me in the editing phase, and I always have a look at the manuscript in the proofreading stage because there are sometimes things we've missed. Be assured, going through a publisher doesn't mean you hand over your manuscript and that's the last say you have in it.

When self-publishing, whether you make a profit or not could come down to how much you've had to pay for services. I swap services a lot when I self-publish. I get friends to beta-read and fix up mistakes before I send it to an editor. And in return I will do the same for them.

An editor is *never* someone you can compromise on. You must have an editor, and you must pay them a decent rate. For a novel, I will contract the services of *two* editors, because the amount of work that goes into a novel is huge, and you don't want to get it wrong and waste that effort.

Cover art is a tricky one. Never attempt it yourself, but there are a lot of artists out there who will work for cheap rates. More expensive cover artists definitely give you a polished product, but sometimes you just can't justify that expense on a short story.

For proofreading, I have people who are willing to do it for free in order to get their hands on one of my books before anyone else, and I reward them with a copy when it's all finished. So far, I've done all the formatting myself.

What technology/services/programs do you use as an author? (email subscription services, Dragon software, editing software, etc.)

Not enough. That is the truth.

I hear people talk about what they use, but my advice is use what you're comfortable with. Start small.

At minimum, I think an author needs to have an email address and website. There are many, many programs that will assist you to get these—both paid for and free. But remember to think big. It is possible that your email and website will be printed in the back of a paperback novel. Ten years down the track, you want that email and website to still be a viable tool people can use. Choose a provider that isn't going to go out of business next year. And choose a handle that is your author name.

You need to know your audience. If you are writing text books or non-fiction, perhaps a newsletter like Mailchimp will keep your audience informed. If you write steampunk, perhaps you need to maintain a gaming avatar on certain sites.

Talk to other authors and ask them about what they use. Many of my colleagues use Scrivener. I've looked into it. However, Scrivener's strength is helping authors plan out a novel, plan out chapters, drop and change sections of the story, etc. As a "pantser" writer, I like my characters to be a bit of a mystery to me, and their outcome uncertain. I think Scrivener works well for some, but it's not for me.

As a writer, I pretty much use Word and Excel . . . and my own brain. But I will be looking at new tools to help me all the time.

What are your thoughts about ebooks vs. print books?

Ebooks are the way of the future. There will always be a place for print books, but eBooks are where fiction writers need to put their effort. 99% of my sales are in eBook form. People are no longer using book stores as their main source of purchasing.

As an author through a publisher, my royalty payment per eBook is only slightly less than my royalty per printed copy. In the self-publishing realm, I've heard that print actually *costs* the author in some cases.

I plan my books to be in eBook. If they make print or audio or foreign language or any of the other forms, then it's a bonus.

What are your thoughts about self-publishing vs traditional publishing?

Both are needed and can be done successfully.

Publishers can be wonderful because they weed out the stories that are not worth it, or are offensive. A reader picking up a book from a publisher can have a level of confidence in the story that it has been edited and vetted.

Publishers are also great for genres were there are definite lines. Submission details will be very specific. However, not all readers want authors to color inside the lines all the time. Some publishers allow this. Sometimes your story is so "weird" compared to the usual genre, that you can't find a publisher to take you.

Self-publishing has its pros and cons too. For authors who like control, it is wonderful. But it's also hard work. Time spent working on formatting, editing, covers, promotion, ARCs, etc, is all time that has been taken away from you writing your next novel.

Some people say that self-publishing is where the money is. I think it can be a good thing and a bad.

If you traditionally publish, and you sell 2000 units of your novel at $5 a pop, and you get 40% of the royalties, you would make $4000. (This scenario doesn't take into account any fee the seller takes, like Amazon's percentage and fees. It's just an illustration.)

With self-publishing you can possibly get to earn a lot more, as you get 100% of royalties, not 40%. *However* you may not reach as many people as a publisher, so your sales are only 1000 units. You may not sell at the price of $5, because people often expect self-published books to be less — so let's say you drop the price to $4. You may also shell out $2000 on costs because you've paid for the cover, editing, formatting, promotional copies, ARCs, etc. So you would earn $4000 (1000 x $4) in royalties, but you've paid $2000 in costs months prior to its release.

So you could possibly sell 2000 units at $5, less $2000 costs = $8000 profit to you. But you could also have to drop the price, settle for less sales, and only make $2000.

It's a gamble.

So my thoughts are that I like *both* forms of publishing. I think both forms are needed. It does create a buyer-beware scenario, and there are some shady authors out there. From the huge profits that eBook sellers are making, I do think they should take more responsibility than they are currently doing in checking eBooks for plagiarism and basic editing.

I think there will always be a niche for publishers and always be a niche for self-publication. I've found in the last 5 years there's been a huge shift to self-publication. My gut feeling is there will need to be an equalization along the way, as readers will revolt against lack of quality from certain sectors. The big thing will be the when.

How often do you write, and how do you find or make time to write?

I try to write daily. But this is not always feasible. Just like a "real" job, authors need to take time off when they're sick, and have weekends and holidays. To keep "on track" I log my daily word count, then average it over the month to allow for days I'm just too busy with other stuff. Remember — garbage in, garbage out. Taking a trip to the beach or hanging out with friends feeds the writer brain and gives them information and ideas. These are just as important as the actual writing time.

As a mother, my biggest chunk of writing time comes when the kids are at school. But, of course, I need to do grocery shopping, housework, catch up with friends occasionally, etc.

If you want to be a full-time writer (or even part-time) you need to make sacrifices. One sacrifice I made was to give up TV. Once the kids are in bed, my husband will head off to watch his shows, and I'll head to my writing room to get another 2–3 hours worth of work done before bed. During the day, I condense my housework into 15 minute blocks, and write for the other 45 minutes of the hour. I've given myself extra time to write by spending part of my royalty check on a robotic vacuum which frees up my writing.

Do you plan your whole book out in advance, or just let it flow? What does your writing process look like?

I'm a "pantser" — I write a book flying by the seat of my pants. My stories are character driven, so I often simply get a particular character and/or scenario in my head to start with. Then I write them on the page, and see how they react to each other, or the situation I've set them in.

For example, I had an idea to write a story about a gay shearer who was in the closet. I constructed his whole history in my head — his physical looks, his attitudes, how he talks and dresses, his family, his experience, his dreams. I mentally plotted until I had him as a solid person.

Then I created a scenario for him that would interest the readers. What would happen if he met someone in the small town he lived in, and their attraction was too much to hide?

I place the two characters into the scene, and work out from there what they will do or say. I think it brings authenticity to the characters, because since I don't know what's going to happen, *they* don't know what's going to happen either. They sometimes say or do the wrong things. Just like in real life.

From a subconscious which grew from reading thousands of books, I have a feel of writing the rhythm of the story: a lot of small conflicts building to a larger one, the energy, timing and tension, the symbolism and themes. Some of writing is natural talent, some is learned behavior. What you don't know, you fake until you get it.

What's a typical working day like for you? When and where do you write?

My typical day is to work between the hours of 9am and 2pm—if the housework allows me. I try to write while the kids are at school. I will also work after they've gone to bed.

Work involves checking emails and replying to publishers, readers and other mail. There is social media to involve yourself with, blogs to write, friends to respond to, sales to track and research to do. I've found my peak writing comes early in the day, so I will write before doing the boring stuff.

So a normal day may involve checking emails and Facebook for half an hour, before turning off the internet for 3 sprints. Sprints involve 45 minutes of writing without stopping, then breaking for 15 minutes where I put the washing on the line, grab something to eat and then dive back in.

By 1pm my energy is failing, so I may Facebook some more or do research. It is very fluid, which fits with the other parts of my life.

Do you ever get Writer's Block? If so, how do you deal with it?

There are days (weeks) I can't write because I'm too worked up about something—like the week before a release and the couple of weeks after. I have trouble relaxing enough to write then. I'm usually prepared for it and work on other things, like getting my website in order or writing blogs.

Sometimes I hit a wall with a story and I have no idea of how to resolve it. I find it beneficial to put aside the story and work on something else for a while. The "stuck" story will chug along in the background of my brain and something will eventually come to me.

Personally I find gardening a great tool for working out stuck stories. The peacefulness of the work, plus the fact you are doing something useful calms me.

Writer's Block where you can't think of a story never happens to me. I literally have over 15 stories in various stages of completion and over 400,000 words written on them. I have so many stories I want to write, but time and the viability of the story sometimes works against me. There are stories I want to write, but I know won't work well with my audience, so they're often put aside for me to concentrate on those I know will work.

Do you read your own reviews? If so, how do you deal with bad reviews?

Yes. I don't read every single one, but you can often tell within the first two lines of a review whether the personal is articulate enough to voice their appreciation or concern with aspects of your story. The in-depth ones I read.

Bad reviews are funny. People are unaware of how much of their own insecurities they are revealing with some of their reviews. How petty they sound. I've had bad reviews because people didn't like the fact that my MC had a Chinese housekeeper, because my character mentioned the words "AIDS" and "rabies" in the same sentence, because they don't like femme guys, because my book was set in Australia, because my MC was overweight, and even because they liked the story so much, they wanted it to be longer, so rated it badly because it was short.

In some not-so-good reviews I appreciate their honesty, and they often point out parts that I found weak when I was writing, but couldn't work out what was wrong with it and how to fix it. I take that as honest feedback and try to work on that.

Some bad reviews you can tell are simply "frustrated wannabe authors." Their reviews say something along the lines of "I didn't like this story, because I think it should've ended *this* way." You can't please those people, because obviously nothing is ever going to satisfy them because they *didn't* write the story.

The hardest reviews to take are the personal attacks on the author. The name calling, the sick messages, and the ones who get angry at your fictional characters. I have one character who is admittedly a bit of an idiot. The story is about him *learning* and *growing* as a person, realizing his point of view was wrong. Some readers did not take kindly to his initial stance, gave up reading because they thought he was homophobic, and so assume that the author holds the same view as the character. Their reviews contain personal slights to me as an author, as they think I have the same views and stances as my character. I often wonder what these readers think about mystery and crime novels. Do they think that the author is a murderer because they wrote about a murderer? Do they think that the authors of fantasy novels are actually wizards and fairies?

Bad reviews hurt. Yes. But being objective helps. Discard the ones that are plain offensive, have problems with your genre, or haven't even read your book and wish to comment. Then, at a time you are calm and relaxed, have a look at the other bad reviews. You may find the reviewer is just a "hard marker" on their star rating and actually enjoyed your book.

As a personal thing, I never comment on reviews—good or bad. I will thank a reviewer of a professional review site, but any comment on Amazon, Goodreads, etc. are not the place to engage your readers. Never argue a point with a reader. If they took away the "wrong" message from your story, then that's on you. As an author you need to either make your character clearer, or accept people will read them in differing ways. Authors who demand bad reviews be removed, or defend their book are often frowned upon by the readers. It's not always fair, but that's how it can be.

Other than reviews, do you hear from your readers very often? What kinds of things do they say?

Oh, wow. My readers are just the BEST. Being active on social media means that they have the ability to easily contact me, and feel comfortable in contacting me.

On the release of a new book I will get a number of emails of people who have tracked me down to tell my they liked/loved my book, or sometimes to tell me how they really resonated with a particular character.

Others will comment through my website, which is good, because hopefully they have a look around at my other stuff while they're there. Most often I will be tagged on Facebook or Twitter when they are singing my praises, or a private message through Facebook.

Usually it's good things they will contact me with. Those who have a problem with my writing will simply leave bad reviews and not bother to contact me personally. I have had a couple of people write to me about certain aspects of my book they're unhappy with, but usually they're not mean about it.

I have heard from people who are visually impaired, or their family is, and have thanked me for writing a blind character with empathy but not pity. I've heard from victims of sexual abuse who wanted to thank me for writing a character who had experienced this. I've heard from people who have nursed their loved ones through Alzheimer's and have thanked me for reminding them about the good things that they've forgotten. They are the special messages I love.

The best thing is people who write to you about books they've just discovered, that are years old. Today I received a message via Goodreads thanking me for my story and my character development. They told me my book has rekindled a passion for the genre in them. That book was released 16 months ago.

I will also get emails asking me if I'm planning to release more books in a series, and sometimes fans asking to beta read my work, hoping to get an earlier look at a book. Truly, my readers are the best.

What are some ways in which you promote your books? What have you found most or least effective?

Being published through a traditional publisher means I "borrow" their reader list. This is the payoff for going with a publisher. A lot of people will follow a publisher's new releases list because they trust that publisher, or know what sort of books they publish. Being able to herald yourself as a member of that publisher is sometimes wonderful. This gives you a leg-up on your first lot of promotion.

The *best* promotion for me however, is recommendations. The genre of M/M has a strong on-line community, and recommendations are golden. You can have the website, the Facebook page, the twitter handle . . . but if no one knows who you are, you won't be followed. Of course, reader recommendations rely on you writing a good solid book that people *want* to recommend, and also rely on your genre being one where people gather to discuss the genre.

Online Book Tours can also make an impact. Visiting a lot of review sites and reviewer blogs can help you be seen outside your usual audience. Cross promotion with other authors are good too. If you have a following on my blog of 400 people, and your author friend has a following of 300 *different* people, by writing a guest blog on your friend's website, you can contact a new audience. You must then extend the favor to your friend on their release though — please don't forget that.

Writing a blog can help. If you have a weekly blog where you talk about issues, you can gather followers to your blog. So every eight weeks or so, you can slip in a "this is my new novel" blog and it's promo for you. If your blog is *only* promo, you won't get followers. You need to blog about something people want to read about.

Least effective promo for my genre is in-person meets. Bookworms rarely venture out in public, and those who follow LGBT don't always wish to be seen to do it. Book signings, author conferences, etc — fun, but don't reach a large audience or make the bucks.

How easy or hard is it to make a living as an author?

It is not easy. It's never easy. Each person who is working full-time as an author probably puts in more than a 50-hour week to their writing, has gone years without pay while they are building their career, and continues to work it hard. Those who think that authors pop out a book by working 40 hours, then are set for life, are dreamin,' mate.

But it's also not impossible. A lot of people I know have done it. You must make sacrifices and smart decisions. There is hard work, constant work, and doing the itty bitty things. There are two things you need—dedication and tenacity. It is easier if you have a natural talent for writing, but not impossible if you're willing to work it hard. You need to research your market, and make sure you're writing in a genre that *can* let you make a living as an author. Don't fool yourself. If you want to write dystopian vampires who meet aliens, solve a few mysteries, hang out with the mermen, then time travel to the Victorian era to do it all over again, you probably will struggle to find an audience to support your career. By all means write it, yes, I'd never say no, but if your market it not there, then you can't cry and ask why doesn't anyone read your novel. A recent article I read showed that the greatest number of full-time writers earning over $5000 per month wrote in the romance genre. In the genre of "Literary Fiction," the number was so low it didn't register on the graph. Other genres that did well were erotica, mystery and sci-fi.

The last piece of the puzzle is the hardest—dumb luck. You need *something* that will pip you over the edge and bring you to the attention of your audience. And *that* is something no one can predict.

What advice would you give to someone aspiring to be an author?

Go for it. But be prepared.

I began writing in January 2013. Serious writing. My first book was published April 2014. My first quarterly royalty payment that was substantial hit my bank account February 2015. That's two years lag time. Two years of effort, pain, determination—and yes, upfront costs. By that time, I had written seven full-length novels, and had various other stories half completed. There is no quick buck to be made with writing.

Also be prepared for long hours without support. It's all up to you. With writing, there are no cheerleaders behind you, no boss breathing down your neck, no expectations of word counts apart from what you make for yourself. And of course, no guaranteed reward. People don't *have* to buy your book, just because you've written it. And just because you write a book, don't expect instant accolades.

And lastly, be honest with yourself. Just because your mother likes your book, it doesn't mean that everyone will. YA doesn't sell as well as adult fiction. A pen name like Pussy Galore may work well in erotica, but probably won't do you any favors in selling mystery. And yes, people have read Twilight, Harry Potter and 50 Shades. If you have the exact some storyline, people will immediately notice.

How can readers find out more about you?

Website: www.renaekaye.weebly.com

Facebook: www.facebook.com/renae.kaye.9

Rosanne Dingli

How long have you been writing, and how did you become involved in writing?

I was living in the country in NSW in 1985, writing many letters a week to my mother in Europe. It was second nature to fall into writing poetry [all the tools were there, lots of paper, especially after putting myself through a self-taught, intensive course of Australian Literature—I thought at the time that all immigrants did that! The brilliant introduction to the *Penguin Book of Australian Women Poets* was what probably did it. I observed everything it said, read another two or three instructional books, and submitted all I wrote. In a year, I was well published, so I went on in that way until—when I moved to Perth in 1988—I had quite a collection of published and awarded pieces. My collected poems came out in 1991. Called *All the Wrong Places,* it was published by the Literary Mouse Press, now defunct. My first novel *Death in Malta* came out in 2001—through Jacobyte Books in South Australia, now also closed. They sold me onward to BeWrite Books in England, who went on to publish two more of my novels. They also shut down in 2012.

What are you working on at the moment?

This is a rest year for me. I wrote and published three novels in 2015, so I'm ahead of myself. 2016 is a year of recovery! I am putting my house in order and only writing two or three potboiler short stories to submit to literary magazines.

Did you have any goals with writing, and if so, how well do you feel you've achieved them? What do you hope to achieve in the future?

Although people tell me I seem all organized and determined, I must admit do not set conscious goals. I just have amazing spurts and productive periods that I know will result in something worthwhile. If I do not feel the urge, I simply do not bother. If my year seems to indicate working at something other than writing, that's what I do.

Despite this reluctance to set goals, I have managed to attract almost two dozen accolades for my writing, including the Patricia Hackett award. I have something like 16 titles out there right now (of which only about eight sell significantly and regularly.)

So for a writer like me, goals and targets are not useful, but I chalk up successes anyway.

The future? We'll see when it comes.

How long does it take you to write a book?

It depends on the book—a novel takes about six weeks to set down as a first draft. That opens the way for several months of redrafting, editing, revisions and re-thinks. Although my novels come out more or less fully formed, they require a lot of tweaking, which is the most enjoyable part. I have been known to go over drafts more than just two dozen times. A year is about what it takes, if it's longer than 100,000 words. Doing three 60,000-word novels in just over a year is a marathon effort, and I'm tired now.

What are the hardest parts of being an author for you?

That first draft. I find it the hardest thing in the world to tackle because I need to let it all out in one big effort if possible, abandoning all else. Life doesn't allow that, and interruptions are inevitable, but I do wish the world would leave me alone when I'm in drafting mode; it's incredibly hard. Argh!

What do you enjoy most about being an author?

I like it when people buy my books. What a question!

What books or authors have had the most influence on you as an author?

My reading choices are narrow and some would say predictable, highbrow, and perhaps boring. But it's not books and authors that have had the greatest influence on what I write. International literature, as a whole, has formed the background to all I think of.

What did you find most useful when you were learning to write and expanding your skills?

Being left alone. Having the ability to immerse myself in thought even when ostensibly doing something else. Understanding Aus Lit, after half a lifetime of European and English Literature. That's what informed my writing.

Expanding my skills meant adding to my rough store of knowledge of the publishing world, printing, typesetting, and design. Working on magazines and newspapers, and for a short period as a graphic artist, and helping out in my uncle's printing press as a child meant I had a very useful background. I added and added to the basic set, and I continue to upgrade as I go. I can't emphasize enough how important these skills are. Today's independent author needs to have a full and up-to-date toolbox.

What author services do you pay for, as opposed to doing yourself? Things like cover design, formatting, editing, proofreading, etc.?

Because I'm already equipped with a nice useful skill set, I do almost everything myself. My computer literacy dates from the early nineties, and I ensure I learn as things change—it's essential, because they do change with alarming frequency. I farm out my finished draft to beta-readers, and pay for a professional edit. I also occasionally employ a cover artist. That's about it.

What technology/services/programs do you use as an author? (email subscription services, Dragon software, editing software, etc.)

I can't stress enough how important it is for an author to understand their word processing program. I use MSWord — and I mean *use*. It works very well for me, and I do all my drafting, editing, typesetting, and formatting on Word. I could not possibly work without Foxit Reader, a free download that manipulates PDFs, by far my most important tool. And a simple imaging program such as Paint or Gimp does the rest. I occasionally use Autocrit to ensure my editor gets nice clean copy. The names of these things are not as important as my wholehearted efforts to learn and understand what they can do for me, and to continually upgrade my skills.

What are your thoughts about ebooks vs. print books?

There is no such *versus*. Just as there is no "buttons versus zips," or "tin cans versus jars," or "escalators and lifts versus stairs," or "ballpoint pens versus pencils," or "cars versus motorbikes," or "wooden spoons versus metal spoons." They all have a parallel existence, and provide parallel uses for more or less similar tasks.

What are your thoughts about self-publishing vs traditional publishing?

There is no such *versus*. In 2008 / 09, publishing met a fork in the road, and everything split into slightly different directions. There are now more than one major publishing streams. (Some say there are four, but I don't really know, since I can only see two major ones.) There is the commercial stream, which uses the old tried and tested model of "agenting-contracts-publishing-printing-retail-returns-remaindering-pulping." The model has worked for many decades, and — although flawed — will continue to work for a while. (*Why* it works is another very long argument.)

Independent publishing uses a vastly different model that dispenses with agents and most of the rest, and is borne by the efficacy of digital tools and online interaction and sales, whether it's paperbacks or ebooks.

I hasten to add there is *some* overlap.

Because readers rarely care *who* publishes what, or *how*, they can straddle these two models and buy their reading material where they will. They can. And they do.

If authors fail to understand the striking differences between the two publishing models, and have unrealistic expectations from independent publishing, thinking it mimics traditional / commercial publishing, they are doomed to be disappointed. All authors owe themselves the comfort of knowing the industry . . . and its different streams, and what each one can and *cannot* do.

How often do you write, and how do you find or make time to write?

No set pattern, no set time. I often go for months without writing a creative word. And also often write for months without coming up for air.

Do you plan your whole book out in advance, or just let it flow? What does your writing process look like?

It doesn't look like anything sane, cogent, sensible, ordered, or thought-out. The miracle is that it produces perfectly readable, logical fiction.

What's a typical working day like for you? When and where do you write?

All I want is a darkened room with an excellent computer that's available at all hours, whether I decide to use it or not.

Is there such a thing as a typical day?

Do you ever get Writer's Block? If so, how do you deal with it?

There is no such thing. It's not a virus. It's not bacterial. It's not an ailment. It's probably anxiety—but how would I know? When there's nothing to write, don't write it. You can quote me.

Do you read your own reviews? If so, how do you deal with bad reviews?

Of course I read reviews. They always say such nice things. I've had possibly two bad reviews for all my sixteen titles — but they make the others look good.

Other than reviews, do you hear from your readers very often? What kinds of things do they say?

My band of true and loyal readers are fantastic, and I get frequent little hints and badges of encouragement from them in the way of heartfelt praise. It's what an author like me loves.

What are some ways in which you promote your books? What have you found most or least effective?

The most effective by far is being an interesting person with a store of entertaining anecdotes to tell; when it comes to real-life interaction. Online, it's about being helpful, willing to share information, lively, and generous. And consistently present. Stay away for a month, and everyone forgets you.

Keeping well away from contentious issues has worked for me. No politics, religion, sex, money, or family issues online. I do have opinions, but I keep them to myself and my family. My cat is the only one that gets a rare mention. Everyone and everything other than books, reading, publishing, the book world, and books, books, books is conspicuous by its absence. Did I mention books?

Appearing to be knowledgeable about the book world, offering advice, sharing news, displaying interesting images and articles related to the topics in my fiction, and taking an interest in the work of other similar authors is vital.

When people think you're interesting, they become curious about your work — could I perhaps have written something interesting? They go and look.

The big publishers found out long ago that advertising does not work for books. You rarely see book adverts on the sides of buses. No book ads on TV or the radio. There's a reason—visual and audio media do not really sell print or ebooks.

What does sell books is two things . . . other books, and word of mouth. I can't begin to tell you what mileage one can get out of a book club buying just nine copies of a novel . . . those nine people will love it or hate it, but they'll tell their families and friends. They will want more, and go looking for more by the same author, so the clever writer makes sure to keep producing more and more books for the band of true and faithful followers, which grows a little every year. It's much easier to keep supplying the same people with new reading material, than to continually seek new readers for the same book.

How easy or hard is it to make a living as an author?

It's impossible. Next question.

Seriously—I have always had to do something else to support my writing habit. I have done some weird things for money; like teach, lecture, read slush for a university press, review books for a newspaper, freelance as a journalist, edit, paint, and cook. Travel writing, heraldic art, and feature writing can be fun. It helps to have a willing spouse. Willing to pay the bills, that is. Since 2012, my sales have trended upward, and I'm now paying for a few things. But it's not the kind of industry to rely on. It might all go to zero tomorrow.

What advice would you give to someone aspiring to be an author?

Are you crazy? Don't even think of it.

How can readers find out more about you?

Website: www.rosannedingli.com
Facebook: www.facebook.com/rosannedingli

Russel Proctor

Tell us about yourself and your books!

I am an Australian writer of horror, science fiction and fantasy. I have also been a lawyer, teacher and professional actor. I now tutor part time which leaves my mornings open to write in. My other interests include cats, astronomy and hiking, the last of which has taken me on extended walks in Africa, Australia and Papua New Guinea. I have several books out, the latest being a horror/fantasy mash-up series based on Alice in Wonderland and The Wizard of Oz, in which Alice and Dorothy join forces to fight supernatural enemies in Edwardian London and World War One. That series is called *The Jabberwocky Book,* the first volume being *The Red King* and the second *An Unkindness of Ravens,* both published by Permuted Press. The third volume, *The Looking-Glass House,* is due out this year. I also have volume one of a science-fiction series Days of Iron, out with a sequel due soon and a science-fiction/humor novel *Plato's Cave.* As well as these, I have several short stories in various anthologies and have written a number of stage plays.

How long have you been writing, and how did you become involved in writing?

I have been writing since as long as I can remember, but in the last few years have I found the time to keep at it every day. I always wanted to be an author, but the necessity of earning a living and getting on with life sort of got in the way.

What are you working on at the moment?

At the moment I am writing the first book of a new time-travel/horror series, tentatively titled *The Scream of Years.* I am working on the first volume now, with at least two more to follow. It tells the adventures of a woman who is one of a race of time-travelers called the Maegri, caught up in both a civil war and an invasion of monsters from some as yet unexplored part of the universe. The first book ranges from 250 BC to 6,000,000 AD. There are no time machines involved; the Maegri have an innate time-travel ability which is not always handy to them. The heroine, April Tooms, is a synesthetic musician caught up in things very much against her will.

Did you have any goals with writing, and if so, how well do you feel you've achieved them? What do you hope to achieve in the future?

I think my goal with writing is simply to tell a good story. I like it when people are reading what I've written. I don't aim for any real goals other than that.

How long does it take you to write a book?

It takes about a year. I'm not one of those writers who can pump one out in a few weeks. The first draft takes about six months and then the other six months is spent in redrafting and getting it right. Since I don't actually plan my stories a lot of rewriting is involved once the thing exists as a first draft.

What are the hardest parts of being an author for you?

Getting noticed. There is a lot of marketing involved in being a writer these days, which I don't think is entirely fair. Just because someone writes a book doesn't mean they know how to sell one. But even legitimate publishers expect writers to do part (or most) of the promotional aspect as well. I'd rather be writing the next story.

What do you enjoy most about being an author?

Finding out what it is I'm writing as I write it. I'm not a planner, which means I don't sit down and plot out my stories.

So basically it's like I'm reading the story myself for the first time as I write it. I don't know how it will end (or maybe I do, but I don't know how the story will unfold to get there), so I am like a reader myself. That's exciting. I also enjoy doing the research. In my Jabberwocky series a lot of research was necessary to get the 1901 setting right, and it's been great to have comments from readers that they found the setting authentic.

What books or authors have had the most influence on you as an author?

My three big influences are Mervyn Peake, Roger Zelazny and William Hope Hodgson. As for books themselves, I put *Moby-Dick* and *Wuthering Heights* up pretty high. Both are gothic horror stories mistaken for other genres. I like authors who break out of traditional genres and strive for something new.

What did you find most useful when you were learning to write and expanding your skills?

Listening to other writers is important. Then, when they have said all they want to say, go and do what you want to anyway. But still remember what they said, because in the end they will be right and you will be wrong. But that shouldn't stop you.

What author services do you pay for, as opposed to doing yourself? Things like cover design, formatting, editing, proofreading, etc.?

I have paid for some editing services, mostly during the drafting stage. One of my novels still to be released, *Shepherd Moon*, was read by an editor after the first draft to give feedback on plotting and characters. My book *Plato's Cave* was self-published, and I paid for everything there—cover, editing, interior layout etc. It also helps to have some writer friends prepared to be beta readers and give informal (and free!) feedback.

What technology/services/programs do you use as an author? (email subscription services, Dragon software, editing software, etc.)

Microsoft Word. I also find OneNote a fabulous note-keeping and research tool. I subscribe to a website called The Horror Tree which is a weekly online newsletter listing publishers taking submissions for horror and science-fiction.

What are your thoughts about ebooks vs. print books?

They are both good. I read both, and my works appear in both. I can't understand the prejudice against either form that some people have. "I love the smell of a real book." What does that mean? I don't go around smelling books. I read them.

What are your thoughts about self-publishing vs traditional publishing?

They both have strengths and weaknesses. It's very hard to get published traditionally, and the publishers and editors might change your work until it matches what they want. On the other hand, self-publishing means there are a lot of poor stories out there, and a lot of competition.

How often do you write, and how do you find or make time to write?

I try to write every day, and usually do, at least a thousand words. My goal is two thousand a day but that isn't always achievable. If I don't write, I edit or do research. Always the research!

Do you plan your whole book out in advance, or just let it flow? What does your writing process look like?

My writing process is all over the shop. I will have a scene or an idea in my head and start writing. Where that takes me is something I find out on the way. I certainly don't plan my stories, they just sort of unfold and then have to be patched together. I also use notebooks, a different one for each book, where I take research notes and jot down ideas so I don't forget them.

What's a typical working day like for you? When and where do you write?

I write at an antique writing desk with a fold-down front. I look quite incongruous with my laptop on it. I spend about two or three hours a day, early in the morning. I can't write later in the day, and I work in the evenings so I have to get my words down while the sun is still coming up.

Do you ever get Writer's Block? If so, how do you deal with it?

I do get writer's block. Dealing with it isn't always easy. Generally, I just go and do something completely unrelated to writing until guilt sends me back to the computer.

Do you read your own reviews? If so, how do you deal with bad reviews?

I do read my reviews. I don't "deal with" bad ones. They are people's opinions, although sometimes they disappoint me. But one of the best "bad reviews" I ever got was for a play I'd written called *Lucifer*. It was being performed on stage and an audience member near me got up and walked out, loudly shouting out that he'd been offended and the play was a load of crap. I loved that feedback, because it was exactly the result I'd hoped for. My intention had been to offend certain people, and it worked!

Other than reviews, do you hear from your readers very often? What kinds of things do they say?

Mostly nice things, which is good. When I was an actor I was taught never to ask for an audience member's opinion. If they complimented the show, I would just say "Thanks, I'm glad you enjoyed it" and if they didn't like it I'd find something else to talk about. There is an old saying in the theatre: "If the show is a success, everyone congratulates the actors; if it's a flop, everyone blames the director."

What are some ways in which you promote your books? What have you found most or least effective?

I have never found an effective way to promote a book. What works for one doesn't work for another.

How easy or hard is it to make a living as an author?

I don't make a living as an author. It would be nice, but it hasn't happened to me.

What advice would you give to someone aspiring to be an author?

Don't expect anything. Don't expect to be published, don't expect to make a living out of it, don't expect that people will praise your work. On the other hand, don't expect that sudden success, don't expect your sudden fanbase, don't expect the great review you receive. Writing is the craziest job in the world, and one of the loneliest.

How can readers find out more about you?

Website: www.russellproctor.com

Facebook: www.facebook.com/writerproctor

Sally Odgers

How long have you been writing, and how did you become involved in writing?

I've been writing for nearly as long as I can remember. Writing was the subject I was best at in Primary School, and when I was in Year Four my teacher entered a story I wrote into a state-wide contest. It won. After that, there was no stopping me. I felt very lucky to be good at something I enjoyed, possibly because I wasn't so good at a lot of other things I enjoyed.

What are you working on at the moment?

I spend much of my time editing and manuscript assessing, but I have several WIPs. Most of these are fantasy or sci-fi for older readers.

Did you have any goals with writing, and if so, how well do you feel you've achieved them? What do you hope to achieve in the future?

I always wanted to write full time and for quite a while I did that. I'd love to write more than I do at present.

How long does it take you to write a book?

How long is a bit of string? One book took me ten minutes, and another one four weeks. If you count the hiatuses that sometimes happen, the time can stretch enormously. It really depends a lot on the length. The most I ever wrote was 10,000 words a day for a three-week stretch in 1999. That turned out to be a mistake because it set off tendonitis which continues to plague me to this day.

What are the hardest parts of being an author for you?

By far the most difficult is finding markets. It used to be much, much, much easier than it is now. In those days, the hardest part was the split between what *I* wanted to write and what publishers wanted me to write. Now finding any publisher that wants anything is the problem.

What do you enjoy most about being an author?

I love creating stories, especially the part which is world-building.

What books or authors have had the most influence on you as an author?

When I was starting out, Monica Edwards and Anne Farrell were influences in that they wrote books set on farms or around characters boating, swimming, riding and acting. Since that was *my* world I was happy to follow suit. Soon after I got my start, farm-and-family stories went out of fashion, so I turned to fantasy and sci-fi.

What did you find most useful when you were learning to write and expanding your skills?

I have always been grateful for my solid primary and high school education in spelling and grammar. Without it, I'd have made far more errors than I do. Having a solid foundation allows me to write without worrying about the grammar. I know it just the same way I know how to make a sandwich or walk down steps.

What author services do you pay for, as opposed to doing yourself? Things like cover design, formatting, editing, proofreading, etc.?

I occasionally pay illustrators, but only in my self-publishing ventures. Most of my books are traditionally published, so the most I ever paid there was postage for the manuscript.

What technology/services/programs do you use as an author? (email subscription services, Dragon software, editing software, etc.)

MS Word. I tried with Dragon on and off for years, but it seems peculiarly non-suited to writing fiction, especially dialogue.

Consider this.

"Are we going home first, or did you want to go to Shaddie's?" asked Jane.

To do that with Dragon, you must say; TAB OPEN QUOTES Are we going home first COMMA or did you want to go to Shaddie's BACK Shaddie's BACK Shaddie's BACK SPELL THAT S-H-A-D-D-I-E-APOSTROPHE- S QUESTION MARK CLOSE QUOTES asked Jane FULL STOP TAB

Even then it is likely to miss words such as OR. TO and GO.

What are your thoughts about ebooks vs. print books?

I prefer audio books to "read" because I do so much reading for work. I love walking and gardening, and I can read while doing those with audio books. If I had a Kindle or some other small device (other than my laptop) I might read more ebooks. My only argument with ebooks is the pricing. They are priced so low it seems to me we're devaluing writers' work. If a paperback costs $15 and the ebook edition costs 99 cents, are we REALLY saying the author's input is worth less than a dollar while the paper and ink and so on is worth $14?

What are your thoughts about self-publishing vs traditional publishing?

Traditional publishing wins hands down when it comes to distribution and sales in my experience. However, self-publishing can allow one to bring out that book-of-the-heart that isn't seen as commercial by publishers. I know of some very capable authors who have never offered their work to traditional publishers because they could never find any open to submissions, or else because they wanted to see their books out NOW and not in two or more years' time. Another reason to self-publish is to keep a book in print. When my books Picture a Poem and Story Strategies went OOP I had several calls from teachers wanting to buy more copies when their originals wore out. I couldn't sell them any, so I wrote brand new books called Reason to Write and How to be an Awesome Author with the idea of keeping them updated and permanently in print. Alas, teachers wanted the old titles. They seemed uninterested in the new ones. I still think it was a good idea in theory though.

How often do you write, and how do you find or make time to write?

I do writing-related work almost every day. It's usually editing or assessing. If I'm working on a new book I usually put other things on hold.

Do you plan your whole book out in advance, or just let it flow? What does your writing process look like?

I plan everything and write to the plan. I make notes. Every day I read over the previous day's output and roughly edit it before writing today's scenes.

What's a typical working day like for you? When and where do you write?

I work every day, so most days are the same. I wake lateish and check email, listing any new editing jobs. I get on with whatever the current job is. I take some of our dogs for a walk with an audio book and get the mail and do necessary shopping.

After lunch I get back to writing/editing or sending receipts / accounting until 2pm when I take over care of my old dad from my sister. I keep working, but go to check him every hour or two. I sometimes get another walk at 5pm, and then get Dad's dinner at 6pm and get him to bed. I come home to have my dinner with my husband at 7 pm and we feed the dogs and watch a DVD or so. My husband goes to bed and I check Dad between 9–11pm, then work until midnight or 1am and check him again. I go to bed about 2am and then the cycle begins again. I do almost all my writing sitting in an armchair with my laptop and a dog or two sprawled on my shoulders or at my feet. That's one of the reasons for all the walking. It keeps me from getting too unfit.

Do you ever get Writer's Block? If so, how do you deal with it?

Never. As I have been known to say to mentees . . . do teachers get teachers' block? Do farmers get milker's block? If you have a job to do, you do it, even if you may not especially feel like it that day. Imagine the chaos if people who were "blocked" just didn't work? This sounds unsympathetic, but it's not meant to be. I have no doubt some people genuinely suffer from this and I'd say if it happens often they would be much better off with a different occupation. After all, people with chronic back pain don't usually work in an environment that calls for frequent heavy lifting and people with poor eyesight are usually not micro-surgeons.

Do you read your own reviews? If so, how do you deal with bad reviews?

I read them, but I don't get many. I'm a mid-lister, so when I write a book it's not all that much of an event. Most reviews seem to be blurbs anyway which is a trifle disappointing.

Other than reviews, do you hear from your readers very often? What kinds of things do they say?

Kids and teachers and parents often email to say how much they loved the Jack or Pet Vet books and to ask if we are writing any more, or to ask if I can sell them (insert OOP title).

What are some ways in which you promote your books? What have you found most or least effective?

When I started out in the 1970s authors didn't promote books; publishers did. These days my promoting consists of business cards listing titles and websites, interviews, as many workshops and talks as I can get, custom-printed tee-shirts, blog tours and so on. I don't know how effective this is. I'd say one of the least effective methods is joining on-line groups because we're trying to sell to other writers who usually are more interested (and why not?) in their own work. One thing I have just done is to put out the Ramses Rat Activity Book as a companion to the Adventures of Ramses Rat series.

How easy or hard is it to make a living as an author?

I used to do it easily, but now it is getting so difficult to place manuscripts that it's getting much harder.

What advice would you give to someone aspiring to be an author?

Learn your craft before you ever submit a thing. Polish your manuscript and/or get an assessor/editor to have a look at it. (Prices vary, so shop around. One client told me another editor quotes him $350.00 for a job I do routinely for $25.00.) If you don't love writing for its own sake, find something else to do instead. If you DO love writing for its own sake, then look at all avenues (including self-publishing) and treat it as any other activity you love. Maintaining a day job is a good idea, so you don't have to worry about the financial side too much.

How can readers find out more about you?

Website: www.sallyodgers.com

Facebook: www.facebook.com/Sally-Odgers-46649730940/

Scott Medbury

Tell us about yourself and your books!

I'm a self-published author, husband and dad of four from the lower Blue Mountains of Sydney. My first novel, After Days-Affliction, is the first of a post-apocalyptic trilogy of books that I began in 2014. It was a #1 bestseller in its genre on Amazon.com and was followed by books 2 and 3, Sanctuary and Attrition. I've also released a short story set in that world about 20 years after the events of the trilogy.

How long have you been writing, and how did you become involved in writing?

I've been righting since I was a kid. I handed my first unsolicited story to my grade 1 teacher at age 6 and I have continued on and off for over 30 years. I always knew I that could write to entertain and that I had a novel or two in me, but life always seemed to get in the way and I began many novels but never followed one through to completion until age 45.

What are you working on at the moment?

I'm working on a sci-fi novella right now, kind of a cross between Blade Runner and Goodfellas. Its tentatively titled *Pleasure Machine 676.*

Did you have any goals with writing, and if so, how well do you feel you've achieved them? What do you hope to achieve in the future?

I never had any goals for my writing before I began to do it seriously, and even now goals are mostly shorter term rather than longer term and tend to focus on what I'm writing at the time. One longer term goal I did set was to write the entire After Days trilogy in two years and I achieved that with 6 months to spare. In the future I hope to be able to write full time and my goal is to write two novels every year until I achieve that.

How long does it take you to write a book?

A novel takes me around 6 months from start to publication.

What are the hardest parts of being an author for you?

Working full time, and being a busy dad, hands down it's TIME.

What do you enjoy most about being an author?

Without a doubt, its bringing pleasure to readers. The satisfaction of hearing things like "gripped me from the start and kept me reading long into the night" and "once I started I couldn't put it down until I finished it" inspires me to keep going and assures me I'm doing something right!

What books or authors have had the most influence on you as an author?

Everything that Stephen King wrote in the 70's and 80's, particularly "The Stand.' William Golding's 'The Lord of the Flies' also influenced me greatly and throw in the fantastic authors John Christopher, Raymond E Feist and David Wingrove.

What did you find most useful when you were learning to write and expanding your skills?

Believe it or not it was writing erotic short stories. They were my first successful foray into self-publishing and gave me the discipline to write every day, even if it was just a few hundred words. Not only that, writing that in that format enabled me to hone my skills and cut the fat out of my writing. My style is spare, to the point and story focussed and its thanks in part to writing around 150,000 words worth of short stories before I wrote After Days.

What author services do you pay for, as opposed to doing yourself? Things like cover design, formatting, editing, proofreading, etc.?

Before I started my own publishing company I would pay external providers to do editing and sometimes covers. Now of course, I employ editors and cover designers but the principle is the same, for things that really count like covers and editing, don't be afraid to invest, it will pay off in the end. You can check out the services we provide at Anscotpublishing.com

What technology/services/programs do you use as an author? (email subscription services, Dragon software, editing software, etc.)

Microsoft word, Freebooksy, Kindle Nation Daily, E-reader News Today.

What are your thoughts about ebooks vs. print books?

Ebooks are where the money is. They have changed the face of book publishing as we know it. That's doesn't mean there isn't a place for print books though. In fact I urge any self-published authors to have a paperback version of their novels available-they are great for promotions and people WILL ask you where they can get a hard copy. From a marketing perspective, they also offer a nice price differential to your ebook.

What are your thoughts about self-publishing vs traditional publishing?

Both have their place, however good luck on the traditional publishing route. My novel After Days was submitted to three agents with a view to obtaining a traditional publishing contract before I self-published. Only one responded and told me it wouldn't sell. 20,000 self-published copies later it's still going strong.

How often do you write, and how do you find or make time to write?

Every day. Early morning and late at night. It's a matter of taking every free minute you have and making it count.

Do you plan your whole book out in advance, or just let it flow? What does your writing process look like?

For me, I find planning my books kills the creative process. I basically begin with a first scene and the main characters and a general idea. I have a rough notion of the ending, but I basically let the story flow and the characters take on a life of their own and decide where it's going to go- often the end will be very different to how I envisaged it when I typed those first few words.

What's a typical working day like for you? When and where do you write?

I rise early and write for an hour or two, then will do the same I the evening after the family has settled for the night. I write in my study at a big beautiful old desktop computer.

Do you ever get Writer's Block? If so, how do you deal with it?

Occasionally the dreaded affliction will strike, usually part way through a novel. I get around it by going back to the beginning and starting a second draft. I don't know why, but this works for me and by the time I get to the stage in the book where the writer's block began I have, momentum again and it gets me through to the end.

Do you read your own reviews? If so, how do you deal with bad reviews?

Yes, I do read my reviews. Depends on what you define as bad. I've had 4 star reviews I thought were bad, and I've had 2 star reviews that I learnt from. To me a bad review is one that offers no constructive criticism just throwaway lines like 'do not waste your money!' or 'poorly edited' with no qualifiers.

Good "bad" reviews are great. I recently had one that said I used foreshadowing too much in a particular book. And do you know what? I did! I used that advice to go back and edit the book which made it a much tighter story.

Other than reviews, do you hear from your readers very often? What kinds of things do they say?

Occasionally through submissions through my websites or via social media a reader will reach out and tell me how much they've enjoyed a book. In my experience these have all been positive.

What are some ways in which you promote your books? What have you found most or least effective?

My author mailing list is the most effective. Other than that some promotional services are great, and I mentioned them above -the most effective for me was Kindle Nation Daily.

How easy or hard is it to make a living as an author?

Hard but very doable.

What advice would you give to someone aspiring to be an author?

Just do it! Don't waste time with traditional publishing — self-publish and build a following then have a crack at the big boys.

How can readers find out more about you?

Website: www.Scottmedbury.com

Facebook: www.facebook.com/AfterDaysTrilogy

Sunanda Chatterjee

Tell us about yourself and your books!

I grew up in Bhilai, a small town in central India, and like everyone else in my family, chose a career in science. I joined the India Air Force as a physician for five years, before coming to the United States for a PhD in cancer research. But I always loved to write. My favorite genres are women's fiction, suspense, and thrillers, although I write only women's fiction. My first book The Vision is about a pathologist whose wish for a 'good eye' to make diagnosis comes true, but she starts getting visions about things that are yet to happen. My second book Shadowed Promise, released in 2016, is about an orphan growing up in Bombay, who makes a promise to her dying cousin to protect the baby, a promise which returns to haunt her years later when she settles in Los Angeles and is married to a politician.

How long have you been writing, and how did you become involved in writing?

I've been writing since a young age. I was always a shy person, and felt that I expressed my views best through the written rather than the spoken word. I used to write short stories and got published in online journals, but my inspiration to write a novel came after I read Jhumpa Lahiri's Interpreter of Maladies.

What are you working on at the moment?

I'm working on another story with a strong female protagonist, from teen to YA, overlapping with women's fiction genre.

Did you have any goals with writing, and if so, how well do you feel you've achieved them? What do you hope to achieve in the future?

I want to write stories that resonate with my readers, which make them laugh and cry, make them cheer for my protagonist and celebrate her wins. With Shadowed Promise, I've got reviews from readers which tell me I have achieved that. I want to keep writing stories that strike a chord in my reader's hearts. During my journey through the little town where I grew up, the five years in the Indian Air Force, and the years I spent in America, I've realized that while situations may differ, our reactions and issues remain the same. An American reader can relate to an Indian orphan growing up with mean relatives, and an Indian reader can relate to an American going through life issues unique to the western world.

How long does it take you to write a book?

My first book took me ten years to write, because I had no idea what I was going to do with it. I had no outline. I had no plans to hopes to ever get it published. When I finally did, it was ten years already. But now I write stories with an outline, with a clear framework about how to proceed. I discuss the storyline and character names with my daughter, and write out a detailed outline before I start typing. Each sentence becomes a scene. Now it takes me about a year to complete a book.

What are the hardest parts of being an author for you?

Finding time to write. I have a full time job. I write when I can. So when I do find time, the creative juices may have dried up. I need outlines jut for that.

What do you enjoy most about being an author?

Making characters go through what I'm afraid to go through. Putting difficulties in their paths. Finding creative solutions. And when a character becomes too interesting for the book, making him or her disappear through relocation or (gasp!) death.

What books or authors have had the most influence on you as an author?

Somerset Maugham, Thomas Hardy and Jhumpa Lahiri.

What did you find most useful when you were learning to write and expanding your skills?

I took writing courses and read about ten books on creative writing. I read about screenwriting, plot and structure, dialogue, character arcs, and the works. It was a lot of effort, but my stories are 'tighter' because of the tricks I learnt.

What author services do you pay for, as opposed to doing yourself? Things like cover design, formatting, editing, proofreading, etc.?

For Shadowed Promise, I outsourced cover-design and editing. But I did my own formatting for paperback. I used Vellum for the ebook formatting.

What technology/services/programs do you use as an author? (email subscription services, Dragon software, editing software, etc.)

For editing, I use prowritingaid.com. My website is hosted by Weebly. I use mailchimp for email subscription services.

What are your thoughts about ebooks vs. print books?

I personally like to hold a book in my hands, but I'm getting used to reading ebooks on my iPad now. I can see how it becomes easy to download five books for a long trip, rather than take a chance with one paperback which you may hate.

What are your thoughts about self-publishing vs traditional publishing?

If you're writing for the fun of it, I think self-publishing is a great option. It gives you freedom and flexibility regarding release date, price, categories, etc. But indie authors should invest in a good editor and cover designer and make the book the best it can be before subjecting unsuspecting readers to it. Traditional publishing is great if you can break into the market. But the author has no control over the process.

How often do you write, and how do you find or make time to write?

I write almost every day. If I don't have time or the creative energy to write, I'll read over what I wrote the previous day and make little corrections as I go along.

Do you plan your whole book out in advance, or just let it flow? What does your writing process look like?

I think of a plot, and talk to my daughter and my husband. I take their advice about whether the story is even interesting. If it passes their threshold, I write out a plot outline and show it to them. I take their advice and the advice of readers for character names. I copy and save the outline as a separate document. Whenever I have time, I convert a sentence from the outline into a scene. If I'm not feeling creative, I go over the previous day's material. Often the storyline changes, and I make adjustments as I go along. Once the first draft is done, I leave it alone for a few days. Then I go over it again, make changes in the story, cut out some things, add others. After the second or third round, I show it to my daughter. She's a high school student and has a really busy schedule, so sometimes it doesn't happen. Then I send it to my beta readers. I make changes as necessary. Then it will go off to the editor.

What's a typical working day like for you? When and where do you write?

I work full time, so I can write only on my days off, afterhours, and weekends. I have a favorite spot in my dining room, where the sun hits my back in just the right doses. I have a cup of coffee beside me, which often runneth cold. I have Google open for any quick references and searches. The room is quiet. No music. Just the clak-clak of my five fingers flying over the keyboard. I'm one of those people who can't type while looking at the monitor. I use two fingers on my right hand and three on my left. It looks awkward, but it's very fast.

Do you ever get Writer's Block? If so, how do you deal with it?

Rather than calling it writer's block, I call it 'not in a mood to write new stuff' time. I read other people's books. I write poems and short stories. Or I read the previous chapters I've already written. Sometimes I go on a long walk just to clear my head. I meditate for an hour every morning. That helps me focus, I think.

Do you read your own reviews? If so, how do you deal with bad reviews?

I read every review. I share the good ones with my family, and hurt over the bad ones. My son told me never to read reviews. But who can help it? After a while I tell myself, a bad review makes it authentic. Not everyone likes Picasso. So I move on.

Other than reviews, do you hear from your readers very often? What kinds of things do they say?

I've had readers connect with me on Facebook and through my blog and website. They tell me about themselves, about what event or character in my book resonated with them. The best compliments I've got are that they would read my future books.

What are some ways in which you promote your books? What have you found most or least effective?

Listing my book through James Mayfield and bknights when it was free. Then a few other promotional sites like buck books and fussy librarian and Ereadernewstoday when my book was 99c. Both free promos were effective. Among the promos when my book was 99c, Ereadernewstoday was the most effective.

How easy or hard is it to make a living as an author?

I haven't yet recovered the cost of editing and cover design. If I didn't have a full time job, I suppose I would write much more and publish more and become more successful. But for the moment, I'm keeping my day job.

What advice would you give to someone aspiring to be an author?

You want to be an author? Then write! Take writing courses, especially for fiction. Read extensively, including books about writing better. Write and edit multiple times before springing your book to the world.

How can readers find out more about you?

Website: www.sunandachatterjee.com/

Facebook:

www.facebook.com/SunandaChatterjee_Author-515705275228760/

Tabitha Ormiston-Smith

Tell us about yourself and your books!

My function is to entertain. My published novels are both contemporary humor, and that's my home genre. However, in short fiction I do like to experiment with different genres. I've written short stories in SF, fantasy, horror and general fiction, and my two novellas are romance/crime and children's fiction. The one non-fiction, Grammar Without Tears, is as funny as a book on grammar can be. Which I have to say is pretty damn funny, actually.

How long have you been writing, and how did you become involved in writing?

I pretty well always wanted to write, but somehow in my teens and twenties I lost sight of that. I started writing in earnest by accident one day in my thirties, but didn't publish anything until 2009.

What are you working on at the moment?

A novel that will knock your socks off. It's a combination of police procedural, humor and urban fantasy. I have various other projects in suspension—an historical novel set in the twelfth century, a third contemporary humor to round off a trilogy with the two I've already published, a YA fantasy novella and a handful of short stories are in progress. But this police novel is the only thing I'm actively working on just now.

Did you have any goals with writing, and if so, how well do you feel you've achieved them? What do you hope to achieve in the future?

Really to me writing is like education—an end in itself, not something to be used as a means to an end. I suppose the one dream I had was that someone I didn't know might come up to me one day and tell me how much they'd enjoyed one of my books. And that dream has come true for me. Of course, writing is really performance art and we all crave the applause. But as to actual goals—of course there's no achieving if you don't set goals, but for me they tend to be concrete things. Finish this draft. Get that paperback edition proofed and ready to go. Things like that. Things that I myself can control.

How long does it take you to write a book?

Well, both my published novels, Gift of Continence and Dance of Chaos, took about a year to draft, and then of course there was more time spent in revisions. My historical novel would have been about the same except that I got stuck with it, wrote myself into a plot corner and so it sat in the 'too hard' basket for years. I've been working on the current book for about six weeks and it seems to be about half done; of course, though, I can work at it full time now.

What are the hardest parts of being an author for you?

Working alone as we do, I find it's terrifyingly easy to let oneself get sidetracked and let the days and weeks drift away. To combat that, I tend to set myself fixed working hours and track my progress in a spreadsheet. Having spent twenty years in Information Technology, the use of tools such as Excel and Microsoft Project comes naturally to me and I do use them a lot and find them very helpful.

Another thing that I think can be very hard is the way one tends to be working in a vacuum. I know a lot of people are constantly interacting with writer's groups and getting people to help them with their plots and characters and so on. Me, I don't believe in that. If I may use a coarse expression, I think it's bullshit. It's my book and I am the one who has to write it. So I don't show anything I write to anyone until after first revisions. But that, of course, leads one very vulnerable to crises of confidence—those dark days where one looks at the manuscript and thinks, this is utter crap, I should scrap it and do something else. It generally happens to me between a third and two thirds of the way through a book, when I am doing the 'hard yards'— the first flush of excitement about the new project has worn off, and I'm not close enough to finishing to be able to smell the stable. The only thing that gets me through those times is the discipline of the set working hours and the daily word count target.

The third thing that makes a writer's life difficult, I think, is lack of support. It's usually not intentional, but so many people seem to equate working from home on one's own stuff with not working. I'm lucky in that in many years in I.T. and later, in credit control, I've learned to say 'no' pretty well, but still my day does get nibbled at. A case in point is the time when I was frantically working to a looming deadline—a short story I'd promised for an anthology—and a 'friend' turned up on my doorstep, saying she'd travelled down from Ballarat to take me out shopping for the day. I wanted to ask her how she'd have reacted if I'd turned up at her workplace at the beginning of her shift saying that (she's a nurse). You just don't get the respect for your work and its demands that a person in paid employment can take for granted. And so, unless you're prepared to get quite tough with people, your work days can be nibbled away until there's nothing left.

What do you enjoy most about being an author?

Most of all, the peace and quiet. Mind you, in my later years in the workforce I was important enough to have an office where I could close the door and have my calls held, and people would respect that, but throughout my time in I.T. it was all open plan, and that's given me a lasting aversion to noise, to interruptions, to mindless chatter and to having a lot of people around. Just to be left alone is a wonderful thing.

Another thing that I love is that there is no time wasted on commuting. When I was going into the city every day, I wasted at least two hours a day on this, plus all the fribbling about with makeup and other rubbish. Now, all I have to do is walk into my office.

Another thing is being able to have my animals with me, of course. But these things are all peripheral. You asked what I enjoy most about being an author, so I've focused on the job-type things. But if you were asking what I enjoyed about being a *writer* — ah, that's another matter. The rush of excitement as a new story idea falls into place. The no-mind bliss of the flow state, when you're writing as fast as you can type and you can almost see the threads of imagination being drawn from the sky and woven into your manuscript, and the almost orgasmic pleasure when you read your own finished work — really finished, I mean, not a first draft — and find it good. Those are the things that make up for everything else.

What books or authors have had the most influence on you as an author?

That's always a difficult question for a writer to answer, and my readers may have a very different idea than I have about who's influenced my work. I can really only guess, as I've never consciously tried to imitate any other writer. But here's my best guess: they are all writers whom I particularly admire for their mastery of specific aspects of the craft.

Jane Austen

Anthony Trollope

Rumer Godden

Stephen King

What did you find most useful when you were learning to write and expanding your skills?

Short stories, without a doubt. They are like a laboratory, where one can experiment with different genres, different techniques and all without a major commitment. Before starting my current book, I spent about the last eighteen months writing short fiction, and I feel I have learned a great deal and really grown as a writer as a result.

What author services do you pay for, as opposed to doing yourself? Things like cover design, formatting, editing, proofreading, etc.?

Professional cover design is a must, as is editing. I'm not going to go into detail about the commercial arrangements I have, because those things are private.

What technology/services/programs do you use as an author? (email subscription services, Dragon software, editing software, etc.)

Everything I use on my computer is from the Microsoft suite. Word of course, Excel, MS Project and Outlook to keep track of projects and tasks. I find those programs and my use of them to be perfectly adequate for everything I want to do. Recently, though, I've started to use Pinterest a little bit—I collect pictures that relate to parts of what I'm writing on a board for each project, and I go and stare at it from time to time. I've found it helpful sometimes, especially if I need to describe something, such as a room or a house.

What are your thoughts about ebooks vs. print books?

One thing that always amazes me is the level of passion and anger one sees in online writers' groups about this. I cannot understand the problem. Most keen readers have a preference for one or the other. They both have their uses. I do feel, however, that to be taken seriously you need to be in print, and preferably in hardcover as well as paperback, despite the extra work and lack of profitability. It is hardcover that will get your book onto the main stacks in the libraries, instead of those little twirly stands where the low-status paperbacks are still relegated.

What are your thoughts about self-publishing vs traditional publishing?

Again, I don't really care. I self-publish myself, because I just can't be bothered going through all the submissions and messing about trying to get picked up by a publisher. To anyone who succeeds at it, though, I say good luck to you.

One very sad thing, though, about self-publishing is the number of people who equate self-publishing with just shoving it up there. No revisions, no edits, no critical second looks—finish writing the first draft, format and publish. These fools have made it a lot more difficult for the rest of us.

How often do you write, and how do you find or make time to write?

It's easy to make the time to write. You do it just as you make the time for anything else that's important. We don't see policemen turning up in their pajamas because they didn't have time to put on their uniforms. As I've said, I assign set hours, and those hours are my working hours, just as if I were a cop rostered on from seven till three. If you're serious about your work, you will be doing something like this.

Do you plan your whole book out in advance, or just let it flow? What does your writing process look like?

I find that varies greatly depending on what I am writing. With my novels to date, I have started blind and discovery written until about half way, or two-thirds; after that I will sit down and knock out a brief outline of how to bring it to resolution. I've departed from that with the current book, because of the nature of it; there's a mystery, and like anything similar to detective fiction, I feel a plan is vital, because all of the clues need to be given throughout the book.

What's a typical working day like for you? When and where do you write?

I have one room in my house set up as my office, and in it I work five hours a day Monday to Friday, two hours in the early morning and three hours in the afternoon. During those hours there is no messing about. The phone rings, I don't answer it. If I'm not dressed in time for the morning session, I write in my robe.

So usually I get up a bit before seven and write from seven till nine. Then I do housework, get dressed if I haven't already, feed the kids and go out with my dog. After lunch I generally take a brief nap with the cats, and I might read or watch a little television. At three I am back in the office until six. I have found this works very well for me, although I may adjust the timings a little.

Do you ever get Writer's Block? If so, how do you deal with it?

Well, I don't actually believe there is any such thing as Writer's Block. Like the 'muse,' 'inspiration' and all that fluff, it is just an excuse for not dealing with whatever problems one is having. As I've said, I have been known to get stuck with something; but as soon as I took that book out of the 'too hard' basket and said, the buck stops here, I finished it without difficulty in about two months.

That said, one can always get stuck, and I find that outlining can help one to unstick oneself, as can stopping in the middle of a scene to make it easier to get into the flow the next day.

Do you read your own reviews? If so, how do you deal with bad reviews?

I do if they are brought to my attention, but I don't particularly go looking for them. I haven't had any really bad ones. When I do — and I am sure it is when, not if, I should think I will first have a think about whether there's actually something wrong with the book, and of course if there is more than one review saying the same thing, or if the reviewer is someone I think has a lot of credibility, I would give more weight to it. Otherwise, I expect I will just ignore it. I certainly won't be throwing a tantrum on social media as I see some people do.

Other than reviews, do you hear from your readers very often? What kinds of things do they say?

Mostly people say how much they laughed. Sometimes they say they stayed up later than they wanted to finish it. That makes me so happy, when I hear that.

What are some ways in which you promote your books? What have you found most or least effective?

Honestly, I'm not the person to ask. I don't give much effort to promotion, I know nothing about it, and I don't see it as being my job. My job is to write excellent books, and I think that's enough for one person.

How easy or hard is it to make a living as an author?

Again, I really don't know. Personally, I am in the happy position of not needing to work for the money.

What advice would you give to someone aspiring to be an author?

That would depend on whether he could actually write or not. But in general, I think I'd say, aspire instead to be a good writer, and leave the 'author' business for another day.

How can readers find out more about you?

Website: www.tormistonsmith.wix.com/tabitha

Facebook:

www.facebook.com/Tabitha-Ormiston-Smith-137637486306612

Tom Morkes

Tell us about yourself and your books!

I'm the founder of Insurgent Publishing, a creative advisory firm that helps professional bloggers, startup founders, and CEOs launch bestselling books and 6-figure digital products.

Insurgent Publishing's portfolio of projects includes the record-setting Kickstarter campaign for "The Freedom Journal," which raised over $450,000.00 in 33 days, "The 7 Day Startup" which sold over 20,000 copies in the first 12 months of release, and current project "Scaling Lean," which is set to be a NYT and WSJ bestseller, among many other notable books and products.

I've personally written several books:

The Art of Instigating

Notes from Seth Godin's Revolution Conference

The Complete Guide to Pay What You Want Pricing

and most recently: Collaborate: The Modern Playbook for Leading a Small Team to Create, Market, and Sell Digital Products Online

How long have you been writing, and how did you become involved in writing?

I started writing in my spare time while in the Army. I officially launched my blog end of 2012.

What are you working on at the moment?

Personally, I just finished Collaborate: The Modern Playbook for Leading a Small Team to Create, Market, and Sell Digital Products Online.

Insurgent Publishing is now working on about a dozen book and product launches slated for 2016 and 2017, including "Scaling Lean," "The Growth Hacker's Guide to the Galaxy," and many others.

Did you have any goals with writing, and if so, how well do you feel you've achieved them? What do you hope to achieve in the future?

The only goal was to get over my fear of writing, which I did. I have no goals around my writing in the future, but I intend to make Insurgent Publishing the industry leader in strategic book and product launches.

How long does it take you to write a book?

From months to years.

What are the hardest parts of being an author for you?

The writing part.

What do you enjoy most about being an author?

Having written.

What books or authors have had the most influence on you as an author?

G.K. Chesterton and C.S. Lewis for writing style; Seth Godin and Steven Pressfield for inspiration.

What did you find most useful when you were learning to write and expanding your skills?

Writing as consistently as possible.

What author services do you pay for, as opposed to doing yourself? Things like cover design, formatting, editing, proofreading, etc.?

I own a publishing company, so I don't have to pay for anything personally ;-)

What technology/services/programs do you use as an author? (email subscription services, Dragon software, editing software, etc.)

I write using Word or Google Docs. No fancy tech needed. I use ConvertKit for email marketing . . . here's why I think it's the BEST for authors and self-publishers: http://tommorkes.com/email-marketing-service-for-authors/

What are your thoughts about ebooks vs. print books?

If you have an ebook, you should have a physical print variation—if it's a good book to begin with, that is. The one caveat is if the book is a lead magnet for your business—in which case ebook is fine.

What are your thoughts about self-publishing vs traditional publishing?

They are both good in their own rights. Depends on your goal. Either can be right or wrong depending on your goals, assets, circumstances, etc.

How often do you write, and how do you find or make time to write?

I am writing every day for my business, just not always for the same project. I find the time to write because it's my job and I have no choice ;-)

Do you plan your whole book out in advance, or just let it flow? What does your writing process look like?

I plan out everything as best I can, then I write, then I rework, then I write, then I rework. And hopefully I only have to do this a few times before it's finished.

What's a typical working day like for you? When and where do you write?

I wake up at 5am, give or take, and I knock out key tasks for the day. Around 8 or 9am, I do a team standup. The rest of the morning I work on projects. Afternoons are usually booked from 1pm — 6pm with calls, Monday -Thursday. I try to keep Friday-Sunday clear so I can catch up on all our projects.

Do you ever get Writer's Block? If so, how do you deal with it?

I do. I usually stop writing and do something else. Writer's block is a symptom of forcing something you don't understand. Getting clarity removes the block.

Do you read your own reviews? If so, how do you deal with bad reviews?

I do, but I don't care. There are a lot of people who are full of hate in the world and they're not worth your time or mine.

Other than reviews, do you hear from your readers very often? What kinds of things do they say?

Depends on the book, but I've heard all sorts of nice things. The Art of Instigating was called one of the most powerful ebooks ever when I released it back in 2012 — that's pretty high praise and I was really grateful to hear that.

What are some ways in which you promote your books? What have you found most or least effective?

That's what Insurgent Publishing does — we sell lots and lots of books.

Most effective: strategic outreach.

Least effective: Twitter

How easy or hard is it to make a living as an author?

It's not hard for me because the majority of my income is from books we publish or launch. My books only make up a small portion of my income — if that were it I wouldn't be doing great. Luckily, it's just a portion of what I do.

What advice would you give to someone aspiring to be an author?

Write your book, then learn how to market and launch it so you didn't just waste years of your life on something that no one cares about. If you have to, pay to learn from the best or hire someone very good at marketing to do it for you.

How can readers find out more about you?

Website: www.tommorkes.com

Wayne Roux

Tell us about yourself and your books!

My name is Wayne Roux, and I am the second youngest of eight children. (My parents lived next to a railway line?). I have authored and self-published three thriller novels, "The Days Beyond," "December Dead" and "The Trembling," as well as a non-fiction book on Bankroll Management.

How long have you been writing, and how did you become involved in writing?

I was always an avid bookworm growing up. I excelled naturally at school essays, and the transition from that to writing novels occurred at around age 14, when I penned my first unpublished novel by hand in two Croxley notebooks. I lost the writing bug after finishing school and military training, but it recently took hold again, thankfully.

What are you working on at the moment?

My current project is a psychological thriller titled "Apartment Five." I'm taking a completely different approach to this one, and putting myself slightly out of my usual comfort zone. It's coming along slowly, but with three novels already out, I'm not feeling the need for urgency, so slow is the way to go this time around.

Did you have any goals with writing, and if so, how well do you feel you've achieved them? What do you hope to achieve in the future?

I think all authors have goals, whether they'd admit it or not. Obviously, being 'discovered' is one of them. The elusive dream of the right person at the right time reading the right book . . . and the 'unexpected' explosion that follows. Of course, in reality the odds of that actually happening are miniscule. So realistically I guess my goal is to get to 10000 downloads across all my novels at some point in time. I'm currently 25% of the way there. Once that is achieved, I'll move the bar.

How long does it take you to write a book?

Well, my first novel, "The Days Beyond" was finished in 6 months, from start to finish. I repeated this immediately with "December Dead," finishing it in 6 months as well, resulting in my first two novels completed in 1 year. The third novel, "The Trembling" took a bit longer, almost an entire year. And I'm estimating a year for the new project too. Luckily I type 65 wpm so that helps.

What are the hardest parts of being an author for you?

Finding the time to write, of late. I work full time and author part time, so getting the energy levels up to the point where I can either be up at 05h00 each morning, or writing till 22h00 in the evening is the biggest challenge.

What do you enjoy most about being an author?

The freedom to create. The magic that happens when thoughts and ideas in my head become tangible and real. And, of course, the ability to touch perfect strangers in different ways, and the intense value of their feedback, regardless of how small.

What books or authors have had the most influence on you as an author?

Dean Koontz, Stephen King and Wilbur Smith. Koontz for his style of writing, King for his brilliance and ability to make you fall in love with characters, and Smith for the local flavor that came with reading something about your home continent or country. Stephen King's "IT" was definitely my biggest influence and inspiration to write.

What did you find most useful when you were learning to write and expanding your skills?

Having a 'sounding board' in the form of a few close friends, who got samples of the books as I wrote them, allowing me to edit 'on the go.' I also experimented with various techniques, including writing the final chapter somewhere near the first quarter of the book, and then having a direction in which to work.

What author services do you pay for, as opposed to doing yourself? Things like cover design, formatting, editing, proofreading, etc.?

I paid for none of those, using people close to me with the relevant skills, free of charge.

What technology/services/programs do you use as an author? (email subscription services, Dragon software, editing software, etc.)

Microsoft Word, and Google, lol.

What are your thoughts about ebooks vs. print books?

I think both have a space in the world. Surprisingly, ebooks have not REPLACED print books, and I doubt that they ever will. It's a lot easier to get an ebook published than it is to get a conventional print book published, unless you do it yourself through services such as CreateSpace. In the same breath, a large print bookstore has recently shut down in my town, so is this a sign of things to come? I guess only time will tell.

What are your thoughts about self-publishing vs traditional publishing?

I believe it's a very small percentage of self-published authors that actually earn anything halfway decent from being an author, in my personal experience. The prestige and marketing that comes from traditional publishing is hard to beat, but also harder to get a foot in the door.

How often do you write, and how do you find or make time to write?

With my first two novels I was up at 05h00 daily, Monday to Friday, writing for an hour a day before heading off to work. My third novel I wrote as and when I had free time, which is why it took a lot longer. I'd definitely stick to a set schedule in order to ensure the book is done on time going forward.

Do you plan your whole book out in advance, or just let it flow? What does your writing process look like?

I have a very basic idea of what I expect to happen, but very little specific character development. This I improvise as I write, and around 25% of the way through the book I find that writing the ending helps. This gives me a compass of sorts. Of course, the ending can always change, and it most likely will, but having that goal in sight definitely helps to maintain order in the chaos. With this method, the book tends to write itself, going in directions that were least expected, which is probably what the reader prefers in any case. ☺

What's a typical working day like for you? When and where do you write?

Writing: 5am to 6am daily.

Do you ever get Writer's Block? If so, how do you deal with it?

I got writers block while penning my third novel, "The Trembling." I was stuck at a particular scene for months, and just couldn't write my way out of it. And then one day, I sat with my cousin and we tossed around some ideas, and before I knew it I was writing again and steamed through to the end.

Do you read your own reviews? If so, how do you deal with bad reviews?

Definitely! For me, the review is more valuable than any financial compensation. I value each and every word written by those who took the time to actually read my work, and I respond where possible. Bad reviews are part and parcel, and must be used as fodder for improvement.

Other than reviews, do you hear from your readers very often? What kinds of things do they say?

I have several 'fans' who followed me on Twitter and Facebook, and I still communicate with them often, sometimes daily. There is always an excitement in the air when they hear of a new release, and I get private messages and "I can't wait's." I love interacting with my readers.

What are some ways in which you promote your books? What have you found most or least effective?

I've tried promoting via Twitter and Facebook, mostly. What I've found is that Twitter has been more effective, especially when offering 'FREE' promotions. I find Facebook limited to more immediate circles, whereas Twitter is more random and far-spread. The best success I've had with promoting is offering free copies to those who Retweet a specific post on Twitter, by means of a lucky draw.

How easy or hard is it to make a living as an author?

Initially I thought that it would be an easy money-making sideline, but I've since come to realize that this is far from the truth. I have since relooked at my strategy, and what I want to achieve, and I am more focused now on building a solid repeatable fan-base instead.

What advice would you give to someone aspiring to be an author?

If you're just starting out, you are about to venture into a very vast ocean, filled with millions of others just like you. The key is to get yourself to stand out from the rest. Bring something unique. Bring something people are looking for. Research the markets and genres. And when you finally step into that ice-cold water, keep paddling or you may just find yourself disappearing below the surface and forgotten like so many others.

How can readers find out more about you?

Website: www.waynerouxauthor.com

Facebook: www.facebook.com/waynerouxauthor/

William Reimer

Tell us about yourself and your books!

Hello! My name is William Reimer, I'm a 22-year-old from Adelaide, Australia.

I published my first children's book "A Ferret Named Phil" in September 2015.

I've had around 12 different jobs in my life, from tending bar to door-to-door sales, and I quit my cafe job early last year to focus full-time on writing.

My book is about a small ferret who overcomes a big bully without resorting to violence. So far I've sold over 2,500 copies and it's receiving wonderful feedback.

How long have you been writing, and how did you become involved in writing?

I've been writing since I was a kid. I still have some print-out of an Indiana Jones rip-off I wrote when I was 9 . . . Apart from that there have been terrible lyrics, a song for a musical production in high school, and a few other things. A few years ago I became obsessed with Hemingway and the self-indulgent writer cliché so I stayed in Paris for a few months playing up to that stereotype, but ended up with hardly anything worthy of publication!

What are you working on at the moment?

I'm currently working on the sequel, composing music for a sing-a-long audiobook and working on a premise for a comedy series!

Did you have any goals with writing, and if so, how well do you feel you've achieved them? What do you hope to achieve in the future?

My goal has always been to get A Ferret Named Phil into each and every primary school, kindergarten and daycare center in Australia. So far I feel like I'm on the right track, many teachers have reached out to me letting me know how they have taken on my book as an anti-bullying resource. In the future I hope to expand the series and take it overseas!

How long does it take you to write a book?

It took me about 3 months to completely finish my book—I went through about 16 rewrites along the way. I hope to one day publish a full-length novel but at this stage I'm really enjoying being a children's author.

What are the hardest parts of being an author for you?

Self-doubt can strike at the most inopportune times. Apart from that—whenever you put something out in the public eye you invite anybody with an internet connection to make a comment. These people can be absolute saints who support everything you do, but on the other side of the coin you can get some pretty nasty stuff . . . Some of the messages I've received have shocked me! Things you would never imagine an author of a children's book would get . . . But I take it all in my stride and keep it in my back pocket for another book down the line. I think when you're able to cause such an extreme reaction (positive OR negative), it means you might be on the right track.

What do you enjoy most about being an author?

I enjoy so many aspects of it—From the sense of fulfilment I get when I receive a heartwarming message from a parent, to being able to work wherever I wish. I love the freedom that writing affords me, and I'm so grateful for it.

What books or authors have had the most influence on you as an author?

Not exactly a children's book, but Nick Hornby's "High Fidelity" is a real favorite of mine. I can relate so well with his dry, self-deprecating style of humor. It's a personal bible of sorts—I must have read it about 15 times. The movie is also a personal favorite, and the audiobook is terrific. Oh man I hope to meet him one day. When it comes to writing children's books however, you can't really go past Mem Fox and her contemporaries. She's written a staggering amount of books in her time which gives me so much motivation. I'm also a huge fan of Tony Robbins, his books are incredibly inspiring.

What did you find most useful when you were learning to write and expanding your skills?

Reading my favorite books/authors helped me without a doubt. The internet is also such a powerful tool—there are thousands upon thousands of informative articles and research you can do, it's all out there if you use your initiative. When it came to self-publishing my book, I spent a lot of time at local bookstores just browsing through all the books that were of a similar genre to the one I was writing. I agonized over fonts, font sizes, colors and themes.

What author services do you pay for, as opposed to doing yourself? Things like cover design, formatting, editing, proofreading, etc.?

Hiring an editor and a graphic designer is of incredible importance. I think a lot of writers believe that they are infallible but editors are fantastic. Even the smallest things are so important!

What technology/services/programs do you use as an author? (email subscription services, Dragon software, editing software, etc.)

I'm still finding my feet with the tech side of things. Only recently have I started up an email subscription service (Which has been fantastic). I like to keep in touch with my readers to see how my book is faring with their schools/children, plus I've been working on a coloring book so on occasion I send out some complimentary sheets as a way to show my gratitude for their continued support.

What are your thoughts about ebooks vs. print books?

At the moment I'm focusing more on print books due to the nature of my book. I've found that parents and teachers are far more inclined to read a physical copy of my book to children as opposed to an eBook. However, with technology advancing the way it is I'm sure eBooks in the classroom will only get more traction.

What are your thoughts about self-publishing vs traditional publishing?

I'm so grateful that the self-publishing route is becoming more and more accepted. On a personal level I feel if one if savvy enough, they can make a huge success with self-publishing. I never really set out to be picked up by a publisher because frankly I'm impatient—Even if my book WAS picked up by a publisher it can take months, years even until the book is distributed. By that stage who knows what has happened to your story!

My opinion is that if you're a self-published author, you are required to be an entrepreneur. Whether you like it or not.

You need to solve problems, think creatively, come up with interesting marketing strategies and have a genuine passion for your mission. If you don't have a burning desire to see your book become a success, why should anyone else care? The only trouble is that when you set off on the journey of self-publishing, you're walking a path that doesn't necessarily have a detailed map.

You're not clocking on at 9am and having your superannuation looked after for you, I suppose, the buck stops with you.

When you do find guidance, you need to be vigilant. A small dose of paranoia can sometimes help, there's a lot of charlatans out there willing to make a quick buck out of a naive writer.

How often do you write, and how do you find or make time to write?

I write every day. I'm a big fan of journaling—it's often cathartic. When it comes to writing I find that if I can commit to a solid 30-45 minutes (No matter how dreadful it is) I have faith that I will eventually stumble onto a gem. So I keep this in mind when I'm on my fourth long black and my hands start shaking.

Do you plan your whole book out in advance, or just let it flow? What does your writing process look like?

I try a combination of everything. Structure is very important for children's books so I do my best to outline my stories with dot points and the themes I want to convey—then it's a mad scramble coming up with the rest of it.

What's a typical working day like for you? When and where do you write?

A GREAT working day for me consists of the following: Wake up at 7, go to the gym and then drive out to a cafe. I'll spend a couple hours at various restaurants taking up their precious table space until I've outstayed my welcome. This is what I set out to achieve anyway—Sometimes I'll come up with one or two great rhymes. Sometimes I'll have a soup.

Do you ever get Writer's Block? If so, how do you deal with it?

I encounter writer's block a lot. It took me over three weeks just to answer these questions. My only solution is to just push through it—and that will usually involve writing utter garbage until I stumble upon a phrase, or a rhyme that I like. Then the process starts all over again.

Do you read your own reviews? If so, how do you deal with bad reviews?

I always read my reviews, and make an effort to get back in touch with as many readers as possible. As for the bad reviews — well I tend to only focus only on the ones that are positive. Those are the readers I care about.

Other than reviews, do you hear from your readers very often? What kinds of things do they say?

I get emails from my readers daily! They've been very generous and positive to me. Recently I heard from a lovely mother named Tara who told me that since reading my book, her daughter in kindergarten has experienced a really profound change in her self-confidence. Tara told me that her words were "I'm going to be brave like Phil and nobody can scare me anymore." When I received this message initially I thought this was one of my friends winding me up . . . There comes that self-doubt again . . . but of course it was genuine! I was so proud to get that feedback. It was incredible to hear that my book has impacted a child in such a way! I also found out that a boy in year one had chosen his first ever book report on A Ferret Named Phil. I haven't read it yet but I hope his analysis was fair and considered.

What are some ways in which you promote your books? What have you found most or least effective?

I'm loving Facebook at the moment. It makes it so easy to reach out to the people who want your story the most.

How easy or hard is it to make a living as an author?

I think it's as easy or as hard as you make it. Getting back to a point earlier, if you're a self-published author you need to be an entrepreneur. You're not handed out a monthly royalty check from Penguin just yet so you need to get out there and spread the word!

What advice would you give to someone aspiring to be an author?

In 2016, anybody can be an author. I think the answer is to just get started on your story. I get emails from some lovely people asking me what the best way to get started is — (I used to send out the very same emails) — The answer always comes back down to "just get it started." I have a belief that if you commit absolutely 100% to something — You will find a way to achieve it. You'll simply have no other choice!

How can readers find out more about you?

Website: www.aferretnamedphil.com.au

Facebook: www.facebook.com/aferretnamedphil

Y.K. Willemse

Tell us about yourself and your books!

My name is Y. K. Willemse (Yvette to those who know me best), and I'm the author of a YA epic fantasy quadrilogy that I hope to turn into a seven-book saga before long. My books are entitled Rafen, The Sianian Wolf, Servant of the King, and The Fourth Runi. My target age group is between twelve and seventeen for these books. I adore epic fantasy fiction and have for a long time.

How long have you been writing, and how did you become involved in writing?

I'm a young author, born in 1993. I started writing my first book at age ten and was signed by Spanish-based international literary and film agency Pontas at eighteen years old. All in all, I've been writing seriously for twelve years. I began writing because I felt I had a story to tell. It wasn't a good enough reason, and I gave up for a while in my late teens. I resumed writing because it helped me make sense of life. It became a type of prayer to my Creator. Writing is my therapy, a way of deepening my understanding of God and a way of reaching out to others and touching their lives with the truth.

What are you working on at the moment?

I'm currently writing the seventh book in my epic fantasy series The Fledgling Account.

Did you have any goals with writing, and if so, how well do you feel you've achieved them? What do you hope to achieve in the future?

Ever since I can remember, I've wanted to be an author and get my books traditionally published. I was signed as Pontas Literary and Film Agency's youngest ever client at age eighteen. When I was two weeks shy of twenty-one, Permuted Press, an offshoot of Simon and Schuster, offered me a multi-book publishing contract. Permuted Press is a bit of a hybrid publisher—independent and traditional in some ways. At the moment, they are veering more toward traditional. They paid me advances for each of my books. When they first published me, they had a POD (Print On Demand) system for their paperback books. For those who aren't familiar with the term, Print On Demand refers to the practice of printing books one by one as there is demand or a sale.

As of March this year (2016), Permuted Press is transitioning their print books to Simon and Schuster's catalogue, meaning that each one will now receive a print run, which results in better quality books than a Print On Demand system. Hence, I will now effectively be traditionally published, God willing. My publisher has a good link with Simon and Schuster, which is a large company. Hence, I've been really happy with the experience overall. In the future, I hope to secure a publishing contract for the remaining three books in my Fledgling Account series. If I can't, then I'll try self-publishing. But for now, I want to do everything possible to secure a publisher that I trust.

How long does it take you to write a book?

Two and a half months approximately. I'm a fast writer and slow editor.

What are the hardest parts of being an author for you?

Facing rejection time and time again is really tough. Also, editing and revising is ceaselessly difficult. It's impossible to make a book perfect, so an author can spend a lifetime trying. I'm a perfectionist, meaning criticisms after I'm published can drive me nuts, because the book is out there and there's precious little I can change. These are the things I find difficult.

What do you enjoy most about being an author?

Writing. I love writing and I love being able to experience the world from someone else's point of view. I also love being able to see the bigger picture of life, and I can only do that when I write. When I write, I feel close to God.

What books or authors have had the most influence on you as an author?

As a Christian, I've been strongly influenced by the Bible. I also adore Shakespeare, Mansfield, Hardy, and Galsworthy. Galsworthy's The Forsyte Saga was perhaps literature's most incredible exercise on character development. Just extraordinary. Shakespeare's Macbeth has all the drama and intensity that I like in a story. Mansfield and Hardy were innovative with their beautiful descriptions. I've also enjoyed the Harry Potter series and found Destiny Unfulfilled: A Critique of the Harry Potter Series very instructive while writing my own saga.

What did you find most useful when you were learning to write and expanding your skills?

Getting my book professionally manuscript assessed by Tina Shaw was one of the smartest things I ever did. She was just so helpful and told me the things that really mattered when it came to getting published. I'd had a lot of criticisms from others up until that point, but quite a bit of it was not necessarily the most important stuff. Tina Shaw gave me the big picture of the publishing world. She also checked both my contracts with me, giving me advice over the phone. So my big piece of advice is to find an author to mentor you. Creative writing courses are actually not that brilliant in my opinion, as you learn someone else's opinion of creativity and they give you very few practical hints on how to break into the market with your work. In my experience, few people at uni teach you how to get a literary agent or a publisher. Hence, getting an author to mentor you is a better alternative.

What author services do you pay for, as opposed to doing yourself? Things like cover design, formatting, editing, proofreading, etc.?

I paid for manuscript assessment and for my own domain for my author website, just prior to getting published. My publisher paid for cover art and editing and formatting. Other than that, I have a "no pay" promotion policy. Everything else I've done has been free. Authors don't earn a lot. It also pays to remember that very few people know what marketing actually works. Even if you pay them, their work may not actually be that beneficial. I've been an opportunist and contacted papers to help get my name out there. The New Zealand Herald did an interview with me, which wound up on page three of their weekend paper in October 2015.

What technology/services/programs do you use as an author? (email subscription services, Dragon software, editing software, etc.)

I use Microsoft Word for writing, Weebly for my website, and Mailchimp for my newsletter. I keep things very simple overall.

What are your thoughts about ebooks vs. print books?

While some publishers believe in the power of the ebook over the print book, I beg to differ. In my experience, I have seen many readers who are keen to get their hands on print copies of my books. Those who purchased the ebooks were fewer. There seems to have been a resurgence in the popularity of print, meaning that Simon and Schuster are doing print runs of many of Permuted Press' books. I personally believe that print will never go out of style. There is something special about a paperback volume as opposed to a kindle. If people truly care about your book, it is my belief that they will want it on their shelf.

What are your thoughts about self-publishing vs traditional publishing?

After I received over forty rejections in the literary world, I was almost ready to try self-publishing my first book. In the end, however, I held out a little bit longer—and it turned out to be a good decision, as I received a deal. I believe traditional publishing is economically safer for a new author and also means that the overall package should be more professional. On top of this, it gives the author more of a chance of getting the book professionally reviewed and potentially getting it into bookstores. Some people have done very well with self-publishing, so I hold nothing against that system either. But for me, I knew the job would be worse if I published it myself. Pushing myself to get traditionally published meant that the books were better in the end—and it's made me a better and more competitive author. However, I do agree it's not for everyone, and one day in the future I might try self-publishing.

How often do you write, and how do you find or make time to write?

I write anywhere from three to five days a week in any time that I can. I'm a self-employed music teacher, meaning I can choose to keep a day or a day and a half free to get ahead on the writing. This is typically what I do. Other than that, I try to write between lessons or in the evenings. I guard my writing time pretty jealously and always have weekly goals for myself, so that I keep on top of it.

Do you plan your whole book out in advance, or just let it flow? What does your writing process look like?

I'm not a planner. I've tried it—meticulously even—and my characters ruin the whole thing. So I tend to write and let them run the plot these days. My opinion is that it makes for a living, breathing book, in which the characters choose what happens and the word processor does not drive their actions. I've noticed that those writers who follow their plans to the letter typically write somewhat dull characters who act in predictable or irrational ways, because they're following a plotline and not their own desires. Then again, this is just my opinion.

What's a typical working day like for you? When and where do you write?

A typical working day for me normally involves some music teaching and a little bit of writing. I write anywhere I can. Anytime is good. I don't have to be in the mood, as I've trained myself to be able to write under most circumstances. I can write in libraries, cafes, parks, and most anywhere one can think of, as long as I have my laptop with me.

Do you ever get Writer's Block? If so, how do you deal with it?

I get what I think of as Writer's Despair. I get to a stage where I think what I am doing is useless and dumb and I just want to stop. Every word feels like a giant effort. I put on CDs and write until the CD is finished. I have daily goals and a reward system in place for when I reach them. For example: write a thousand words and then goof off on the internet for ten minutes. As a Christian, I also pray a lot to God to provide me with ideas and words. Even when I don't pull through, He always does.

Do you read your own reviews? If so, how do you deal with bad reviews?

I do read my own reviews. I tend to sulk a little over bad reviews, but I never reply. The way I figure it is "if you can't take the heat, get out of the kitchen." When your book is published, you're going to get criticism, because it's out in the market. Don't stew unnecessarily over reviews. Bad happens. Get on with the good.

Other than reviews, do you hear from your readers very often? What kinds of things do they say?

Sometimes I do hear from readers. Sometimes I even met them at writing talks that I do. Typically, they only come up to me if they really like it and then they compliment me and I become all awkward. I've had other Christians mention that my books contain heresy. I don't let it bother me. I don't mind if people burn my books, so long as they buy them first!

What are some ways in which you promote your books? What have you found most or least effective?

Nobody knows what works with promotion. Literally, nobody. I've contacted newspapers, radio shows, and writing magazines, asking for reviews or interviews. In a number of cases, I've gotten them, and it's resulted in sales. This is effective around the time of a book release. I've also contacted libraries and school libraries personally, as I write YA literature. Hence, there will be a market for it in schools. I have found that this sort of direct marketing has resulted in sales too. I've decided Facebook pages are very ineffective. I've also found blogging helps get your name out there but doesn't necessarily result in sales. Twitter is not good for sales, but rather for connections. You can find authors who might do an endorsement for your book in exchange for a free digital copy. Blog reviews are not always effective. Guest posts are cute, but don't always do much. Overall, my policy is to start with the crowd of people I have some connection with. I market the book to them and then try a wider audience I don't know. Marketing via relationships typically works better than marketing to the masses. At least, it does for me.

How easy or hard is it to make a living as an author?

It's abysmally hard. I don't let it bother me, as I enjoy music teaching as well. Authors get paid pittance. Anyone who tells you otherwise needs to do their research. From what I've seen, there are two ways to make a living as an author: write a book and publish it every other month or hit the big time. Hitting the big time is difficult; and besides requiring much talent and hard work, it depends a lot on your connections and a healthy dose of luck. Writing a book every other month is also challenging, and often the frequency of the book releases will mean that the products are of a lower quality. Certainly, keeping writing will help. I don't deny this. But don't quit your day job in a hurry.

What advice would you give to someone aspiring to be an author?

Pray often. Write often, and don't wait till you're in the mood. Edit until your brain is panting on the floor like a winded starfish. Never give up. And don't forget to feed yourself with quality literature.

How can readers find out more about you?

Website: www.writersanctuary.net

Facebook: www.facebook.com/fledglingaccount

Ashton Cartwright

Tell us about yourself and your books!

My first book was a facetious parody of a relationship advice book. I thought it was extremely amusing (a perspective that is shared by the grand total of 3 people whom have read it since then.)

After that, I decided to try my hand at another genre: I wrote a romance short story which did a great deal better than I expected. I started co-authoring romance novels with a friend of mine, and they did a great deal better than I could have possibly hoped.

After writing several romances, I went off on another tangent. Before I started writing, I made my living as a professional poker player, so, naturally, I decided to combine those two interests, and published several instructional poker books.

Somewhere during all this, a friend asked me to help publish their book. It sold quite successfully, and he offered to split the profits with me. Since then, at least as much of my time has been spent on the publishing side of things as the writing side of things.

How long have you been writing, and how did you become involved in writing?

I actually started back in 2012. My housemate at that time had often professed a desire to be an author, and being of the ilk that will try anything once, I thought I'd give it a go myself. I honestly never expected to make any money from it, but I thought I'd try my utmost to perform every step of the publishing process as though I was already a professional author. I figured that would be the best way to learn, as well as being the most interesting for me.

After I'd finished my first book (the comedy) a friend of mine mentioned that he'd been making a bit of extra money writing stories and selling them through Amazon. He was happy to give me some pointers, and I went from there.

My housemate never ended up completing a manuscript, having moved on to other things, but now my entire income is based on writing and publishing. If I'd never lived with him, I doubt I would have ever chosen this path . . . but I'm extremely glad I did.

What are you working on at the moment?

As well as putting together this book that you're currently reading, I'm spending most of my time working with some new authors. My little brother is writing now, and has just gone part-time at work to focus on being an author.

Both my mother and my father have also written books that I've published, so I've got my hands somewhat full. I also publish and promote another half a dozen other authors as well, so there is always plenty to be done.

As for my own writing, when this book is complete (as it must be now if you're here reading it) I'm going to be focusing more on instructional writing for the publishing industry. My website www.PaidAuthor.com is where I've been compiling everything. It's an interesting change from writing entire books, and I generally enjoy writing in a new genre/style.

Did you have any goals with writing, and if so, how well do you feel you've achieved them? What do you hope to achieve in the future?

When I first started writing, my only goal was to finish my book. Once that happened, I opened a bottle of wine and felt very proud of myself for a day or two! I had only partially thought that I'd ever finish it, so when I did I kind of didn't know what to do next.

Soon enough I made a new goal to make it available for sale, so that others could enjoy what I felt was the best book ever written. I published it myself, using Kindle Direct Publishing for the digital version, and Createspace for the paperback versions.

After I had a few more books under my belt, I made a new longer-term goal of being able to make a living from my own books, as well as the books I'd published for other authors. It took a couple of years of pretty dedicated effort to get to that stage, but it was well worth it.

How long does it take you to write a book?

I'm not a very fast author. The reason I say this is because it takes me a reasonably long time to write a very small amount of text. My first book (the comedy) was no more than 30,000 words, and it took me 3 months of solid effort to complete it. There are plenty of authors out there who could have done something like that in two weeks.

I'd have days where I'd spend all day and write a single page that I was happy with. It's all well and good to say I was a perfectionist . . . but the truth is there are perfectionists who can still pump out a couple thousand good words in a full day's writing. Stephen King writes 2,000 words every day . . . but sometimes 2,000 words takes a week for me.

I'm not a natural writer. I never have been. But when there is something I feel that I should write, or more likely NEED to write . . . then it has to be done, even though it takes a long time. If I don't write it, then it's like having an itch that can't be scratched . . . a story that you need to tell MUST be told . . . and that's all there is to it.

What are the hardest parts of being an author for you?

For me, I have a lot of trouble staying focused when I'm writing. I've played poker for a living, which requires a huge amount of focus. I've even been a professional kickboxer (albeit not a hugely successful one) and that obviously takes a huge amount of focus as well. But for writing . . . for whatever reason . . . I struggle to stay focused.

I know that I'd be more successful if I was able to dedicate X hours a day to writing . . . but I just can't do it. I write when I almost force myself to write . . . and that's about it.

Like I said, I'm not a natural writer. Which is okay; I'm not a natural NBA player or a natural Astronaut, or a natural anything else. I chose what I want to spend my time and effort on, and for me, right here, right now, that's writing.

I know it seems odd to say "Oh, I make my living as a writer" and also say that I'm not very good at it, but it's still the truth. My dad's a better writer than I am. My brother's a better writer than I am. My mother's a better writer than I am. That makes me the fourth most talented writer in my four-person family. It's odd, but it's true.

What I lack in natural talent however, I make up in persistence. I make it up in dedication. I make it up in effort. It's hard for me to complete a book, but I do it, no matter what. If I decide a book is going to be written, then I write it, even if I want to give up part way through. Even if I decide it's terrible and nobody is going to buy it. Even if I think I must have been insane to think I could ever finish a book . . . I finish it no matter what.

And some of the time it DOES prove to be an unprofitable story that I wrote. Some of the time it DOES appear to be a terrible decision. But the rest of the time my story or book does pretty well, and that's where my living comes from (along with promoting other authors of course).

If I'd trained myself to accept failing to finish a story, I never would have made it to the stage where some of my stories did very well . . . and that's what's made me successful.

What do you enjoy most about being an author?

As I write this, I'm 33 years old, and I haven't set my alarm clock for several years.

It seems like a very small thing, but it makes a world of difference to me.

I spent many years working in a government job, where it was all about clocking in on time, not doing anything wrong, and then just waiting until your seniority gave you a promotion.

As an author, there is no schedule, there is no automatic career advancement. If you get ahead as an author, it's based on your talent as a writer, and your ability to market yourself (or your publisher's ability to market you).

Being able to be successful working on my own schedule, on my own terms, is definitely what I enjoy most about being an author.

What books or authors have had the most influence on you as an author?

There is a book by Stephen King called 'On Writing' which is sensational. As one of the most successful authors of all time, I'm keen to learn anything he's happy to teach. I can't recommend it enough.

Also, there is a book called 'The Four-Hour Work Week' which is essentially a business book, but the concepts translate so well to being a professional author, that I think it's well work reading if you're hoping to become a full time writer.

What did you find most useful when you were learning to write and expanding your skills?

For me, talking to other authors was invaluable. I can't count the number of mistakes I would have made were it not for another author being willing to guide me in the right direction.

Also, I spend a lot of time on the internet, reading articles and learning from authors who have gone before me. Even now as a moderately successful writer, I still dedicate a large proportion of my time to studying other authors, and how they achieved their successes.

Study the authors who write the way you want to write. Study the authors that you look up to. Study the authors that you want to emulate. You don't have to copy them, but be aware of the things they do that make you want to read more, and see if you can incorporate that into your own writing style.

What author services do you pay for, as opposed to doing yourself? Things like cover design, formatting, editing, proofreading, etc.?

I'm a TERRIBLE cover designer, formatter, editor, and proofreader.

A lot of authors run into the problem of thinking that because their story is good, they should do every aspect of their book themselves.

They think that because they understand their artistic vision better than anyone, that they should download some free image software, and slap together a cover.

I once fell EXACTLY into this category.

The cover for my first book was absolutely horrible . . .

. . . and I loved it.

Foolishly.

It was a horrendous cover. It was badly drawn stick figures (which featured in my book) and some very basic Microsoft Paint artistry applied for the fonts.

I thought it was incredible at the time, but the truth was, I was HUGELY biased by how great I thought my book was.

Even if you think your book is amazing, having a cover you've done yourself is a really bad idea unless you're a professional designer. Being good at story telling doesn't mean you're a good cover designer, just as it doesn't mean you're an amazing mechanic or carpenter. These skills are almost completely unrelated, and an amateur cover design is probably the biggest handicap to success as an author that you can ever encounter.

Don't waste this chance to make a good first impression: Have an amazing cover.

P.s I also hire professionals for editing and formatting . . . but cover design is definitely the minimum that you need a professional for.

What technology/services/programs do you use as an author? (email subscription services, Dragon software, editing software, etc.)

I use SO MUCH software to make my life easier as an author and as a publisher.

I use Aweber as an email subscription service for all my authors, as well as myself. For some of my authors, when we release a book and send an email message through Aweber, we sell $1,000 dollars worth of books the very first day . . . and that's more than enough reason to use them.

As well as that I use Dreamhost to host all of my authors websites, along with my own. A good website that doesn't have .blogspot or .web or .wordpress after it shows that you're serious about your writing. I've encountered so many talented authors who've sold themselves short by using a free website when a professional one would cost no more than a few dollars a month.

I don't use any editing software when I write (other than the spell checker in MS Word).

For promotion, I use two services quite a lot: One is Hootsuite, which lets you schedule posts and images for all of your social networks (such as Facebook, Instagram, Twitter, YouTube, and LinkedIn). Hootsuite is free (unless you use more than 10 social media accounts) so I think it's one of the best services for authors.

The second service I use is from Book Marketing Tools. This is pretty much just for promoting myself and my published authors. It's a service that helps you pre-fill the forms for over 30 free Kindle promotion websites. In general, it saves me probably 2-3 hours for every free promotion we run, and costs less than a few cups of coffee.

What are your thoughts about ebooks vs. print books?

Anyone who says print is dead is a silly little bumblebee.

For my own books, I make just as much from print (through Createspace) as I do through digital versions.

That's not to say it's an even playing field however: there are many genres in which digital does better, just as there are many genres in which physical versions do better. One of my poker books for example generates as much revenue as a paperback as it does as a Kindle book. My dad's instructional watercolor book makes more money as a paperback then it does digitally. Other genres (such as romance) seem to sell more than 5 times as much as a Kindle download than they do as a paperback.

The truth is that the digital book industry is still so new, that if you base any long term decisions on what is happening now, you're probably going to be incorrect. Any serious author should be aware that things change in the blink of an eye in publishing . . . and if you aren't able to keep up to date, you need to make sure you have a publisher that can.

What are your thoughts about self-publishing vs traditional publishing?

I run a small publishing company, so my perspective should be biased . . . but here is it anyway:

If you're good at marketing, cover design, promotion, and so on and so forth, then you can be very successful without dealing with a publisher.

If you're a good writer . . . then that's the most valuable talent in the world, and wasting your time on marketing and promotion is almost sacrilege.

For myself, I'm no J.K. Rowling . . . but I'm pretty solid businessman, and a moderately successful publisher. I can't pretend every author I've published has done well, because that's just not true. What I can say is that all the authors who work with me that have had at least a few books published, are doing quite well. My own books are also doing quite well, far beyond what I ever expected before I moved into this industry.

One thing you avoid by publishing "traditionally" is that you don't have to spend all your time trying to work out how Facebook Ads work, as well as how various forms of marketing for books works. You generally don't need to schedule promotions yourself, or deal with cover designers and formatters. All that is done by the publisher.

One issue you could face by publishing "traditionally" is that unless you get a solid advance, your publisher may be terrible . . . and unable to make your books profitable (which is actually a very different thing than it being a good book).

As an author, and also as a publisher, I can't give you a simple answer. I'd be doing you a disservice if I told you that there was one solution that fit all authors. It would be a barefaced lie.

If you're book is in a genre that MIGHT be made into a TV series or a movie, AND if you're completely inexperienced at promoting your own work . . . then a publisher might be the right choice for you.

If your book is even a little bit niche, then there are few, if any, publishers that will be able to promote your book to the maximum.

And lastly . . . (I can't stress this enough) if a publisher offers to publish your book only if you pay them money . . . then run away as fast as you can. Any publisher than does this (which is quite a lot of the marketplace I must admit) is likely to be more focused on the amount you pay them, rather than the potential for you book to do well in the future . . . and that's certainly not a recipe for success.

This is of course very different from hiring a publisher or publishing firm to perform a specific service: If you hire a publisher to be your editor or proof-reader for example. In that situation, you're paying up front for a particular service. If someone wants a percentage of your book sales though, then it's much more like a traditional publishing deal, and you shouldn't have to put money up front.

How often do you write, and how do you find or make time to write?

I struggle quite a lot to find time to write. The only solution I've found is to set aside a particular time each day/week that is your writing time, and not to let anything interrupt it.

If I dedicate a particular day to writing a particular number of chapters, or a particular article, then I do my best to make sure that happens. I make sure that the people around me know that this is my writing time, and that I'm not available for regular issues or conversations.

It seems a touch excessive, but I even turn off my mobile phone and take the house phone off the hook. The truth is that writing is my occupation . . . and nobody would expect you to be able to chat all day while you're meant to be working, so why would they expect an author to be like that?

Do you plan your whole book out in advance, or just let it flow? What does your writing process look like?

I'm a hugely analytical person, which is both a curse and a blessing.

For me, I can't complete a book unless it's planned out in advance. I know many other authors who treat it entirely differently and will do extremely well by just typing things out and then finding out what's going to happen to their characters. It doesn't work for me though, so I plan things out in advance as much as I can.

What's a typical working day like for you? When and where do you write?

My working day goes in pulses. Perhaps a third of the time, my day is dedicated to writing, and two thirds of the time my day is dedicated to promoting either my own books, or my other authors.

Generally, I wake up at about 10am. I grab some food and a coffee, then I work on either writing or promotion for 3 hours . . . then I get some more food, and go back to writing or promotion for another few hours. I very rarely work more than 6 hours in a day, and I very rarely wake up before 10am.

I know my own strengths and weaknesses, and I know that I do my best work in the first 4–6 hours of my day, and I also know that if I don't get LOTS of sleep, then I'm of no use to anyone. I spend a lot of time at the gym, or kickboxing, or doing yoga, so if my body doesn't have time to rest, then my brain gets sluggish and I'm extremely ineffective.

Do you ever get Writer's Block? If so, how do you deal with it?

I definitely do. Writer's block is a constant irritation for me . . . but here is my solution: push your way through it. When I get writer's block, I turn off the music, I turn off my phone, I turn off Facebook . . . I leave myself with nothing except a keyboard and a Word file . . . and then I don't have any option but to type.

Do you read your own reviews? If so, how do you deal with bad reviews?

When I first started writing, I would read every review like my life depended on it.

But now that I'm a touch more experienced, I know that not everyone's opinion is going to mesh with mine, nor is everyone's opinion relevant as I progress as an author.

Sometimes, reviews are very helpful. If someone says "The book was good, but the motorbike referred to in 1962 wasn't invented until 1968" then you can make legitimate adjustments to the details of the book.

In other situations, though, people rejoice on the anonymity of the internet, and may say things that are a little bit excessive. I once had someone leave a review that said "This author is so terrible he should be charged with a crime!" which, though it may have been that particular individual's perspective, is unlikely to fall under the category of constructive criticism.

I'm a tremendously emotional person, and I've struggled with depression at certain points in my life. I've found that if I get four 5-star reviews in a row, followed by a 2-star review . . . the 2-star review will dominate my thoughts, and handicap me significantly when it comes to writing more.

These days I make it a point to only check my reviews every month or so. This is something that probably isn't necessary for everyone, but for myself, I find that I stay more focused when I'm not busy checking reviews every day to see if someone likes my work or hates it.

Other than reviews, do you hear from your readers very often? What kinds of things do they say?

I hear from readers all the time! Generally, they'll hit me up on Facebook, or send me an email to say that they enjoyed such-and-such a book. Often they'll have questions about the book, or about when my next one is coming out.

I always enjoy chatting to people who've been kind enough to read one of my books. Without the readers, I wouldn't be able to make a living from my books, and so I'm very thankful whenever someone takes the time to get in contact.

What are some ways in which you promote your books? What have you found most or least effective?

I think there are two main types of promotion: passive and active.

Passive promotion includes things that make you book able to be found, and establishing a presence for yourself online. Things like setting up a Facebook Author page, a website, an email subscriber list, and a Twitter account, are the basic (but essential) aspects of passive promotion.

Will having a dedicated Facebook page or Twitter account suddenly skyrocket your book to #1 on the Bestsellers list? Of course not. But what it WILL do is it will make it easier for readers to find you. It will make it easier for them to keep in touch with you. It will make it easier for them to find out when you have a new book coming out, or even to find out about a previous book you'd published that they weren't aware of. At the very least, it will make you seem more professional, and if you want readers to take your writing seriously, then looking like a professional online is very important.

For a new author, these passive aspects of promotion might only result in a few extra sales each month, but as you become better and better known, having that passive promotion in place will pay dividends.

The other type of promotion is active promotion. This type of promotion includes things like discounting a book, running a competition, paying for advertising, scheduling a book tour, running a book signing event, attending festivals, and so on.

Over the last four years I've tried just about every type of promotion, and most of them have their place.

For myself, I've found that the most effective method for getting new readers to discover you is to run a discounted sale on a book, or even to give a book away free for a limited time.

This strategy, if it's done properly, can get so many new readers it's incredible.

All my own books, as well as the books I publish on behalf of other authors, are exclusively with Kindle Direct Publishing. There are pros and cons with having your book exclusive, and whether or not it's worth it is a question that always sparks a heated debate among authors.

The first benefit you get by being exclusively with KDP is that for 5 days out of every 90, you can make your book free, or, alternatively, you make it 99c and still get a 70% royalty on sales at that price (usually you only get 35% if the book is priced at 99c).

If you have several books, then making one of your books free can get your work in front of a huge number of readers, who may not have taken a chance on your book if they had to pay for it. Even a small free book promotion will usually get several hundred downloads, and a very dedicated promotion in a big genre can expect 40,000 to 50,000 free downloads over a 5-day period. Our most successful free promotion garnered 63,000 downloads over 5 days, and sales of the other books by that author went through the roof.

The free promotion itself even showed a profit, and the reason for that has to do with the other main benefit of being exclusively with KDP, which is as follows:

The other benefit of being exclusively with Kindle Direct Publishing is that your books can be borrowed by readers through the Kindle Unlimited program (kind of like Netflix for books) and this can account for a substantial amount of your royalties. Particularly for genres which seem to do well in Kindle

Unlimited (romance and erotica are probably the biggest of them) then not having access to this pool of readers is a huge handicap.

When you have a very successful free promotion, it's very common to see a surge of people borrowing your book through Kindle Unlimited. There are several probable reasons for this:

Partially it's because your book will start to show up on other pages on Amazon, under the "Customers who bought this, also bought this" section.

Partially it's because of word of mouth (thousands of people reading and hopefully enjoying your book generates its own momentum).

And partially, (and perhaps most importantly) Amazon's algorithms detect that a book is popular, which then makes it more likely that that title will be discovered or recommended to people on Kindle Unlimited.

Obviously I'm not privy to the internal workings and calculations of Amazon, but what I can say categorically is this: in the month following the free promotion of the novel that had 63,000 downloads, we had over 1,000,000 pages of that novel read through Kindle Unlimited alone. At half a cent per page read (which was the approximate amount we were receiving at the time), that equated to about $5,000 in extra royalties, for a book which generated no more than $300 the month before. Our paid sales for the book also went up, and we saw an increase in sales of that authors other books of between 50% and 100%.

Obviously this is an extreme example; that particular book hit the #1 spot on the free list for all of Amazon with that promotion, and that certainly doesn't happen for every book. But the one thing I'd like you to take away from this is that giving your book away free for a few days can be an excellent way to start "getting your name out there."

If you only have a single book and can't face the thought of giving it away, then running a discounted promotion works well too. A discounted promotion (or a Kindle Countdown Deal, which is effectively the same thing with a fancier name) can generate you plenty of extra readers as well, although the absolute number will be much less than if the book was free.

For most 99c promotions, I expect to get perhaps 5% as many sales as I would have free downloads, assuming that I spend the same money on the promotion as I would have if it were free. If I would expect 5,000 downloads for a small free promotion, then I'd expect to sell about 250 copies at 99c using the same promotion methods.

I've compiled a list of the promotion sites I use: www.paidauthor.com/best-ebook-promotion-sites/

For any serious promotion, I try to schedule my book in with as many of those groups as possible. The effects of promotion are not just cumulative, they're synergistic. If you get 100 sales from one promo group, and 100 from another group on the same day, that doesn't equal just 200 sales; it pushes you so much higher in the rankings, that people will start to see you on bestseller lists for your category, or the overall bestseller list if you've done particularly well, and that translates to additional sales.

If you combine promotions with 5 or 6 groups all for the same day, then it can well and truly skyrocket your sales to a point where you're sitting at #1 in a category.

Having said all that . . . the single best form of marketing you can do as an author is to write another book. The more books you have out, the more chances that somebody will decide to read one, and if they enjoy it, they'll likely read all your other books. When I find a new author I like, I read all of their books one right after another, until I've read them all. I know I'm not the only reader out there like that, which is why writing more books is one of the best ways to promote.

How easy or hard is it to make a living as an author?

The first thing you should know about this industry is that it's nothing like it seems in the movies, or in the news.

A lot of first time writers hear about people like J.K. Rowling or E.L. James, and think "That'll be me! I'll write a book and make hundreds of millions of dollars! Sounds like fun!"

The truth of course is that for every author who becomes that successful, there are thousands of authors who never sell more than a handful of books, and then of course there are all the authors that fall somewhere in between those two extremes.

I've been lucky enough to be able to make my living from books, and I've been honored to help several other authors bridge that gap between getting a few extra bucks a month, and turning writing into a full time occupation.

Making a living from writing can DEFINITELY be done. It can be done whether you get an agent and find a publisher, or whether you self-publish. It can be done no matter what genre you want to write in. It can be done no matter your age, or your experience, or anything else.

Becoming an author as a career is definitely possible for most people, but it's very rarely easy, it's very rarely a quick process, and it's almost always more work that you would expect.

Obviously if you're a single 21-year-old, fresh out of college, no kids, no major debts, then generating enough royalties to live off is going to be a fair bit easier for you than it would be for someone in their mid-forties, with three kids, credit cards, and a mortgage.

If you're expecting to write one book and make a living from that, then I'd say your chances are less than 1 in a 1000.

If you write 5 books, then your chances of making a living from them is perhaps 1 in 15.

If you write as many books as Stephen King has (618 titles listed on Amazon at time of writing) then I'd say your chances of making a living from writing is 1 in 1!

Most authors will fall somewhere between those numbers, but if you're serious about authorship as a career, you have to plan on writing at least half a dozen books before it's likely to generate the equivalent of a full time income . . . and even then "likely" is a very strong word.

What advice would you give to someone aspiring to be an author?

Having published for a dozen authors, and worked with 100 more in various capacities, I believe the number one piece of advice I can give is this:

Keep writing.

Your skills as a storyteller will always be improving as long as you keep writing, and your income from royalties will go up as you get more and more books out there in the marketplace.

Like any skill, it needs to be practiced often to stay sharp. If you get distracted and don't write, your skills will atrophy, and that will make it harder to start writing again.

There will always be things in life that get in the way of your writing. That's completely normal, but you need to push through them and keep writing anyway. Write as often as you can, write as well as you can, and eventually, success in this industry will become inevitable.

How can readers find out more about you?

Website: www.paidauthor.com

Facebook: www.facebook.com/AshtonCartwright

So, what now?

We hope you've enjoyed this glimpse into the lives and careers of 36 real authors.

Every author has a different story to tell, and no doubt your story will different as well.

If you haven't written your masterpiece yet, then we all wish you the best of luck completing it, and sending it out into the world for readers to enjoy and benefit from.

If you're already an author, perhaps you were able to glean some new information from the people in this book; either some different writing concept, or a marketing strategy that you haven't yet tried.

In the end though, the most important thing, beyond anything else, is that you write.

Best wishes,

Ashton Cartwright.

www.ingramcontent.com/pod-product-compliance
Lightning Source LLC
Chambersburg PA
CBHW071329280526
45787CB00001B/41

9 781533 528780